The Donald Trump Turkey Shoot

Humorous, Caustic, and Satirical Observations on the Immoral, Ignorant, Incompetent, and Dangerous Occupant of the Oval Office

John R. Scannell

Wutherwood Press

The Donald Trump Turkey Shoot
Humorous, Caustic, and Satirical Observations on the Immoral, Ignorant, Incompetent, & Dangerous Occupant of the Oval Office
All Rights Reserved.
Copyright © 2020 John R. Scannell
v3.0

This is a work of fiction. The events and characters described herein are imaginary and are not intended to refer to specific places or living persons. The opinions expressed in this manuscript are solely the opinions of the author and do not represent the opinions or thoughts of the publisher. The author has represented and warranted full ownership and/or legal right to publish all the materials in this book.

This book may not be reproduced, transmitted, or stored in whole or in part by any means, including graphic, electronic, or mechanical without the express written consent of the publisher except in the case of brief quotations embodied in critical articles and reviews.

Wutherwood Press

ISBN: 978-0-578-23215-7

Cover Photo © 2020 www.gettyimages.com. All rights reserved - used with permission.
Interior Designer: Laura Edding

PRINTED IN THE UNITED STATES OF AMERICA

This book is dedicated to the 65,844,610 American voters who had the good sense to vote for Hillary Clinton.

This book is also dedicated to those with the courage to oppose a president so manifestly incompetent, immoral, and ignorant.

*This book is also dedicated
to my partner in satirical observation
&
in life,
Wendy Kelling.*

The Donald Trump Turkey Shoot is a work of political analysis, commentary & satire. The opinions, beliefs, and political perspectives expressed are the author's alone—although he hopes they are widely shared.
Copyright © 2020 by John R. Scannell

Contents

Acknowledgements i
Preface.. iii
A Letter to My Sister on Trump's Inauguration Day 1

Week 0: Orange Trump and the Three Bears 5
Week 1: Trump, the Ignorant & Unqualified 17
Week 2: Let the Autocracy Begin.. 22
Week 3: Chaos Born of Stupidity 27
Week 4: Russia's Best Friend 33
Week 5: Pledging Allegiance 37
Week 6: The Trump Reality Show. 41
Week 7: *from* The Desk of Your English Teacher.. 46
Week 8: Chaos Is My First, Last, & Middle Name 50
Week 9: First Rule of Trumpcare: Don't Get Sick. 57
Week 10: The Dolt Who Walks & Talks. 62
Week 12: Ironic Juxtaposition.. 67
Week 13: Stupid & Evil 72
Week 14: One Hundred Days of B.S. 81
Week 15: Saying Makes It So.. 89
Week 16: Liar, Liar, Pants on Fire 96
Week 17: Trump Limericks 101
Week 18: Will Rogers Never Knew Donald Trump 105
Week 19: A Letter to OMB 110
Week 20: Only You Can Prevent Global Climate Change. 116
Week 22: Not Feeling the Love 120
Week 23: Letters, We Get Letters 126
Week 25: Twitter-Pated 132
Week 26: A Family Affair 136
Week 27: Savior McCain 143

Week 28: Ode to Trump 152
Week 29: The Sock Song 157
Week 34: A Child's Bedtime Tale 160
Week 36: Trump's Letters to Losers 168
Week 63: The Doctor Is In 177
Week 64: Trumpian Truthiness 183
Week 71: New Word: Kakistocracy 186
Week 72: G.U.I.L.T 191
Week 73: Layperson's Guide to the Madness of Donald Trump. .. 199
Week 74: Trump Theater at the Border 203
Week 75: Loyalty is the Thing 211
Week 76: The Scott Pruitt Edition 216
Week 77: Trump Overseas Edition 222
Week 78: Scary Trumpins 225
Week 79: Scary Trumpins, Part 2 228
Week 83: Duncan Hunter, The Swamp Thing 232
Week 85: Only Duh Best Woids 240
Week 89: Lies & Damn Lies…Sorry, No Statistics 248
Week 92: The Country Bumpkin and The City Trumpkin 253
Week 95: An Un-Armistice Day in France 257
Week 99: Piggy-Bank Government 259
Week 103: Stuck on the Wall 267
Week 104: The State of the Miserable Union 272
Week 109: Fantasy Becomes Reality 281
Week 122: The Nicknamer-in-Chief 287
Week 130: Ignorance is (Presidential) Bliss 293
Week 140: Songs from the Optimist's Heart 296
Week 146: Lying: It's What Republicans Do 300
Week 159: "I'm Like, A Smart Person" 305
Week 170: Theater of the Absurdest 309

Epilogue: The Morning After 322
Appendix / The Trump Nursery 323

Acknowledgements

Few, if any, contemporary presidents have inspired as many books as Donald Trump. The list is already long—and growing. From books like *Win Bigly: Persuasion in a World Where Facts Don't Matter* by *Dilbert* cartoonist, Scott Adams [2017] to books examining Trump's mental deficiencies, *The Dangerous Case of Donald Trump* edited by Bandy X. Lee [2017]. Some books, like Matt Taibbi's *Insane Clown President: Dispatches from the 2016 Circus* [2016], view the president much as I do, while others like Philip Rucker and Carol Leonig's book, *A Very Stable Genius* [2020] offer a deeply researched and very disturbing portrait of the president's erratic behavior. Republicans have written some of the most scathing books about Trump. Consider Rick Wilson's *Everything Trump Touches Dies: A Republican Strategist Gets Real About the Worst President Ever* [2018] or *A Warning*, penned by that well-known White House insider, Anonymous [2019]. I'm assuming Mr. or Ms. Anonymous is Republican.

The Donald Trump Turkey Shoot, however, provides an outsider's perspective—dare I say, an unhappy voter's perspective?—one predicated on what I've read in books written about Trump, or on contemporaneous newspaper and magazine accounts concerning Trump, his policies, and his administration, or on what I see and hear televised nightly. What I've seen, heard, and read appalls me, maddens me, and saddens me. I am not alone.

While I've attempted to formulate my own theory of Trump, always attempting to understand—and satirize—our Twidiot-in-Chief,

I've been heartened and gladdened by the support of so many people with whom I share a thoughtful, humanistic, and empathetic view of the world. I would like to acknowledge some of those wonderful people here. First, I want to offer my deepest thanks to my wife, Wendy, whose political views are completely in synch with my own, and whose research skills and advice have proven invaluable. Our daily political conversations have found a voice in this book.

I also want to acknowledge many of my friends who have offered me encouragement and been a source of emotional energy for me. That group includes Celeste DeCuir, AJ Edwards, Eve Gordon, Harold Gross, Elaine Harper, Sam Kelling, Larry & Kathy Kershaw, Roger Ledbetter, John Markowski, and Judie Weaver and a host of other people who shall remain nameless. I hope they realize how much they've sustained me in my efforts.

Preface

Now that Donald Trump has been impeached by the House of Representatives and acquitted by the Senate, I decided it was time for someone outside the halls of government—someone like me who can only judge our president from afar on what is reported about what he says or doesn't say and what he does or doesn't do—to speak up and declare what the whole world already knows: our President has no clothes.

I've come to understand that Donald Trump is simply the most powerful, naked man ever to occupy the presidency.

As someone who reads newspapers and watches the news broadcasts, as someone who weighs the evidence as objectively as possible, I fear we are witnessing our slide into a malignant autocracy. Be assured, I take no comfort in the pyrrhic knowledge that Trump was acquitted but not exonerated. So what? Exonerated, exschmonerated, Trump doesn't care. Emboldened by a sycophantic Senate, Trump has actually concluded that he can indeed do whatever he wants. And that's bad for me, for you, and for all the people we love. Bad for the United States. Bad for the world.

Is this hyperbole? I'm afraid not.

That's why I've compiled this book.

I began writing a Trump Journal for my own amusement a few months before the 2016 election—foolishly believing that Donald Trump could never be elected. Certainly not by an American populace as intelligent and freedom-loving as I thought they were.

I was wrong.

Twice.

Once by underestimating the candidate Donald Trump; and the second time by overestimating the intelligence of the American electorate.

Trump won the Electoral College even as he lost the popular vote by 2.86 million votes. And now we have a malignant narcissist at the helm, a man who lacks the character, competence, intelligence, and morality to be the "leader of the free world."

The man is despicable in almost every way it is possible to be despicable. He lacks all personal discipline, places incompetent and corrupt toadies in vitally important cabinet posts—despite claiming he knows "all he best people"—insults anyone who thinks differently than he does, and brazenly disparages American citizens and foreign leaders with equal enthusiasm. He proposes policies that threaten to upset long-standing alliances—like NATO—even as he schmoozes our arch nemesis, Russia, in the person of Vladimir Putin. All that and he's a bully, too.

And he lies. Perpetually. About things great and small, important and superfluous. The tally for lies, deceptions, misrepresentations, and other sorts of verbal misdirection will likely surpass 20,000 by the end of his first term. When it comes to presidential lies, Trump has no equal. No other president—even those who served two terms—is even close.

Making matters worse, Trump governs without thought, without advice, and without any purpose except his own. He issues edicts that foment chaos because he thrives on chaos. Chaos is wonderful theater, and Trump relishes theater, not governance.

With theatrical flair, Trump has petulantly and foolishly withdrawn from the Iran Nuclear Agreement and The Paris Climate Accords, as well as a host of important environmental policies that affect clean air and water, making all of us less safe—in both the short and long term.

And then, on September 24, 2019, Trump renounced globalism

before the United Nations General Assembly. In a world being transformed by global warming, at a time when international cooperation may well be the only avenue for survival, Trump essentially said, "Count me—and my United States of Selfishness—out." That's when I decided I'd like to add my voice to the wider anti-Trump chorus. I cannot stop him, but I've done my utmost to diminish him.

I've been writing my weekly Trump Journal—*Solum Optimis Verbis*: "Only the Best Words"—for over 150 weeks. I've taken a few weeks off from time to time because the Trumpian nonsense makes me weary and overwhelms my sense of reality. But I always return. Evil must be opposed. A good friend once said that she "laughs [at Trump] because there just isn't enough alcohol."

She's correct. I write, but drinking remains my second option.

Between the covers of *The Donald Trump Turkey Shoot* you will find my attempts at critical analysis, caustic commentary, satiric observation, and creative satire dressed up as dramatic sketches, mocking poetry, imagined letters, nursery rhymes, and adapted song lyrics. There's also a few children's stories—strictly for adults—with an anti-Trump sensibility.

Nothing here is classified.

Finally, and truly most compelling of all, I write because I believe Trump is a traitor—both literally and figuratively—to all things American. To our values. To our beliefs. To our institutions. And to our international friends. A traitor to everyone except himself.

This book aims to both understand and sarcastically insult, mock, and demean the anti-democratic, lying, narcissistic, ignorant, traitorous bully named Trump—who is a genuine stain on America's reputation.

I hope I've hit my target.

John R Scannell, May 2020

A Letter to My Sister on Trump's Inauguration Day

Friday, January 20th, 2017
Dear Sister,

    I had a dream last night that I was a journalist working under deadline, and I kept wondering how I could best characterize the inauguration of someone as unseemly and infantile as Donald Trump. After all, virtually every possible negative descriptor has been applied to our new president—with good reason, if you ask me—and still he persists. Trump won the Electoral College—even though he got clobbered in the popular vote by 2,864,903 votes when the final figures were tallied. So why does he still act petty and small-minded? Despite winning the national election, he takes to Twitter to insult his former opponents. The man has neither grace nor class—just ask the women he groped or walked in on as they stood in all manner of undress.
    Here's the headline from my dream that woke me up early this morning:

Traitor Trump's Triumph
Dooms Democracy

    I worry that it's true. So I got out of bed and walked my dog Beau across the back of our property while my Boston terrier, Luigi, chased rabbits and squirrels. I came back in to feed the animals, and made myself a cup of coffee. Later while shaving, I wondered if I was being too over-reactive and too melodramatic. Then I listened to Trump's brief—sixteen minutes???—dark and foreboding inaugural address. Two themes emerged for me—fear and selfishness—and I suspect those will be themes that set the tone for his entire presidency. According to him, the USA is weak and in tatters. We are a wreck. Wow. Who knew? Apparently, those dystopian movies and television series can't hold a candle to the true dark days that have befallen the good old USA. And rather than forging alliances and working to build friendships with other countries, Trump wants America's military to stand as a warning to every other nation.

After listening to Trump—and being grateful that his dark, deluded, platitude-driven, and simple-minded inaugural speech was mercifully brief—I wonder if you realize his speech was more suited to 1950 than 2017. We live in a global economy and Trump hypocritically advocates protectionism and tariffs? While his shirts and ties are manufactured in Asia, Trump wants to punish other manufacturers for having the audacity to produce their products overseas, too. He's the "Do as I say, not as I do" president. Unfortunately, protectionism and tariffs only punish one group—the American consumer—through higher prices. We'll either pay higher costs for manufacturing goods in the USA, or pay the additional cost of the tariff. It's *Economics 101*. Of course, the principles of *Economics 101* don't apply if you decide to NOT pay your vendors who provided you with products and services. That's called *Trumponomics*.

Even as Trump delivered an inaugural address out of step with reality, I wonder if you agree with his vision of a crippled America. How much of what he says rings true for you? After all, he is your guy. And if it does ring true, should I contemplate emulating him by adopting my own personal, mirror version of Trump's *America First*? Should I adopt a policy of *Me First*?

Surely adopting the *Me First* policy could save me a ton of money. Imagine if I made no more charitable contributions to the ASPCA, The Humane Society, American Cancer Society, The Alzheimer's Foundation, or even Toys for Tots. Imagine if I no longer worked for social justice issues—access to voting, equal pay for equal work, equality for women—by writing to my senators or congressman? Are we better off with every person for himself? Or herself? Trump thinks so.

I've always resisted a *Me First* policy, but perhaps I should just surrender to the same selfish inclinations Donald Trump does. Don't pay taxes. Don't contribute to charitable causes. Of course, that would mean the next time you needed money, you shouldn't call me. A *Me First* policy simply means I've got mine and everyone else is on their own. A *Me First* policy would have kept me from contributing several thousands of dollars your stepdaughter needed for her divorce. That was back in 2003 if I remember correctly. That kind of generosity wouldn't fit with a *Me First* policy. Mom's expenses at the Funeral Home would never have been paid for in advance if I'd implemented a *Me First* policy four years ago.

If I worried about myself first, last, and always, other concerns—like family and friends—would always be lower on my list of priorities. But I have this habit of worrying about people—unlike Donald Trump who sees most of us as useful tools for his own selfish ends. Do you think Trump will have time for automatic weapons, voting rights, racial discrimination, the minimum wage, food stamps, affordable housing, healthcare for all, clean energy, the preservation of our forests and lakes, the meddling by Russians in American politics, or massive ethical violations when there are billionaires waiting for tax cuts or massive dollars to be earned personally?

"I can do it all," says Donald Trump. "Run my businesses and run the country. I'm the only one who can." And I thought Superman was dead. Silly me. But there is a silver lining. On November 13, 2016, Trump said he'd forsake the $400,000 annual presidential salary and accept only one dollar per year. What a guy! Still, at only a dollar per year, I worry that we still won't get our money's worth.

I find your political, religious, and environmental positions so radically different from my own that I wonder at times if we could possibly share any DNA. Just recently, Trump's cabinet picks (EPA, Health, Education, Justice, State Dept.) and NASA's report that global climate change is accelerating, make me wonder what reality Trump and his supporters actually inhabit. And Trump's long-ingrained habit of screwing and scamming the middle class—consider Trump University and his side-stepping taxes—makes him unlikely to be its savior. When I reflect on your positions, positions that are bad for you and virtually everyone we know, I'm stumped; I'm horrified; I'm sad beyond words.

I've never quibbled about being generous with my time and money—and I've always been glad to share, especially with family—but I genuinely feel anger toward people who've put such a thoughtless, dangerous, selfish man in our nation's highest office. I'm saddened most when I realize you are among those people.

I wish you weren't.

Remember the warning we all read in Shakespeare's *Julius Caesar*:

The evil that men do lives after them.

Trump is responsible for far too much evil.
You can help change that in November 2018.

Your Brother,
John

𝔖olum 𝔒ptimis 𝔙erbis

Orange Trump and the Three Bears

January 2017

Orange Trump and the Three Bears
A Modern but Sorta True Fairy Tale
by John Scannell & Wendy Kelling
© 2017

Once upon a time, in the Kingdom of Insania, in the dark and tangled Forest Bannon, in a land badly ruled by the Evil Prince of Orange, there lived a family of three bears. Mama Bear, Papa Bear, and Baby Bear. They were a racially mixed bear couple—Papa Bear was a Black Bear and Mama Bear was a Brown Bear—and they had moved into the deep, remote regions of Forest Bannon because the Kingdom of Insania had forbidden Mixed Bear co-habitation.

Along the dilapidated highways and byways of the Kingdom of Insania, dilapidated due to sustained, long-term inattention to infrastructure maintenance, billboards declared mixed-bear relationships
FORBIDDEN.
REPORT ALL OFFENDERS.

The billboards also forbade mixed cohabitation among foxes, deer, and other mammals that lived apart in the deep woods. Of course, cellphone coverage was spotty in the depths of Forest Bannon—a place, it is said, where demons abound—so reports were seldom made. The Evil Prince, in his distant castle tower, knew nothing of the lives of his peasants or his woodland denizens, and he made no effort to understand.

Papa Bear remained in the Forest Bannon because he harbored a dark secret. Papa Bear had emigrated illegally from the distant Kingdom of Common Sense, a kingdom beyond the Mountains of Learning and across the Sea of Knowledge. The evil Prince of Orange had forbidden his subjects to climb those mountains or cross that sea, insisting that the Kingdom of Common Sense didn't really exist.

"No one's ever seen it," said the Evil Prince. "No one's ever been there. Common Sense is a tremendous lie. A very big lie. But if it does exist—it really doesn't, you know, it really doesn't—but if it does exist, it's very terrible, everyone says it's terrible. That's what everyone says, even the people who aren't talking about it say how terrible it is. The people there are terrible, and they want to hurt us all here in the Kingdom of Insania. We must keep them out."

Despite the Evil Prince of Orange's lack of certainty about the existence of the Kingdom of Common Sense, he took no chances and built a wall at the base of the Mountains of Learning to protect his kingdom from the potential threat of non-existent Common Sense.

Papa Bear had come to Insania because the few bears who had ever traveled there said that the berries in Insania were the best berries in the known world. Rumor had it—and Insania was a kingdom where people communicated almost entirely by rumor—that Insania's burgeoning business in better berries was booming, blossoming because their bountiful bunches of better berries were fed on the swiny swill of the swirling waters of the River Excrement—whose source was the Castle Trump—and visited by the buzzing bees beguiled by the beautiful bouquet of the better berries. Those subjects, living downwind and subject to the salient smell of the swiny swill from the Castle Trump, laughingly referred to the residence of the Evil Prince as the Offal Office.

"Our Evil Prince really knows his shit," one peasant said as he bit into one of the lush berries he was gathering beside the kingdom's dilapidated highway.

"Well, that's all he knows," said his rustic companion shoving berries into his mouth. "He should be glad that the King will be leaving him a lot of money. He'd be a pauper otherwise. He's failed at everything else. It'll be a shame when his father King Congress dies, and he becomes the King."

"I hear that King Congress has grown sicker by the day," said the peasant sympathetically.

'Tis true. Our once noble King Congress has grown weak and cowardly. Once he cared for his subjects, but now he languishes in crass dormancy while his useless son shamefully abuses women as if he had a divine right, and foolishly spends money like a profligate—playing that new game called 'golp'…" The rustic was unsure.

"Methinks it's called golf, and you are right. Our Evil Braggart Prince tells everyone that he can fill eighteen holes in one afternoon."

"When he's king, we'll call him 'Your High-Ass,'" said the rustic laughing, berry juice streaming from the corners of his mouth. Everyone laughed. Throughout Kingdom Insania, everyone laughed to mask the pain of such an offensive sovereign. Their laughter echoed from the Mountains of Learning to the deep dark depths of the Forest Bannon. The Evil Prince had become the Kingdom of Insania's most moronic joke from the first moment he opened his mouth. The Evil Prince was a monosyllabic wonder.

The gossip reaching the shores of Insania from the Kingdom of Common Sense confirmed the impossibility of changing the Evil Prince. The Common Sensors, as the good folks from that fair kingdom were known, proclaimed, "You can't fix stupid." Even the folk from the southern regions of that fair kingdom agreed, saying, "No puedes arreglar estupido." You can't fix stupid.

Although they lived in the kingdom ruled by this empty-headed, spendthrift tyrant, Papa Bear and Mama Bear never let the kingdom's marital restrictions affect their love for one another, and their first born was a lovely brindle bear. They named him Baby Bear.

Years ago, when fairy tales were first written, Papa Bear would have spent his days gathering food for his ursine family and Mama Bear would have spent her days cooking and cleaning and tending to Baby Bear. But this a modern fairy tale. While it is true that Trump Castle was still run like the fairy tales of old, here in the deep woods of the Forest Bannon, duties were shared.

That's because Papa Bear and Mama Bear had heard all the stories from the Kingdom of Common Sense in which women were equal to men. They took them to heart.

The Evil Prince of Orange, of course, had heard all those stories, too, and said they were "Rubbish. Those Common Sense stories are rubbish," he said as he ate his Big Mac and slurped his diet Coke. "Women's equality is another lie. Tremendous lie. No one believes women are equal. How could they be? They're women. Women would have to be men to be equal. And they're not. Most of them anyway." He turned to his servant. "Get me another bottle of diet Coke." He took a swig, wiped his mouth with the back of his incredibly tiny hand, and insisted, "These Common Sense people should go back to that imaginary place they came from."

Once again, the Evil Prince's denial of the existence of something that everyone else knew actually existed didn't stop the Bear family from living and loving as they chose. There in the woods they thrived, helping one another, being kind to one another.

Then one day, everything changed. On this day, all the morning chores had been completed. Dishes done. Clothes cleaned. Sweaters swung on the clothesline beneath the soft shimmering shafts of sunshine. Baby Bear's spelling lesson on the words *nasty, nefarious*, and *numbskull* had concluded with a crayon rendering of the Evil Prince that hung irreverently on the refrigerator. Mama Bear's delicious vegetarian stew simmered slowly on the stove. For dessert, she planned picking pocketsful of plump beautiful boysenberries that grew in bunches by the burbling brook.

"Okay, everyone. Papa Bear. Baby Bear. We're picking beautiful berries for dessert. So out we go. My slowly simmering stew will be ready when we return."

And off they went, beneath the beautiful blue sky alive with birdsong and puffy clouds to pick a bounty of beautiful berries.

Meanwhile back at Castle Trump, Orange Trump, bastard brother of the Evil Prince of Orange—who, rumor has it, was also reputed to be a bastard—left the castle in a huff. His sister-in-law, Mel, from the hostile Kingdom of Rush-here-n-there, had told Little O—that's what everyone called him, Little O—that he had to find a job if he wanted to remain in the castle. As they stood in the Offal Office, the Evil Prince agreed.

"I reopened the coal mines, Little O," said the Evil Prince to his bastard brother. "Just for you. For you. That was a big deal. Very big deal. Everyone said it was a big deal."

"But I don't want to be a miner," whined Little O. "It's a dirty job. Awful dirty. Too dirty."

"Take a bath in the river," said the Evil Prince. "After all, it does wonders for the berries."

"But miners get sick. They get black lung disease. If I get that I'll have a pre-existing condition. And then I won't be able to get health insurance."

The Evil Prince grew angry. "Nobody in the kingdom has health insurance, you nitwit. Nobody. And do you want to know why?"

Little O shrank from his shouting brother and meekly asked, "Why?"

"Because life is a pre-existing condition," the Evil Prince screamed. "Life. If you're alive, you'll probably end up dead. I'm pretty sure that's true. Anyway, that's what my advisors tell me. So nobody has health insurance. Besides, everyone has to die from something."

"But what about you?" Little O asked fearfully.

"Me? Me? I'm different. The rules don't apply to me. Everyone knows that. Ask anyone."

"What about me getting a job rebuilding the infrastructure?"

"Not gonna happen."

"Why not?"

"'Cause I've eliminated all taxes. No taxes, no jobs. Everyone wants to see my tax returns. Everyone. But I'm the Prince, so the rules don't apply. But who listens? Nobody. Nobody listens. So I figured: Easy problem, right? No taxes, no tax returns. Problem solved."

"But what about fixing and repairing our bridges and roads? What about maintaining the wall at the foot of the Mountains of Learning? What about the Berry Defense Brigade who have bravely battled the bold, brazen and barbaric attacks of the Rush-here-n-therians on our beautiful berries?

"Well, something had to go, and I decided it would be tax returns. I can't be bothered by any problems that my solution causes."

Little O's frustration had reached critical mass. He turned, seething at his bastard brother, the Evil Prince. "You're really stupid, brother. Really stupid."

"Wrong," said the Evil Prince. "Really wrong. I'm rich. If you're rich, you can't be stupid. So I'm smart. Everyone tells me I'm smart. I'm, like, a really smart guy."

At that moment, Little O discovered the straw that broke the camel's back. He ran from the castle, ran across the drawbridge, ran along the steaming River Excrement, and ran and ran and ran. He didn't stop until he'd reached the deepest part of the Forest Bannon.

Sunlight filtered through the dense foliage. Completely out of breath, Little O sat on a large rock. Never in his life had he ever been in this part of the kingdom. Only once had he ever traveled to the Kingdom of Rush-here-n-there, and that was when he'd gone with his bastard brother to negotiate an uneasy peace with the kingdom that coveted Insania's beautiful berries—Insania's principal crop. The Evil Prince had bargained away a large part of his country's main product in return for the hand of Princess Mel. It was a bad deal from the beginning.

It was not lost on the Insanians that the Prince, who hated and banned immigrants, was now married to one.

———◆———

But let's return to Little O sitting on the rock.

Apparently, out of breath and exhausted, Little O had wandered even deeper into the Forest Bannon, despairing of ever finding his way back. Just as he was about to cry out in woe, he saw a small cottage in a small clearing illuminated by a small shaft of sunlight. A small hope began to bloom in his small soul, and he knocked on the door.

No one answered. He walked around back and saw the sweaters swinging and smelled the succulent stew simmering on the stove. "Someone must be home," he said to himself.

Little O opened the back door and went inside. "Hello," he called out. "Anyone home?"

Not being the savvy savant like his bastard brother the Evil Prince, he was seduced by the succulent smell of simmering stew and realized that he was hugely hungry. He searched for a bowl in the quaint kitchen. The first bowl he found was a voluminous vessel of vivid violet...and very heavy.

That bowl is too large, he thought to himself. *Besides, if I filled that bowl, I'd need a doggie bag before I left. And I don't have a doggie.*

He pulled out the big bowl and found a second bowl, clearly smaller. He held it up to the light. Pretty, and pink perhaps, but puny.

This bowl is too small, Little O thought as he put it down. *It would hardly alleviate my agonizing appetite.*

Then he found it. The perfect size. A little boy's blue bowl impossibly perfect for quenching his quickening hunger.

This bowl is just right, he thought, and he filled it with the simmering succulent stew.

But simmering stew is hot.

His dead mother's caveats, "Never touch hot things," and "Think before you act," had never been his forte...nor his brother's.

"Hot, hot, hot," he cried as he dropped the impossibly perfect bowl as soon as he'd picked it up.

"Hot, hot, hot," he shrilly shouted as the boy's blue bowl shattered, splashing the succulent stew across the stone floor.

That's not good, he thought. *A broken bowl and burned fingers. Not good at all. And me without health insurance. I need to sit down.*

Little O walked out of the kitchen into the living room. *I need to sit and rest*, he thought as he surveyed the trio of chairs gathered around the homey hearth. The first chair required climbing.

That chair is too tall, he thought as he pulled it around. Yes, it was soft, but he reminded himself, *If I fall fast from fluffy furniture, I'm bound to break some bones on the bare floor. I don't want to add broken bones to burned fingers.* He wondered if there might be an emergency room close by or if there were any good roads to get him to one if necessary. Such thoughts interrupted him only for the briefest of moments.

The second chair drawn up to the hearth was much shorter. Much shorter. He jumped up a moment after sitting down.

This little chair is just too short, I need something with back support, he thought.

The chair closest to the hearth seemed best. It rocked. No really, it rocked.

This chair is just right, he thought and he climbed aboard. And Little O rocked, and rocked, and rocked, and rocked. And he fell over backwards bashing his balding head on the cold, hard stone floor as the rocking chair crumbled and would rock no more.

A woozy Little O awoke. *Now I am dizzy, now I am doomed. I broke the bowl, I broke the chair. Are these things I broke beyond repair?* But thoughts of repair surrendered to a growing headache. *Perhaps I should sleep.*

He waveringly wandered up the stairs to the bare bear bedroom.

Three beds, he thought, *I'll try them all.*

Barely bouncing from bed to bed, Little O hoped to lay his head. He thought, *The big bed's too hard, the small bed's a fright, but this third bed is best, and proving just right.* He settled in, pulled up the covers and fell fast asleep.

Moments after Little O nodded off, Papa Bear, Mama Bear, and Baby Bear returned with buckets of beautiful berries.

"Who left the back door open?" asked Papa Bear.

"Not me," said Baby Bear.

"Not me," said Mama Bear.

"Not me does quite a bit around this house, doesn't he?" said Papa Bear laughing.

The laughing stopped as soon as they entered the kitchen. Papa Bear saw that someone had taken his bowl out of the cabinet.

"Someone's been touching my bowl," he said.

Mama Bear saw her pink bowl on the counter. "And someone's been touching my bowl," she said.

Baby Bear's nose led him around the counter and he saw pieces of his beautiful blue bowl scattered on the stone floor. "And someone's been using my bowl and now it's smashed into pieces along with Mama's succulent stew. What a mess."

"Who could have done this?" asked Mama Bear.

"Could be a wolf or an evil witch," said Baby Bear. "After all this is a fairy tale."

"Yes, but it's not *that* fairy tale," Papa Bear said. "So there has to be another reason. Let's look around. Maybe someone left a note."

They went into the living room. Papa Bear's chair, always facing the homey hearth, had been moved. "Someone has moved my chair," he said

"And someone sat in my chair. Look, there's the impression of a bony rear end," said Mama Bear. "Who here has a bony rear?"

"Not me," laughed Papa and Baby Bear in unison.

But then all laughter stopped. Yes, Papa and Mama Bear were upset by this mysterious and unexplained intrusion, but poor Baby Bear was devastated. "I can't say how, I can't say where, but some awful someone smashed my chair. My lovely rocker that Papa built me is now in pieces…let's find who's guilty."

They looked around the full first floor then went upstairs to the bedroom door. They heard some snoring from Baby Bear's bed, and the thought of entering the room filled them all with dread. They lined up behind Papa Bear's broad shoulders and burst through the door. Papa Bear brandished a candle holder.

Little O snoozed soundly, he was out like a light. But Baby Bear wanted him to make things right. Baby Bear shook him, "Get out of my bed. You can't sleep here," Baby Bear said.

Little O jumped up, he'd heard all about bears, and now he was surrounded and it raised all his fears. "I'm really sorry," he stammered, as he backed down the stairs, then he ran out the door without making repairs. He ran and he ran—lots of running this day—till he ran to the river…and was sadly swept away.

The kingdom officially listed Little O as missing.

"I guess he's gone," Mama Bear calmly noted.

"Good riddance," said Papa Bear. Then Papa Bear turned to comfort Baby Bear. "Don't worry Baby Bear, I'll build you a new chair, one that rocks for my fast growing bear."

"Anyone hungry?" asked chef Mama Bear. "Cause if you are, we have some stew we can share."

The bears lived happily ever after, as bears do.

———◆———

Here is where traditional fairy tales end. With unruly rulers still ruling and subjected subjects still subjected. But this is a modern fairy tale, and modern fairy tales require resolution. No reasonable reader would rally to the reality of a rotten ruler treating his subjects like trash. And while I would like to say that the peasants and the woodland folk from the Forest Bannon rose up and seized control of the kingdom when Insania's Berry Defense Brigade disbanded because the kingdom abandoned its tax base and could no longer pay—I can't. That would be an alternative fact.

I would like to say that the fair folk from the Kingdom of Common Sense, armed with good intentions, competent tax policies, and healthcare insurance, sailed across the Sea of Knowledge and descended upon Insania from the Mountains of Learning, unimpeded by a decaying, unguarded wall. But I can't.

That would also be an alternative fact.

What happened, shortly after the untimely disappearance of Little O, was the colossal collapse of Castle Trump. The Evil Prince of Orange's no tax/no maintenance policy proved to be a catastrophically careless calculation for the kingdom's castle, boldly but brainlessly built above the fetid flow of the River Excrement. The collapse happened suddenly, while the Evil Prince was signing an executive order rescinding rules regulating the registration and sale of longbows to the mentally defective. The Evil Prince and all his rowdy, unreasoning retinue were hoisting a glass of beautiful berry bubbly, literally laughing about his subjects' abject stupidity, when he and his audience all, unfailingly fell, flailing and flinging and flying, you know, as they splished and they splashed to the rank river below. While their fate is unknown, it is now taught in university that they all drowned before reaching the vast Sea of Knowledge.

Common Sensors, waiting and watching from the Mountains of Learning, sent a quick rescue party, a squad quite discerning. When they arrived at the banks of the River Excrement as they were tasked to do, they realized that some people are simply beyond rescue. Those wily wise words, "Some people are beyond rescue," were words that Insanians soon found to be true. The Evil Prince and his rotten, wretched retainers were all beyond rescue.

"Some people are simply beyond rescue" quickly became an apt corollary to "You can't fix stupid."

Sometimes the truth is really scary, helping us all to be cautiously wary.

There's still a sign posted by the crumbling wall, a crumbling wall that once stood ever so tall. It was once a dastardly, daunting, impenetrable fence, keeping immigrants from crossing from the realm of Common Sense…to the Kingdom of Insania. Anyone from the realm of Common Sense was banned. Blocked. Forbidden. The Common Sense sign tells a simple truth that was hidden—from Insanians.

When Stupid Stops, Happiness Happens

Here Endeth the Tale

Solum Optimis Verbis

Trump, the Ignorant & Unqualified

Week 1 / January 20 – 28, 2017

What happens when you combine inexperience, ignorance, incompetence, and arrogance? You get the Trump presidency.

What happens when you combine a complete lack of historical perspective, a failure to grasp the US Constitution, a total absence of core beliefs, values, ethics, empathy, or decency with a monstrous *id* fed by a lifetime of privilege? You get Donald Trump.

I've been in a mental funk since the election, and that funk deepened when Trump took the oath of office. To be blunt, administering an oath to a man with neither values nor ethics is the definition of a fool's errand. Does anyone really expect him to live up to that oath? And should he break it—which I believe he already has in colluding with our enemy, i.e. Russia—will there be any consequences except the dissolution of our democracy?

I don't have the answers to my questions, but I plan to chronicle the man's efforts to dismantle and/or undermine the good of the American people, combining brief synopsis from the news with my personal editorial commentary. The weekly list is not meant to be comprehensive or exhaustive, but indicative of the careless, foolish, thoughtless, heartless, ignorant, stupid, and dangerous actions and words of our new president.

Re: Attendance at Trump's Inaugural

It has been reported—and verified via photographic evidence—that somewhere between 300,000 and 600,000 people showed up on the Washington Mall on Inauguration Day. Donald Trump insists his crowd numbers were record-breaking despite the fact that Bill Clinton had 800,000 in 1993 and Barak Obama attracted 1.8 million in January 2009.

Donald Trump disputes the evidence—and the evidence is based on facts, not opinion. Trump is asking, "Who are you going to believe? Me? Or your own eyes?" He insists the media is lying when, in fact, the only liar is him. Lying is part of his *modus operandi*. Curiously, he lies about things that are easily and immediately disprovable, as well as about things that are of no particular consequence.

WRITER'S NOTE:
Despite what Kellyanne Conway asserted this week, there are no such things as "alternative facts." Alternative facts are lies. One example might help.

FACT: Trump University was a scam operation intended to bilk people out of their money.
ALTERNATIVE FACT: Trump University was an educational institution.

Re: Trump's Inaugural Speech

In the same lying vein mentioned above, Trump used an "American carnage" theme in his inaugural address. His speech, while mercifully brief, was dark, uniformed, and betrayed exactly how unready he is to be America's chief executive. Some facts:

1. We still have a functioning economy because Barack Obama and the Democrats rescued it from the brink when he took office in 2009.

2. The Dow Jones is over 20,000. It hit 19,885 under Obama—climbing from 7,550.
3. Unemployment, that skyrocketed under Bush and climbed to 10% in October 2009, is down. [It was 5.5% as Obama left.] It may not be what everyone wants it to be, but it is down by every measure available.
4. Manufacturing is gone because lower manufacturing labor costs and equally lower environmental concerns make other countries more attractive. Even Trump manufactures his brand-name items in other countries. It's not part of some liberal conspiracy. So how do we ensure living wages and clean air and water in the US? Those are the questions that Trump should be asking. But he ends up with the wrong answers because he asks the wrong questions.
5. So where were the inspirational words? The words of hope? The belief that Americans can—through the good offices of their government—achieve something good together for all its citizens? Oh, I forgot. That's what I believe, not Trump. Trump thinks were all chumps. Unless we agree with him... then we are all useful chumps.

Re: Climate Change Policy

If you were worried about climate change, good news: According to the White House, it more or less doesn't exist. The new White House website was recently scrubbed of any mention of climate change, and as of publication, there are still zero search results on the site for the term.

WRITER'S NOTE:

I sincerely hope the climate deniers have a new planetary address in mind so we can migrate to our new digs when their foolishness has made our current home uninhabitable.

Re: EPA Policy

On Monday, the Trump administration ordered the EPA to freeze all grants and cease public communications. Apparently the future is in burning hydrocarbons and the almost laughable—if it weren't so potentially tragic—belief that oil and coal are our friends. It may have been good for Neanderthals, but if we keep doing what we are doing, we shall follow the Neanderthals into extinction. Unlike Neanderthal man, however, we could actually do things to forestall or prevent our own extinction if the climate deniers would only pull their collective heads out of their collective asses.

Re: Healthcare Policy

Trump insists he wants "insurance for everybody." Those are his words on January 17, 2017. This seems to be in conflict with the Republicans' repeated efforts to dismantle Obamacare. The truth is this. Obamacare, as implemented, is virtually indistinguishable from the Republican-supported Massachusetts healthcare bill that passed when Mitt Romney was governor. The reason Republicans want to repeal Obamacare is because they are racists and don't approve anything that Obama achieved, even if it's good for the American people.

Re: Economic Policy

Trump asserts he wants to rebuild the military, rebuild infrastructure, and lower taxes. For a man who pays NO federal income tax, he's pretty free with our money, and more than generous to his wealthy friends who will 1) get the business contracts while 2) paying lower taxes themselves.

WRITER'S NOTE:

Of course, if the infrastructure comes with tolls everywhere, we'll lose twice. We'll pay to build, and we'll pay to use. What a guy!

Even Nobel Prize winning economist Paul Krugman says what Trump proposes is "dangerous idiocy."

Re: The Wall
Trump keeps saying that "Mexico will pay for the wall. We'll build it, and Mexico will pay for it." Mexico's president Nieto disagrees, and cancelled his US trip to emphasize his "No." Of course, Trump decided that if Mexico didn't pay for the wall directly, he would impose a 20% tariff on Mexican imports, failing to realize that the WTO and various trade agreements don't permit him to unilaterally do that. BUT…even if Trump could impose the tariff, the higher costs created by the tariff wouldn't be paid by Mexico, but by American consumers when they buy the Mexican goods. I wonder how American people will feel when they realize that any wall will be paid for by us—when so many other items demand our attention.

Re: Immigration Policy
Trump banned immigrants from seven countries—Iran, Iraq, Libya, Somalia, Sudan, Syria, and Yemen. He wants to keep all Americans safe. Let's be clear. None of these countries has ever terrorized the USA. This is just the "legal" way for Trump to violate our own First Amendment, i.e. to ban Muslims. Now if he'd banned Saudi Arabians [15], Lebanese [1], Egyptians [1], or immigrants from United Arab Emirates [2]—the countries of origin of the nineteen 9/11 terrorists—that might have made sense. But the Trump immigration ban is an exercise in bigotry, not safety.

Conclusion:
Week 1 ended with Trump demonstrating his wholesale ignorance of virtually everything. I believe him to be a clear and present danger.

Solum Optimis Verbis

Let the Autocracy Begin

Week 2 / January 29 – February 4, 2017

Re: The Muslim Ban
Well, there it is—a Muslim ban done in our name. We are now officially a nation of Bigots.

Re: Military Adventurism
In what an official said was the first military raid carried out under President Donald Trump, two Americans were killed in Yemen on Sunday — one a member of SEAL Team 6, Chief Petty Officer William Owens, and the 8-year-old daughter of Anwar al-Awlaki, the New Mexico-born al Qaeda leader who himself was killed in a U.S. strike five years ago. [from NBC News]

WRITER'S NOTE:
Donald Trump doesn't care who dies. The electorate gave this unthinking braggart the world's most potent army. The words "unthinking" and "potent army" should never appear in the same sentence, but here, in the administration's second week, they are yoked together beneath the banner of our Bigot-in-Chief Donald Trump.

Re: Problems with Failing to Tell the Truth
Because the Commander-in Chief is a known liar—about both minor and major facts—it is hard to accept anything asserted about

the military mission at face value. Therefore, let me offer segments of the NBC News article.

> *The death toll [in the Yemeni raid conducted by Seal Team 6 mentioned above] varies according to the sourcing, with the Pentagon saying 14 militants died, along with "numerous" civilians. Nasser al-Awlaki said Yemenis were circulating a body count of combatants and civilians as high as 59.*

That's some discrepancy. Moreover, Trump's assertion that the families of terrorists should also be killed [December 3, 2015] looks especially bad when US soldiers actually begin doing just that.

> *Yemeni Nasser al-Awlaki also said, "They [the SEALs] entered another house and killed everybody in it, including all the women. They burned the house. There is an assumption there was a woman [in the house] from Saudi Arabia who was with al Qaeda. All we know is that she was a children's teacher."*

Trump, a man who champions the big lie, seems blithely unaware that perception—not reality—drives foreign policy. The paragraph above, suggesting senseless killing, when coupled with Trump's recent ban on Yemeni and Iraqi passport holders, will only swell the ranks of America's enemies. So we must ask: Is Trump stupid or careless…or evil? Or all of the above? His failure to act with integrity or humanity will have grim consequences.

> *Intentional or not…the deaths of three al-Awlaki family members will enhance the al Qaeda narrative. She noted that as part of propaganda efforts, terrorist groups have begun to circulate photographs of children reputedly killed*

by U.S. forces. Photos of Nawar al-Awlaki alive and dead are already circulating widely in Arab media. Al Qaeda in the Arabian Peninsula released a statement via online jihadi media referring to the raid as a "massacre," saying U.S. troops had fired on women and children "in cold blood," and accused the SEALs of having "no human values."

Re: The Separation of Powers, Checks and Balances, and Religious Bigotry

When have we ever really given thought to the US Constitution and the existence of an independent judiciary? Well, we certainly did this week, didn't we? The Muslim Ban, hastily put into effect without genuine and meaningful consultation with agencies that do this professionally, has had wide-ranging consequences for green-card holders, visa holders, foreign students, foreign workers, and many others. Trump's executive order was ill-conceived and created with a woefully-inadequate-eye toward consequences—just like the raid in Yemen.

Fortunately, a federal judge in Seattle—a justice appointed by George W Bush—issued a temporary stay of the Muslim Ban. This perfectly legal action earned the judge the Twitter wrath of Donald Trump. Someone needs to explain the "separation of powers" to President Trump, and tell him that checks and balances are an integral part of our functioning democracy. Naturally, Trump was offended by the court's brazen interference into his reckless authoritarian order. After all, what does it mean to be president if one cannot be a dictator? Trump, always given to hyperbolic statements and insults in his tweets, called the judge a "so-called judge" and declared that bad guys (whatever that may mean) may be pouring into the US. Trump speaks as if US immigration has no vetting process in place—which we do—and his hyperbole serves his dark vision of the current US so clearly articulated in his inaugural address. Clearly, he believes he is "the only one" who can save us from a wide-spectrum of non-existent threats, including Muslims arriving from nations with no terrorist history in the United States. Trump is truly a Twidiot.

Here's the core issue. Donald Trump wishes to rule, not to lead. Democratic and autocratic may both end in "cratic," but they have nothing else in common. Autocrat Trump's bullying, insulting, lying approach got him into office, and there is no reason to believe that he will change his bullying, insulting, lying approach now that he's been inaugurated. His only core principle is personal gain, and that means he'll say or do anything that will keep him in the seat of power which will assure him additional personal gain.

Like all authoritarians, Trump decides what he wants to do without genuine consideration of whether he could or should do it. And consequences? Consequences are of no consequence. Not to him, anyway. That's frightening.

If life were a clever novel or a good movie, this would be the climactic moment when the bad man is turned back, defeated, or overcome so that good (whatever that means) could prevail. But history shows us that sometimes evil wins. We feel it shouldn't, but it does. Ask the American Indian. Ask the Germans under Hitler. Ask the Russians under Stalin or the Chinese under Mao.

And we shouldn't smugly think that "We are a representative democracy. It can't happen here." Because it has. Just how awful it may become is yet to be seen. Numerous questions occur to me:

1. What happens to America—the trusted, reliable partner in NATO, the Geneva Convention, and trade agreements—when it becomes an untrustworthy, unreliable, rogue nation?
2. What happens to the America that asks "Give me your tired, your poor, your huddled masses yearning to breathe free?"

3. What happens when America's president blatantly insults the leaders of our friends and allies?
4. What happens when America restricts minority voting rights?
5. What happens when America's growing white supremacy movement has the president's ear?
6. What are the consequences of a seemingly endless stream of lies ushering from the White House—the president and his minions?
7. What happens when our chief executive is a mindless, ignorant numbskull, thoroughly uninformed with no desire to become informed?
8. What happens when we give the man in #7 the largest military in the world?

There are more questions popping up every day. Disturbing questions. Unsettling questions. One member of my family on the east coast has told me I should take a "chill pill before [I] have a heart attack." Perhaps. But I predict that little good will come from Trump's presidency, and that any good that does arise will be sorely outweighed by the destruction of the genuine American values that we assert we've always had. When he wrecks our world relationships, and destroys the earth's environment, when America's reputation for good things is in tatters, perhaps then the electorate will decided they chose unwisely.

Till then, my only question is: Can we survive him for four years?

Solum Optimis Verbis

Chaos Born of Stupidity

Week 3 / February 5 – February 11, 2017

Now that we've had three weeks—plus the eighteen-month traveling circus called the Trump Campaign—to observe Donald Trump in action, we can conclude certain things about him. None are flattering.

Observation # 1: Trump Wants the Biggest Stage Possible…But Doesn't Understand It.

Trump's a narcissist. Probably a malignant narcissist. That's why he wanted to be president. He has attained the highest office in the United States, and still remains petty and peevish. Someone recently described him as "a sore winner."

Trump is the US president, yet he feels free to insult the leaders of our nation's closest allies. He talks glibly—and carelessly—about other countries acquiring nuclear weapons, abandoning NATO, welching on trade agreements, or banning Muslims. He has no idea what it means to be a responsible president who can look after the reputation of our nation. Worse, he just doesn't know when to keep his mouth shut. His lack of impulse control could well be the death of us all.

Observation # 2: Trump Doesn't Care About the Constitution or American Citizens. The Presidential Gig Is a Game.

The world is now Trump's reality show stage. After all, on a reality show, the producer gets to direct, even create, reality. Let's call it, an "alternative reality." You want a Travel Ban? Go ahead, issue an executive order in the same way you would make a bold declaration on "The Apprentice." You want to change gun regulations so that mentally unstable people can acquire them? Go ahead, issue an executive order. "It's all a game. I get to make the rules. And if there are rules I don't like, those rules don't apply."

Money insulates Trump from any real consequences—even impeachment. "Go ahead, impeach me. I'll just go back to Trump Tower and direct 'The Apprentice.'"

Both the Constitution and the will of the American people are annoyances that others have to reckon with, but not Trump. Reality show folks get to make their own reality. The reason Trump appears to live in a fact-free, alternative universe is because he can. His money has always shielded him from consequences, and that's not likely to change. He doesn't see the world the way most people do, and that's why his tax records reveal virtually no charitable contributions.

Observation # 3: Trump Thrives on Conflict & Chaos

Trump enjoys nothing so much as division. He has zero interest in uniting people, and it is amazing that pundits and commentators seem to be continually amazed that he hasn't "reached out." These are the same people who expected Trump to somehow become "presidential." It's not going to happen. One cannot expect kindness nor decency nor civility from a man who does not possess those qualities. Insulting people is Trump's habitual, ingrained response. He did it to his fellow Republican candidates, to federal judges, to department stores like Nordstrom, and of course, to Hilary Clinton.

I predict an exhausting four years ahead, because Trump does not want things to calm down. His television mentality tells him that conflict is dramatic and garners him the attention that he so desperately wants. [See #1] Peace and quiet are dull and boring.

Observation # 4: Trump Doesn't Care If He Wins or Loses, Because He Always Wins…or So He Says.

A few examples will help here.

1. Trump did indeed win the Electoral College, but he also lost the popular vote by more than 2.8 million votes. Let me reiterate: Trump LOST the popular vote. To hear him tell it, however, he won the popular vote because millions of fraudulent votes were cast against him, and that accounts for that 2.8 million. He has no proof, because no proof exists, but a lack of proof won't stop him. The real truth is that Trump relies heavily on bold lies. And that's how Trump expects to win, even when he loses. Bold, audacious lies will do very nicely, thank you. He'll tell you when he's won. He'll tell you the score—or tell you why the score you believe to be true is wrong. Ironically, Trump could have simply swept aside the popular vote business with a breezy, "It doesn't matter. I won the Electoral College." But he couldn't do that. He has to declare victory even when he loses.
2. Trump's inaugural crowd, by every objective measure, including the eye of the camera, was relatively small. However, Trump disagrees. "Don't believe your eyes," he insists. "Believe me. I'll tell you when I'm winning. And I won on inauguration day when the largest crowd ever showed up to watch me." Really? Trump has no use for facts—except alternative facts. Worse, Trump has no use for the truth.

WRITER'S NOTE: Whole pages could be filled with his lies.

1. "The murder rate in America is the highest it's been in decades." Lie.
2. "Bad people are pouring across our borders." Another Lie.
3. "My people are in Hawaii looking at Obama's birth papers, and you'd be surprised what they've found." A Truly Audacious Lie.
4. Trump University wants students to succeed. A Lie & a Scam.
5. "I never settle." (Referring to legal entanglements.) Demonstrable Lie.

(Is there a need to continue?)

Observation # 5: Trump's Criticisms Are Really Reflections in the Mirror.

When Trump calls someone a liar—"Lyin' Hillary," "Lyin' Ted"—you can be assured that he is speaking of himself. Trump is the liar. When Trump castigates Jeb Bush as "low energy," rest assured that is because he, himself, is low energy…aka Trump the Slug, a man who is intellectually lazy. When Trump asserts that the nominating process is rigged, you can trust that it is…and no one knows that better than Trump. If you don't believe me, ask the Russians. Accusations or slurs made by Trump invariably are reflections of the man who so blithely casts aspersions on others.

Observation # 6: Trump Is Stupid: Part I

Naturally, that is not the image Trump has of himself, but his tweets speak volumes about his empty-headedness, his poor vocabulary, his bullying technique, his lack of information, and his pettiness. He uses the bully of bluster because he lacks the power of information. When I coached high school debate, we used to joke that "If you can't dazzle them with brilliance, baffle them with bullshit." Baffling people with BS is Trump's *modus operandi*. He relies on BS because he lacks knowledge, a problem exacerbated by his twin habits: incessant television watching and his failure to read. Any man who has to continually declare "I know words. I have the best words," [December 30, 2015] or that he's a smart person [December 11, 2016] or that he once humbly declared that he "is one of the smartest people anywhere in the world" [July 21, 2016] is probably a man of limited vocabulary and intelligence.

Observation # 7: Trump Is Stupid: Part 2 / Trump Surrounds Himself with People Who Are As Inept As He Is.

A smart person would surround himself with the best and the brightest. [See #6] But not Trump. He's decided to:

1. Appoint Jeff Sessions, a bigot with a record of bigotry, as Attorney General.
2. Appoint billionaire Betsy DeVos, a know-nothing when it comes to public education, as Secretary of Education.
3. Select Steve "I-Have-Never-Found-a-Conspiracy-I-Didn't-Like" Bannon, former head of Breitbart "Fake-News" News as a chief advisor.
4. Select Kellyanne Conway as an advisor despite the fact that she not only believes that alternative facts are facts—they are lies, not facts—but that she creates new ones out of whole cloth, e.g. the truly exciting, though non-existent, Bowling Green Massacre. That's right Kelleyanne talked about a non-existent incident in *Cosmo*.

I could, and will, detail more about Trump's cabinet choices in the future, but for now we should agree that he has chosen people ill-suited to serve the interests of the American people. They serve only his narrow, money-making, bigoted, short-sighted interests. As I said, it will be a long four years.

Solum Optimis Verbis

Russia's Best Friend

Week 4 / February 4 – February 11, 2017

A Hypothetical Scenario

I am about to take a casual walk down a conspiratorial path. Normally, I resist such journeys because they usually dead end in a dark wood where no light shines. In contrast, I think my stroll will end up in a place where the light may prove unbearable. So…

One of the more puzzling aspects of Trump's presidential campaign was—is?—his on-going, inexplicable "love affair" with Russia and Vladimir Putin. As historically ignorant and chronically uninformed as Trump appears to be about so many things—and who would question Trump's extraordinary inexperience and ineptitude in the foreign relations arena?—why would Trump speak so positively about a country that has been our traditional adversary since the end of World War II? More than that, in the face of Russian military adventurism in the Crimea and the Ukraine over the last decade, why would Trump advocate cozying up to an authoritarian regime like Putin's Russia?

Not only should we ask why Donald Trump would want rapprochement with Russia or why he would be so complimentary of Putin, we need to flip the equation and ask why Putin would be so complimentary of Trump or why Russia would fail to retaliate when Obama imposed increased sanctions on Russia on December 29, 2016?

Some have suggested that Russia appeals to Trump's own authoritarian inclinations. Some have suggested it may be because Russia could help him get elected. Perhaps both those motivations apply, but I'd like to suggest a stronger, more compelling reason for the Trump/Putin connection: Money.

Those investigating corruption counsel their investigative teams to "follow the money." That's because most corruption erupts when personal gain—aka greed—is the motivating force. That's precisely what I am suggesting. Additionally, corruption moves easily along an unimpeded path when the greedy interests of all the partners align.

Let's agree to a few statements. Donald Trump is greedy. His desire to scam, bilk, and bamboozle people out of their money through the use of the Trump name—even when it's involved in shady real estate deals, and fake universities—attests to his own personal greed. His lack of charitable giving and his failure—perhaps legal, perhaps not—to pay his fair share of federal taxes all indicate that greed calls the tune. The same is true of Putin—an oligarch with his greedy, dictatorial fingers in every money-making enterprise in Russia. The man who used to be the "Kremlin's banker," Sergei Pugachev, says that as long the Russian president Vladimir Putin remains in power, he's the richest person in the world.

There is a third member of this conspiracy of greed—a person whose interests in money and Russia align absolutely with Donald Trump and Vladimir Putin's interests: former *Exxon Mobil's* CEO, Rex Tillerson.

Here is the chronology:

APRIL 16, 2012: *Exxon Mobil,* under CEO Rex Tillerson, enters into an agreement with *Rosneft*—the Russian Oil giant—to drill for oil in the Arctic for which Tillerson received the Russian Order of Friendship. Drilling there is enormously expensive, but the financial rewards will be outrageous.

APRIL 2014: After Russia seizes the Crimea and threatens the Ukraine, US sanctions are leveled against Russia. This negatively affects Putin, and it doesn't do *Exxon Mobil*—and Rex Tillerson—any good either.

JUNE 2015: Trump announces for the presidency. As long as the US maintains sanctions against Russia, the huge, anticipated profits from *Exxon Mobil's* investment in Russian oil will be essentially unavailable. Moreover, Tillerson opposes and undermines the sanctions.

JUNE 2015 and FEBRUARY 2017: Sometime during Trump's nomination campaign and his actually being nominated, Tillerson and Putin see that their mutually aligned economic interests will best be served if Donald Trump becomes the 45th President of the United States. They believe that Trump's own greed-driven, financial aspirations might also be served. With this prospect in mind, Trump's on-going commentary about Russia and Putin is invariably favorable. Russian intelligence undertakes a secret cyber campaign to sow sufficient doubt about Hillary Clinton. There doesn't have to be anything "real" because the objective is to create doubt and make the electorate unsure. No American fingerprints would appear on the operation.

Once elected, Trump's administration installs Tillerson as Secretary of State—a reward for his successful role as go-between on Trump's behalf—advocates the lifting of the punitive financial sanctions, and voila, all conspirators will be considerably wealthier than they were previously. We are talking billions of dollars for each of the three principle players here: Putin, Tillerson, and Trump. Keep in mind: Corruption works best when the interests of all the principles—in this case, greed—are mutually served. That's precisely what has happened here.

How have things worked out? So far, so good. Trump has been

elected. Tillerson is Secretary of State. And while the sanctions have not yet been lifted, don't hold your breath…not when billions of dollars await.

Is what I am hypothesizing true? I don't know. But it sounds possible…even plausible. Shouldn't we find out? As I said, greed calls the tune, and now the rest of us are expected to dance. My feet are tired already.

Solum Optimis Verbis

Pledging Allegiance

Week 5 / February 19 – 25, 2017

Trump talks a great deal about unity. I want to congratulate him. That is the one thing he has genuinely achieved so far. In so many ways, he has united Democrats and many Independents by implementing policies that betray both the Progressive agenda and good old American decency.

My wife and I attended the *Amazing Invisible Reichert Rally [AIRR]* in Issaquah, Washington, yesterday [February 22, 2017]. Dave Reichert, our 8th Congressional District representative, has decided he doesn't want to host town halls because he's afraid that people will yell at him. He's right about that. People want to yell at him because he's spineless and unwilling to speak out against injustice or harm. Make no mistake, Reichert is a Republican lapdog, enjoying a cushy job without breaking a sweat or entertaining a moment of independent thought. He's a coward.

Yes, Trump talks incessantly about unity—even though he doesn't understand the concept nor how to bring people together. On Friday, at the CPAC conference, *He said allegiance to the United States is the one thing that brings the entire country together [Washington Examiner, February 24, 2017]*

But it's all talk. Empty rhetoric. I have decided to take Rachel Maddow's advice *[MSNBC]* and turn off the sound and simply watch what is happening. And what is happening is very disturbing. Trump wants to remake America in his own myopic, bigoted image.

I have decided I cannot pledge allegiance to an America that has lost both its moral compass and its claim to be a beacon of freedom to the rest of the world. I pledge resistance not allegiance. My resistance begins by sitting during the National Anthem and the pledge of allegiance. My constitution gives me that right and I claim it. Here's why:

I won't pledge allegiance to a country led by a man who has proven time and again that he is a bigot. Choose your ethnic group—Mexicans, Muslims, Jews, African-Americans—and you'll find a tweet or a comment that betrays his administration's view. It's bigoted, heartless, and thoughtless. Trump and Jeff Sessions, our racist Attorney General, may want to live back in the 80s—that's 1880, not 1980—but I don't.

I won't pledge allegiance to a country led by a man who believes in corporate elitism. Already he has begun rescinding EPA rules curtailing pollution of our air and water because various industries want the freedom to pollute our planet in the name of greater profits. This is our environment—the air we breathe; the water we drink. When clean air and water are gone, we will be, too.

I won't pledge allegiance to a country led by a man who suffers from extraordinary xenophobic myopia. Again, at CPAC, Trump said, *"I'm not representing the globe, I'm representing your country."* [*Washington Examiner, February 24, 2017*] No, he must represent our country as part of a global community. In a satiric vein, let me offer my most articulate Trump-like tweet expressing my view of isolationism.

> *Isolationism is bad. Not good. Very bad. Very bad.*
> *Do we want to be alone? All by ourselves? Do we?*
> *It's sad. Very sad. #LonelyDemocrat*

The advent of the internet, and all its attendant social media avenues, means that we can no longer be isolated. Once again, reality intrudes. Someone should tell Trump that isolationism in not only unwise, it's not possible—unless you live in North Korea.

———◆———

WRITER'S NOTE:
Ironically, I believe Trump is, in his own unique way, isolated. He's demonstrated that he is either isolated or insulated from the world of facts. Consider his bleak assessment of the inner city, or his bloated understanding of the United States' murder rate…his catalog of misinformation and "alternative facts" is incredibly long. Trump's wealth has insulated him from both the world of facts and the world of consequences. That's why he—and so many others—can call something "Reality Television" when it possesses not one scintilla of reality. Insulation is isolation. It appears he wants us to be as mentally isolated as he is.

———◆———

I won't pledge allegiance to a country led by a man who is so amazingly inarticulate—and ignorant and dangerous and narcissistic—that I am actually ashamed to acknowledge that he is our president. I cannot speak for anyone else, but I find him impossible to listen to—or to take seriously, even though I know he's serious. When he's not spewing outright falsehoods, he's arrogantly advancing his own self-image, or saying things that truly display his vast ignorance and thorough lack of information. Everyone should stand up and say: *We have a monumentally stupid president. Sorry.*

Finally, sowing fear to create unity works when there is a common enemy. That's what motivated America during World War II. Afraid of the Nazis and the Japanese, Americans united in a single cause—defeat the enemy, win the war, and win the peace as well. But

Trump is trying to sow fear where there is no genuine threat. We are not threatened by immigrants—legal or illegal. In truth, immigrants take jobs many Americans simply don't want, and immigrants commit fewer crimes than native-born Americans. Consider that former *Florida governor Jeb Bush said...that many who illegally come to the United States do so out of an "act of love" for their families and should be treated differently than people who illegally cross U.S. borders or overstay visas. [Ed O'Keefe, Washington Post, April 6, 2014]*

During the Vietnam War, I objected to the facile but flippant remark, "My country, right or wrong." I believed that comment was misguided then, and I feel the same now. I'll pledge allegiance when I can stop being ashamed to call myself an American living in the Trump autocracy.

Solum Optimis Verbis

The Trump Reality Show

Week 6 / February 26 – March 4, 2017

The Presidency As Reality Show
I hear an endless stream of hopeful comments from pundits and commentators who hope Trump can become a more thoughtful president. *Perhaps today he'll be more presidential,* they say hopefully.

While I believe this is all wishful thinking, I, too, harbor the same hope. If I could have one wish, it would be that Trump cease and desist telling lies and making hyperbolic statements. He slips into lies and hyperbole so often, and with such facility, I wonder if it's pathological. I suspect we've all heard variations of

> *Maybe he'll pivot from the ominous but false 'Obama left me a mess' message to one that is more accurate.*
> OR
> *One can hope that the facts he uses today will be the universally accepted facts which inform and shape our lives. Otherwise, the earth is flat.*

These comments seek to understand Trump, to find out what makes him tick, to be able to determine what policies he will actually pursue.

During the presidential campaign, Trump's party affiliation was endlessly debated, as if correctly identifying his party label—Tea Party Republican? Mainstream Republican? Dixiecrat? Libertarian?—would bring Trump's nature, intentions, and policy inclinations into sharper focus. It wouldn't. It didn't.

I believe we need to observe Trump through an entirely different, non-political lens.

As someone who wears bifocals, I find this metaphor completely apt. Let me illustrate. When my optometrist attempts to find the best lens to correct my vision, he asks me to look through a variety of lenses while saying:

> [Click Lens #1 in place] "Is what you are seeing clearer this way?
> [Click Lens #2 in place] "Or is it clearer this way?

My doctor spends quite a bit of time determining which lens will yield the clearest vision. Correspondingly, I believe the same process—finding the correct lens to bring Trump into sharper focus—is what many of the pundits have failed to find. When they do find the correct lens, they'll finally be able to explain what so many have often found inexplicable.

If you observe Trump as the President of the United States, you are using a political lens—a lens that blurs reality. If, however, you observe Trump as a man playing at being the President of the United States—in the midst of his own, self-produced Reality Show—you are using an entertainment lens. Through the Reality Show lens, Trump's behaviors—from Tweets to Executive Orders to outrageous lies to contradictory pronouncements—will come into sharper focus.

When Is Reality Not Reality?

After Tuesday night's speech before Congress [Feb. 28, 2017], everyone seemed to be excited about Trump's tone. I call that the

"Ask-Me-Nicely" Syndrome. Unfortunately, if you ask someone to do something distasteful with a nice tone of voice, it doesn't change the distasteful task. I heard one commentator explain how pleased he was to hear the change in Trump's tone as if it were somehow a genuine change rather than an apparent one. I wonder why so many people fail to see the ploy—the rank manipulation—that the change is only one of style, not substance. Real change requires much more.

I worry that Trump's administration will continue with its actions, but do it in a less strident voice. Can't you just hear the newer, gentler, kinder approach that the ICE Enforcement folks will employ?

> *Hola, senorita Emilia, that's a lovely dress. Won't you please step into this comfortable government van so we can take you to the local ICE Deportation Center? Watch your head now. You're gonna love Mexico this time of the year. You do speak Spanish, don't you? Have a nice day."*

With Trump, none of it is real. As I've said earlier, the Trump presidency is a reality show. And a reality show is entertainment, NOT reality. Trump's reality—with all its relevant facts—is a construct created anew each day with Trump as its architect. During last night's speech before Congress, he surprised many by adopting a "nice" tone. But his performance was theater, intended to serve the moment. Tomorrow he could easily revert to an authoritarian tone. If needed. Like all good advertisers, Trump will use whatever marketing strategy works, until it doesn't. On the campaign trail last year, Trump declared that women who have abortions need to be punished. Tomorrow? Who knows? He may counsel kindness and forgiveness for the same group. How can Trump change his tune so easily? I can name that tune in one word: *Ratings*.

It's quite simple, really. Trump is a man whose principle desire is to remain the center of attention, which is especially curious when you realize that Trump is a cypher, a man without convictions or beliefs. He stands for nothing except those things that will garner him attention, acclaim, or money. His energies are forever being expended in a never-ending effort to shape a reality that will shine its light on him. And increase his ratings. The brouhaha over the numbers attending the inauguration offers a telling example:

> *Don't trust what you see.*
> [You didn't see a partially empty mall.]
> *Don't trust your own eyes. I will tell you what you are seeing.*
> [You are seeing a mall crowded to overflowing with my well-wishers.]
> *I will tell everyone what is real and what is fake because my reality must be everyone else's reality.*
> [Just listen to Sean Spicer. He knows what's real.]

Here is the bottom line: If you tell a lie in a nicer tone, it doesn't suddenly become a fact. We need to adopt the Gertrude Stein point-of-view:

> *A lie is a lie is a lie is a lie is a lie.*
> OR
> *A fact is a fact is a fact is a fact is a fact.*

Keep in mind, an alternative fact is a lie.

Administrative Caricatures

More than once I have called Trump a Neanderthal. That's because he's a poor example of *homo sapiens* [literally, wise man]. He's unevolved, displaying no capacity for apology or empathy. (My apologies to any Neanderthals insulted by being compared to

Trump.) Curiously, Trump's orange skin tone reminds me of the cave paintings at Lascaux, France. I find it ironic that in a prehistoric horse drawing, sketched in lovely Trump tones by one *homo sapiens* predecessor, its head is small, but the horse's ass is much more prominent. What should we infer from that?

I have a simple question. Has any president's administration been translated into caricature so quickly, and does that tell us anything about the true nature of this less-than-two-month-old presidency? The Trump administration, rife with arrogant incompetence and vast quantities of arrogant ignorance, has been caricatured and lampooned in national newspapers, in tweets, on daily late night TV—Stephen Colbert, Seth Meyers, Trevor Noah—on the weekly shows like Samantha Bee or John Oliver, and on Saturday Night Live. Political leanings aside, every president has been the target of editorial and political cartoonists and comedians, but this administration offers a target-rich environment. It's like a turkey shoot. How could a cartoonist or comedian miss with Kellyanne Conway, Steve Bannon, Steve Miller, Mike Flynn, Betsy DeVos, and others as targets?

We Can Have It All

And finally, I offer an insight from the Reagan years, the era of voodoo economics. The current crop of Republicans will once again try to convince Americans that we can have it all—increased defense spending, massive infrastructure spending, incredible increases in the number of border patrol and ICE agents—and we won't raise taxes, imperil the national budget, or increase the national debt—and we'll be able to do all this and LOWER taxes. The age of miracles is not over.

Solum Optimis Verbis

from The Desk of Your English Teacher

Week 7 / March 5 - 11, 2017

From the Desk of Your English Teacher
That's me. And as everyone knows, English teachers are fond of quotations. So, as I begin this week's journal, I thought of an apt quotation that I'd like to send to the Trump administration. So far they've failed to grasp just what the following quotation means.

> *The secret of happiness is to keep your*
> *mind full and your bowels empty.*
> —the late Leo Buscaglia, Professor,
> *University of Southern California*

As the Trump presidency moves into week seven, the insanity seems to be heightening. Unfounded accusations of wire-tapping leveled at Barack Obama, growing evidence that the Russians played, are playing, and hope to play an on-going role in the current administration, and the anticipation of the "new and improved" Travel Ban, dominate the news.

As I read and watch the news—and the roaring flood of sarcasm from Stephen Colbert, Seth Meyers, Trevor Noah, John Oliver, Samantha Bee, and the cast of SNL—I wonder if I am a skeptical cynic, or a cynical skeptic. Let's turn to the authority on such matters, Noah Webster, who compiled *A Compendious Dictionary of the English Language* in 1806. (Yes, he's dead, but he's still smarter and wiser than Trump. And he has better words.)

Cynic [**sin**-ik], *noun,* plural cynics:
A person who believes that only selfishness motivates human actions and who disbelieves in or minimizes selfless acts or disinterested points of view.

Skeptic [**skep**-tik], *noun,* plural skeptics:
1. *a person who questions the validity or authenticity of something purporting to be factual.*
2. *a person who maintains a doubting attitude, as toward values, plans, statements, or the character of others.*

After due consideration, I think I belong to the cynical skeptic category. Of course, the current administration gives us much to be cynical *and* skeptical about. Without going into detail here, Trump has continually demonstrated that selfishness always motivates him, while he appears to be constitutionally—yes, that's a pun—incapable of telling the truth about anything. When one combines those two character traits—selfishness and pathological lying—one need not wonder how a bigoted, racist southern Senator could be nominated as America's Attorney General. I'll save my wonder for the United States Senate—a heretofore august body whose members have sworn to "support and defend the Constitution of the United States against all enemies, foreign and domestic ~~unless it's the Russians.~~" How could they ever have approved Sessions' nomination and still call themselves men and women of integrity?

And now, it appears Attorney General Jeff ~~Bigot~~…er…Sessions committed perjury during his Senate Confirmation Hearings. That's a felony. I want to see if the old wisdom still holds: *The lie that gets you into office is the lie that will drive you from that office.*

We shall see. If I understand what happened over the weekend, Senator Grassley intends to permit Jeff Sessions an opportunity to un-perjure himself. Something like un-shooting yourself in the foot, I suppose. I didn't know that was possible. Let's see what the Merriam-Webster Dictionary can tell us about Attorney General Jeff Sessions.

Perjury [**pur**-j*uh*-ree], *noun*, plural perjuries. *Law.*
1. *The willful giving of false testimony under oath or affirmation, before a competent tribunal, upon a point material to a legal inquiry.*
2. *False swearing, see Fake News.*
3. *Propagation of alternative facts for personal gain.*
4. *Lies, damned lies, and* ~~statistics~~ *Jeff Sessions.*
5. *A lie told best with a sweet Southern accent—preferably Alabamian.*
6. *A nasty, three-syllable word that, when you rearrange the letters, spells kissyourassgoodbye.*

Recuse [ri-**kyooz**], *verb, transitive,* recused, recusing.
1. *To withdraw from a position of judging so as to avoid any semblance of partiality or bias.*
2. *Running for a dark hiding place hoping the clouds will go away, see Flood, Disaster.*
3. *A word that sounds like "wreck youse" when pronounced with a sweet Southern accent—preferably Alabamian.*

Dullness is the Enemy

Reality Shows thrive in an atmosphere of excitement and mystery. The enemy of good theater is the ordinary and the dull. And Trump loves good theater. What he loves even more is chaos. When turmoil and uncertainty reign, everyone wonders what will happen next. Everyone *worries* about what will happen next. Who can possibly turn away? When things turn chaotic, the first and most important task is to restore order, and that means investigating everything that introduced the chaos. All avenues. Including false ones. So let's expand our vocabulary this week by introducing one of the operating principles upon which Trump and Reality TV depend: the Red Herring.

Red herring [red **her**-ing], *noun*, plural red herrings
1. *smoked herring*
2. *something intended to divert attention from the real problem or matter at hand; a misleading clue.*
3. *a Trump Tweet, Trump is Mr. Red Herring [see example below]*

Terrible! Just found out that Obama had my "wires tapped" in Trump Tower just before the victory. Nothing found. This is McCarthyism! 3:35 AM - 4 Mar 2017

Synonyms: fool's errand, wild-goose chase, false trail, attention-grabber, diversionary tactic

Final Note:
From Paul Krugman, *NY Times*, Monday March 6, 2017
According to Politico, a Trump confidante says that the man in the Oval Office — or more often at Mar-a-Lago — is "tired of everyone thinking his presidency is screwed up."

WRITER'S NOTE:
Not everyone thinks Trump's presidency is screwed up, just those people who are paying attention, and those people who know up from down or right from wrong. Just them.

Solum Optimis Verbis

Chaos Is My First, Last, & Middle Name

Week 8 / March 12 - 18, 2017

This week we begin the annual basketball ritual known as March Madness. Naturally, Trump has upped the ante with Year-Round Insanity, and my guess is that he'll do his best for the next three weeks to steal the headlines from Duke, Kentucky, and Gonzaga—and any other NCAA upstart that might challenge him for air time or print space.

Speaking of madness, isn't it madness to fashion a budget that increases guns while reducing butter? A budget that desires a $50+ billion increase to bolster the world's highest defense budget—exceeding the combined spending of the next eight countries—while cutting the Meals on Wheels program because "it's just not showing any results," according to Mick Mulvaney, Trump's budget director. This assertion is another example of the fact-free universe that Trump and his support staff inhabit. According to a Washington Post article, Meals on Wheels has a terrific track record for doing what it's supposed to be doing: feeding people.

> *A 2013 review of studies, for instance, found that home-delivered meal programs for seniors "significantly improve diet quality, increase nutrient intakes, and reduce food insecurity and nutritional risk among participants. Other*

beneficial outcomes include increased socialization opportunities, improvement in dietary adherence, and higher quality of life."
—Christopher Ingraham, *Washington Post*, March 16, 2017

Mulvaney left the impression that keeping American senior citizens fed is simply not a "result." Like so many other Trump appointees, Mulvaney lies on behalf of his boss.

"Meals on Wheels sounds great," Mulvaney said Thursday, but "to take that federal money and give it to the states and say, 'Look, we want to give you money for programs that don't work'— I can't defend that anymore."
—Christopher Ingraham, *Washington Post*, March 16, 2017

The Meals on Wheels data and statistics tell a story that is 180 degrees different from Mulvaney's assertion. Saying that Meals on Wheels doesn't work is NOT an alternative fact, it is a deliberate, heartless lie. Perhaps almost as heartless as repealing the Affordable Care Act.

Trump's budget also wants to cut "after school programs" that serve more than 2,000,000 kids, the National Endowment for the Arts, the Corporation for Public Broadcasting, and other items that help keep the electorate healthy and informed. All these cuts are predicated on misinformation and justified by lies according to the Los Angeles Daily News, March 16, 2017.

Let's Review

It's easy to get caught up in the chaos that Trump thrives on. But chaos is exhausting, and most of us have lives to live quite apart from Trump's. For the first time in history, we have a social media president. He lives on Twitter, finds incredible reinforcement from his Twidiots, and lives in a fact-free world—or one with manufactured "alternative facts"—separate from almost everyone else. The moniker "blue-collar billionaire," coined during the campaign, was pure invention. Trump hasn't a clue about the real world. Worse, he doesn't care that he doesn't have a clue. He's too busy focusing on himself to learn about the world "out there."

To cut through the noise and the chaos that Trump and his administration create, you'll need to remember four simple maxims that guide our infantile, delusional, greedy president who wants attention...aka, ratings:

A. *It's all about me. [Ratings]*
B. *I want what I want when I want it. [Infantile]*
C. *Whatever I say, that's reality...until I say something different. [Delusion]*
D. *I'm in it for the money. [Greed]*

I offer these four maxims in the spirit of David Henry Thoreau, whose pithiest advice was, "Simplify, simplify." Almost everything that Trump does is a response to one or more of these maxims. Let me offer a few examples:

1. Trump travels almost every weekend to his golf course in Florida. Despite what he said about Obama's profligate spending, Trump has already outspent—in about two months—the annual spending by Obama. He knows he's on the company dime. *[D...Greed]*
2. Obama wire-tapped me. *[A...Ratings; C...Delusion]*
3. The *Meals on Wheels* program because "it's just not showing any results..." *[C...Delusion]*

NOTE: Do you find it as amusing as I do that one of the principle roles given Trump's spokespeople is that of interpreter? Apparently

Trump is incapable of saying what he means, because so many of his spokespeople spend an inordinate amount of time explaining how we all misunderstood or misheard what Trump said, or explain that "he didn't mean that literally." It's as if this self-declared smart person—"I'm, like, a really smart person"[Reported in *The Guardian*, July 12, 2015]—also thinks he has a great vocabulary. "I know words, I have the best words." [Reported in the *Los Angeles Times*, December 6, 2016.] Trump speaks another language which only he understands.

Another Political Vocabulary Lesson
Hyperbole [hī'pər bəlē], *noun*, plural hyperbole
1. *exaggerated statements or claims not meant to be taken literally.*
2. *the modus operandi of all Trump speeches*

Synonyms: exaggeration · overstatement · magnification · embroidery

Trump uses hyperbole whenever he speaks. He can't help himself. Hyperbole is entertaining—far more entertaining than most mundane political statements. The central problem for Trump is that he wants politics to be exciting, even riveting. Trump wants his administration to be the center of attention for four years, maybe eight. Most of us really don't want that. Most of us want politics to be practical—but in the background—so we can get on with our lives. To use an analogy: Trump wants the light switch to spark and scare the hell out of people when they throw the switch. Most of us just want the lights to go on.

Simply, hyperbole is bait for his listening audience. And the more outrageous he becomes, the more attentively people listen. Trump's hyperbole goes from best to worst.

"Obamacare is a complete failure. My health care plan is going to be the greatest ever. It will cover everybody and cost less."

"Biggest crowd ever at my inauguration."

"We must rebuild our depleted military."
[NBC News, 2/6/2017]

"Our inner cities are a disaster. You get shot walking to the store," Trump said. *"They have no education. They have no jobs."* *[The Nation, 11/7/2016]*

"I know words, I have the best words" *[LA Times, 12/6/2016]*

Of course, hyperbole eschews facts because actual facts undermine the statement itself. And when the statement is undermined, one is left with conundrums.

Conundrum [kəˈnən drəm], *noun*, plural conundrums
1. *a confusing and difficult problem or question*
2. *the Republican Party*

Synonyms: problem · difficult question · difficulty · quandary · dilemma
Sentence: Trump is a conundrum and his entire administration are conundrums because they speak out of both sides of their mouths. Adopting two positions at the same time.

1. *Trump says his health care repeal-and-replace plan is better than the ACA—Obamacare—but the Office of Management and Budget, the American Medical Association, AARP, and*

many potentially disenfranchised Americans assert the opposite. That's a conundrum.
2. Trump and Sean Spicer tell us that the inaugural crowd on the Washington Mall was the largest ever, but photographs tell the opposite story. ~~That's a conundrum~~. Sorry, that's a lie. A demonstrable lie.
3. Trump said on February 6th our military is depleted, and then tells a Nashville crowd on March 15th, "This [federal judges'] ruling [blocking my travel ban] makes us look weak, which by the way we no longer are, believe me." [NY Times, 3/16/2017] That's a conundrum.

Isn't that always the problem with hyperbole? It's always way worse than anything in the whole wide world ever was, including Armageddon or our sun going supernova. Or it's always way better than sliced bread, the invention of the wheel, or a guaranteed place in heaven. Trump's hyperbole are fact-free lies dressed up like the truth.

In case you wondered if everyone feels, as so many do, that Trump talks like a child, the answer is yes. The UK's newspaper, *The Independent*, asserts that "Donald Trump Speaks like a sixth-grader;" that's more generous than *Politico*.

Trump isn't a simpleton, he just talks like one. If you were to market Donald Trump's vocabulary as a toy, it would resemble a small box of Lincoln Logs...His comments from an August 11 news conference in Michigan earned only a 3rd-grade score.
—*Politico*, August 13, 2015

Personally, I find that more than unsettling. It's frightening. If that's the way he is perceived, imagine how other countries and world leaders perceive him.

The level of language employed by a person demonstrates not only a good vocabulary but the ability to handle complicated matters competently. Was anyone, other than me, not surprised when Trump said this?

"Nobody knew health care could be so complicated."
—Kevin Liptak, *CNN*, February 28, 2017

This remark is true only if Trump is Mr. Nobody. Otherwise, it shows all of us how stupid, ill-informed, and unqualified Trump truly is. It's never wise to claim that "nobody knows" what almost everyone knows.

Solum Optimis Verbis

First Rule of Trumpcare: Don't Get Sick

Week 9 / March 19 - 25, 2017

Editor's Caution: Republican Healthcare Advice… Don't Ever Get Sick

The Republicans' healthcare plan operates under a very simple and completely valid premise: People should never get sick. As proper subsets of this premise, people are abjured to never have sex because birth control costs money that the AHCA—the American Health Care Act—doesn't want to spend, and because rumor has it that sex—without birth control—can lead to children. And as we all know, children are always sick; a clear violation of the basic Republican premise [See above]. Under no circumstances should anyone ever contract a catastrophic illness like MS or cancer—for these are among the most egregious transgressions of the basic Republican premise. While no one can fail to grow old—unless they have the great good fortune to die early—they should avoid becoming frail and/or infirm—or sick.

    I believe I can say that we all know people who were irresponsible enough to get cancer, or heart disease, or a myriad of other maladies or diseases that sap the public healthcare coffers. We all know people who were sufficiently careless to fall and break hips or arms or legs. Decades ago, I knew one youngster who died at age eight when he fell over a thirty-foot cliff. Some called it an accident, but we all know who was responsible, don't we? We also know people who foolishly, but deliberately, contracted life-threatening illnesses. The wise Republican watchword has always been and continues to be "Vigilance," and regrettably, the sick among us are clearly wearing blinders.

Fortunately for us all, the Republicans acknowledge the well-established fact that getting sick is a personal failure, akin to being poor. After all, the ACA—aka Obamacare—was written specifically for the sick and the poor, as if we are all expected to be our brothers' keepers. While the sick and the poor ought to assume responsibility for their tragic condition, they seldom do. Instead, they plead with healthy Americans for comprehensive medical coverage—as if they deserve it. Ironically, this is the health coverage that healthy people clearly don't need. A question we should all be asking is: Whatever happened to rugged individualism?

Since the ACA is all about the poor and the sick, since it is primarily for them, then why shouldn't they be expected to pay more? That's precisely what the Republican-sponsored AHCA proposes to do, and if they can't pay, they'll be SOL. I have personally suggested that the last line of the Republican-sponsored American Health Care Act should be, "Have you considered suicide?"

No one can deny that the Republicans are merciful.

Healthcare from a Literary Perspective
For you always have the poor with you...
    Matthew 26:11, *American Standard Bible*
Blessed are you who are poor, for yours is the kingdom of God.
    Luke 6:20, *American Standard Bible*
I'm not afraid of death; I just don't want to be there when it happens.
    Woody Allen
[The poor] had better [die], and decrease the surplus population.
    Scrooge, *A Christmas Carol*, Charles Dickens
Ditto.
    Rush Limbaugh and *The Republican Party*

Why Not Universal, Single-Payer Healthcare?

Let me see if it's possible to simplify the whole healthcare morass that has been leading the headlines all week long. Granted, the whole issue of attempting to offer the entire American populace healthcare is extraordinarily complex, but there are certain standards that ought to be met by any attempt to craft a healthcare solution for 330,000,000 people. I offer two straightforward criteria:

1. Healthcare in America should be a non-profit issue.
2. No individual or family should ever be bankrupted by a healthcare crisis.

The Affordable Care Act met one of these criteria—#2 dealing with bankruptcy—and I live in hope that someday healthcare will become less expensive because no shareholders will be getting a piece of my premium. The ACA was all good. The ACA:

1. Eliminated lifetime payment caps.
2. Demanded coverage for pre-existing conditions.
3. Subsidized coverage for the poor.
4. Included the "mandate" so that every person must have coverage thus distributing the "risk" [Consider auto insurance: good drivers mitigate the risk for bad drivers.]
5. Allowed youngsters to remain on their parents' policy.

Additionally, the ACA demanded that all insurance policies include the following ten benefits, calling them absolutely essential. *These are the same benefits that GOP leaders considered eliminating just this week...which is reason enough to make this all italics.*

Here's the list:

1. Pregnancy, maternity, and newborn services
2. Mental health and substance-abuse treatment

3. Prescription drugs
4. Emergency services
5. Hospitalization
6. Outpatient care
7. Rehabilitation (PT)
8. Laboratory and diagnostic tests
9. Preventive and Wellness Services
10. Pediatric Care

Ask yourself, if all of these things were eliminated, what remains? Look carefully at this list, and weep with joy that the Republicans failed…this week. Then weep out of fear that these are Congressmen who say they have the best interests of the American people at heart. You can stop wondering if their program quietly asks, "Have you considered suicide?" The answer is "Yes."

This brings me to the, as yet, unfulfilled criteria # 1: Not-for-profit, single-payer healthcare. Single-payer takes the profit motive out of health care. When anyone—mainly Republicans—insist that we need a market-driven health care system, you must realize that such rhetoric is nonsense. Pure, unadulterated nonsense. That's because market-driven systems are all about choice…and timing.

You want a new car? Here are your choices. Here are the price ranges. If you decide a new car is too expensive, you may go to the used-car market or defer purchasing until a later date. That's how market-driven systems work.

However, healthcare embraces illness and injury and childbirth and children and all form of emergent situations. Healthcare and car-buying are completely different financial issues. A diagnosis of cancer, high-blood pressure, kidney failure, congestive heart failure, macular degeneration, multiple sclerosis or [*insert your malady here*] is never timely nor convenient. A patient cannot simply shrug and say, "I'll see about treatment next year when I can afford it."

There is a reason it's called "Emergent Care." Better they should say, "I'll afford it after I'm dead." And they'd be right.

Universal, single-payer healthcare is the best way to go. The chart [below] offers stark proof that countries with a single-payer system pay significantly LESS per capita than US citizens. Why doesn't every American realize this?

Finally, all other western developed nations offer their citizens some form of universal healthcare. I decided to look up some statistical data that might prove persuasive to any reader hoping to support a universal healthcare argument. The cost of healthcare in the United States is truly out-of-control—largely because the United States has a market-driven healthcare system. The chart I've included is from 2013, nevertheless, it is a genuine eye-opener. [See the chart below]

Comparison of Health Care Costs among First World Countries

	Total health care spending per capita	Real average annual growth per capita 2009-2013
Australia	$4,115	2.42%
Canada	$4,569	0.22%
Denmark	$4,847	-0.17%
France	$4,361	1.35%
Germany	$4,920	1.95%
Japan	$3,713	3.83%
Netherlands	$5,131	1.73%
New Zealand	$3,855	0.82%
Norway	$6,170	1.40%
Sweden	$5,153	6.95%
Switzerland	$6,325	2.54%
United Kingdom	$3,364	-0.88%
United States	$9,086	1.50%

These figures are provided by the OECD—the Organization for Economic Cooperation and Development. [2014]

Solum Optimis Verbis

The Dolt Who Walks & Talks

Week 10 / March 26 – April 1, 2017

Let's begin this week with a variety of reports from pundits on the political right ridiculing and detailing Trump's most glaring and comprehensive failure thus far in his fledgling administration: The astonishing failure to corral the votes even though the Republicans hold a clear majority in the House of Representatives.

First, from the desk of Bernard Goldberg, a right-winger of renown…for being a right-winger on *FOX News*:

Remind me not to ask Paul Ryan or his GOP House posse to ever arrange a one-car funeral — because the odds are good that they'd find a way to foul it up.

On March 23, 2010 President Barack Obama signed the Affordable Care Act into law. Which means that Paul Ryan and his team had seven years to come up with a replacement for Obamacare, a replacement that would get enough votes from fellow Republicans to at least make it out of the House.

He couldn't have said it better if he were a left-wing ideologue. From my perspective, the truly horrendous aspect of Republican behavior over the past seven years following the passage of the Affordable Care Act was not their repeated and futile attempts to repeal the ACA, but their utter indifference to solving the problem(s) that the ACA was attempting to solve. I believe we all have noticed that the Republicans are keen on legislation to solve non-existent problems—like voter fraud or high taxes. Conversely, Republicans are happy to ignore genuine problems—like global climate change or Russian interference in American democracy. I've developed a slogan that I'd like them to use during the mid-term elections in 2018. I promise not to charge them royalties.

**If You've Got A
Real Problem,
We Don't Care…
But
We'll Be Happy
To Solve
Your
Non-Existent Ones.**

There are virtually no instances of voter fraud, and the federal income tax rates are almost the lowest they've ever been. Still, the Republicans labor mightily to address these non-existent issues. I'm reminded of a silly poem my mother used to recite to me when I was a youngster. It embodies the Republican philosophy.

*Last night I saw upon the stair,
The little man who wasn't there.
He wasn't there again today,
Oh, how I wish he'd go away.*

Next, from Tucker Carlson—FOX News sycophant and toady—*The Daily Caller*:

The Donald Trump Turkey Shoot

President Trump told Americans Saturday morning to watch "Justice Jeanine" on Fox News. Jeanine Pirro started her show with a segment calling for House Speaker Paul Ryan to "step down."

Trump publicly expressed confidence in Ryan after the White House-backed Obamacare replacement bill had to be pulled as there weren't enough votes. However, there have been reports that President Trump and his allies are upset about Ryan's performance as speaker.

Trump directed people through a tweet to watch Pirro, a former county court judge and district attorney. Her "opening statement" was, "Paul Ryan needs to step down as speaker of the house. The reason? He failed to deliver the votes on his healthcare bill."

These two articles generate two incredibly different responses from me—both quite visceral.

First, I take solace in knowing that even Republicans believe that a Republican-led Congress with Paul Ryan at the helm is proving itself inept. Thank goodness for that. Who knows how bad things would be if the Republicans were ept?

Most disturbing is realizing that the Republican-heavy Congress has lost sight of their mission as legislators: *Make America a welcoming place that genuinely works for all Americans—even the poor and disenfranchised.* It's a shame that these legislators think their mission is about money—saving it, holding costs down at all costs. They've forgotten—perhaps they never knew?—being a legislator is first and foremost about people, helping as many as we can. More succinctly, legislators must represent people first, and the Treasury second.

The Donald Trump Turkey Shoot

Let's not forget, this is the same gang of legislators who call themselves "Christian." Do I need to trot out words like "irony" or "hypocrisy?" The Christian right supporting Trump strikes me as unfathomable, but they supported him rather than Hillary Clinton. That would be like the Catholic College of Cardinals supporting Satan for Pope. The Christian Right decided to back a known liar… his lies are as numberless as the stars. To back a known bigot… remember the Muslim ban. To back a known womanizer…does the name Stormy Daniels ring a bell? To back a known fraud…let's talk about Trump University. Shall I continue? How many sins would disqualify him?

Second, I find myself loathing Trump more than ever. The man embodies the three Ds of a dolt: duplicitous, despicable, and dumb. Before proceeding to our analysis, let's turn to Mr. Webster for the definition of "dolt." (I've decided to provide ALL the synonyms because they all seem to apply. And they made me laugh.)

———◆———

Dolt [dōlt] *noun,* plural dolts
1. *a stupid person.*
2. *anyone in the Trump administration*

Synonyms: fool · ass · halfwit · dunce · dolt · ignoramus · cretin · moron · imbecile · simpleton[more] · dope · ninny · nincompoop · chump · dimwit · dumbo · dummy · dum-dum · loon · dork · sap · jackass · blockhead jughead · bonehead · knucklehead · fathead · butthead · numbskull · numbnuts · dumb-ass · doofus · clod dunderhead · ditz · lummox · knuckle-dragger · dipstick · thickhead · meathead · meatball · wooden-head airhead · pinhead · lamer · lamebrain · peabrain · birdbrain · mouth-breather · scissorbill · jerk · nerd · donkey · nitwit · twit · boob · twerp · hoser · schmuck · bozo · turkey · chowderhead · dingbat · mook

The Donald Trump Turkey Shoot

Does anyone else wonder about Trump's short-term memory? On Friday, [March 24, 2017] Trump praises Paul Ryan, and by Sunday [March 26] he's indirectly calling for Ryan to step down as Speaker of the House. Duplicitous and despicable behavior? Yes, I think so. Either Paul Ryan is a man who made every legitimate effort on Trump's behalf, or he didn't. Praising him one day and indirectly denigrating him the next is the behavior of a neurotic, insecure individual, besides being a bad example of leadership. After all, isn't the president supposed to be an American role model?

Solum Optimis Verbis

Ironic Juxtaposition

Week 12 / April 9 – April 15, 2017

The word for this week is *incoherence*. It is also Trump's second middle name—after Chaos. The opposite, of course, is coherence, something that Trump does not possess.

Incoherence [in-kō-ˈhir-əns], *noun*
1. *Ideas, statements, or behaviors that are expressed in an incomprehensible or confusing way;*
2. *Lack of clarity or direction*
3. *Lack of connection between statements and behaviors; lack of consistency in statements and/or behaviors*
4. *The quality making Trump so dangerous.*

Synonyms: incongruity, nonsense, unintelligibility, Donald J Trump

Most of us associate with people whose lives display *coherence*. *Coherence* means we expect and anticipate certain behaviors, certain comments, certain ideas from certain people. That is, we know who they are. *Coherence* means we can rely on them to do what we anticipate they will do. In a word, they are predictable. And their actions invariably are predictable because such people are guided by a set of principles and values. Those principles create predictability and coherence. Genuine trust is built on such principles.

Occasionally, such people may speak or act in unexpected ways, and when they do, we characterize those words or actions as being "out of character" for that person. In Trump's case, nothing ever seems "out of character" because there is no character to act "out of." Trump possesses no core beliefs, no core principles, no core values. None. That means that whatever he says he "believes"—believes at this moment—can be overthrown in the next instant for personal gain. Trump possesses neither character nor beliefs. Several pundits have recently resorted to the word chameleon. Trump acts purely on feeling, or whim, or perceived self-interest. Beliefs and values, being less malleable and less capable of instantaneous alteration, don't influence his statements or behaviors.

Let's say that today, Easter, I am feeling happy. Tomorrow, after I visit my father-in-law's home and continue the work of organizing his family home for ultimate sale, I might feel sad. Whether happy or sad, my core beliefs haven't changed. My feelings may fluctuate because circumstances have changed, but the things that motivate me—helping my children and grandchildren, supporting my community, advocating for women's rights, advocating for better education, advocating for free higher education, advocating for equal pay, advocating for the needs of the middle class, advocating for animal rescue, advocating for a single-payer national healthcare system—those things will not change. That's who I am. These are the things that form my character. While I won't claim that these core tenets are beyond changing, I have arrived where I have after a lifetime of thought. I've seen "what happens to a dream deferred" as Langston Hughes asked in his brief but seminal poem.

What happens to a dream deferred?

Does it dry up
Like a raisin in the sun?

The Donald Trump Turkey Shoot

*Or fester like a sore--
And then run?*

*Does it stink like rotten meat?
Or crust and sugar over--
like a syrupy sweet?*

*Maybe it just sags
like a heavy load.*

Or does it explode?

Trump advocates for nothing but his own narrow self-interests. So what was good yesterday may very well be bad tomorrow because it no longer serves his interest. "The greater good" matters not at all if it does not align with his own personal interests. For instance, Trump vigorously opposed any and all intervention in Syria with a series of tweets during the years before he was president. He mocked Obama when Obama suggested that Congress should vote to authorize—or not—military intervention in Syria. Now that he is president, and now that the only time he receives positive press is when he's launching missiles or dropping "daisy-cutters," war in Syria is looking better and better.

Launching 59 cruise missiles at Syria gave Trump a level of machismo that made him feel good, even though his policy on Syria, his military intervention in foreign conflicts, or what thresholds ought to be observed before using the US military are all mysteries—mysteries to the public, to his inner circle, and probably even to himself. Trump does not operate from policy or principle, and I doubt that he will begin now. Both juvenile and infantile in his relationships with people and the world, Trump manifests the infamous quote, "If it feels good, do it."

That's what makes him especially dangerous. A man with authority over the best-armed military in the world needs to be principled, predictable, and peace-minded. Trump is unprincipled, unpredictable, and bellicose. Foreign leaders know this and may feel obliged to respond to him in ways none of us will enjoy.

Ironic Juxtaposition

When I worked at McGraw-Hill, we sold one of the most comprehensive dictionaries available in the high school market. By comprehensive I mean that our dictionary had ALL the words. Frequently customers purchased our dictionary without ever really perusing it before purchasing. *It's a dictionary, after all*, they thought.

McGraw-Hill's dictionary was more than the typical dictionary to which they were accustomed and that caused comedy and consternation. When asked to say a few words about what made our dictionary special, I'd always begin by saying, "In our dictionary, all the words are in alphabetical order." That comment provoked laughter because all modern dictionaries are organized that way. When the laughter faded, I typically asked the teachers in my audience to open their dictionaries to the entry *Mother Goose*—under the letter "M", of course. English teachers, always cooperative at opening-day in-services, turned immediately to that entry. I seldom had to ask them to peruse other entries—like the entry that immediately preceded *Mother Goose*.

I knew they had seen that preceding entry when a symphony of gasps, giggles, and disapproving grunts reached my ears. After they had calmed down—and looked for other potentially incendiary words...like the F word in all its manifestations—I explained they could use our dictionary to teach T.S. Eliot's literary concept: *ironic juxtaposition*. Juxtaposing *Mother Goose* and *motherf**ker*— that is, placing them side-by-side, is comic when one realizes that they represent such opposites on the spectrum of ideas. I'd tell my teachers that those entries embodied *ironic juxtaposition* about as well as any example I could conjure. Thus making our dictionary especially useful. Other examples of *ironic juxtaposition* I can offer from various arenas:

1. Trump is a billionaire claiming to be the champion of the middle class. *[Politics, The Campaign]*
2. Imagine the portraits of Barack Obama and Trump side by side. *[Politics, History]*
3. In the movie Jurassic Park, the main characters are speeding in a jeep away from a Tyrannosaurus Rex when the driver looks in his rearview mirror and sees this message: *Objects in the mirror may be closer than they appear.* *[Film]*
4. A New Orleans billboard exhorts the viewer to "Reach for the American Dream" while all around is the destruction left from Hurricane Katrina. *[Advertising]*

In the interest of full-disclosure, I happily explained that our dictionary was the only one on the high school market that could teach their students the difference between *chickenshit* and *bullshit*. To make matters even more comic, the word *chickenshit* was a guide word at the top of the page. The other guide word for that page was *Chilkoot Pass*—a place made famous during the Klondike Gold Rush. A friend and colleague told me he thought *"From Chickenshit to Chilkoot Pass"* would be a terrific title for a novel. I'm not so sure anymore.

Let me be clear, Trump's administration is making chickenshit policies and attempting to fool the American voter with the biggest load of bullshit ever dumped by any president at one time. Just ask Sean Spicer.

𝔖olum 𝔒ptimis 𝔙erbis

Stupid & Evil

Week 13 / April 16 – April 22, 2017

The publication, *Political Forum*, asked a simple question this past week. Is the Trump administration stupid or nefarious? I believe the correct answer is "Yes." Simply change the "or" to "and." That leads us to the word of the week:

Nefarious [ni-ˈfer-ē-əs] *adjective*
1. *Wicked or criminal*
2. *Trump's ICE enforcement.*

Synonyms: wicked · evil · sinful · iniquitous · egregious · heinous · atrocious · vile · foul · abominable · odious · depraved · monstrous · fiendish · diabolical · unspeakable · despicable · villainous ·[more] criminal · corrupt · illegal · unlawful · dastardly ·Steve Mnuchin · Steve Bannon · Steve Miller · Jeff Sessions · Scott Pruitt · Tom Price · Rex Tillerson
Antonyms: good

We have discussed that Trump does not operate on principles, nor does he possess or seek out accurate, up-to-date information. He is stupid and doesn't care that he's stupid. The argument can easily be made that Trump is the least knowledgeable, least informed, most arrogant, and most intellectually lazy president in my lifetime. I resist using the word "ever" because I'd have no legitimate way to quantify or prove my assertion. According to various historians, the dubious distinction of "dumbest president"—if one accounts for ALL presidents—was a toss-up between James Buchanan and Franklin Pierce, the two 19th century Democrats who immediately preceded Abraham Lincoln.

While I cannot prove it, my money is on Trump as dumbest president…past, present, and future. How else can we account for Trump's never-ending onslaught of incorrect or provably false statements? Let me refresh our memories:

1. Trump claimed to have seen "thousands of Muslims" celebrating in the streets of northern New Jersey on the day the Twin Towers fell. He's alone in that assertion.
2. How else could Trump speak of Frederick Douglass as if he were still alive? Said Trump: *"Frederick Douglass is an example of somebody who's done an amazing job and is getting recognized more and more, I notice."* To which I say, I sure hope we can get that amazing Mr. Douglass on *Good Morning America*. Trump's historical ignorance of history is unparalleled in my lifetime.
3. Current events also elude Trump's grasp. Said Trump: *"Vladimir Putin is not going into Ukraine. Okay? Just so you understand, he's not gonna go into Ukraine, all right? You can mark it down. You can put it down."* He said that well after Putin had already gone into the Ukraine. Is it a short-term memory issue, or stupidity?
4. Remember when Trump referred to Jeb Bush as "low-energy?" Remember when Trump shouted on the campaign trail, *"I think I've made a lot of sacrifices. I work very, very hard."* Remember that? So how does one account for all his days on the golf links? Trump is not only intellectually lazy, he is just plain lazy, a member of the idle rich, interested only in enjoying his own life—and making money for himself

and his friends. He has not yet realized that the Presidency requires a leader, not a ruler.

5. Trump said he could "fix" the country as he "fixed" his country clubs. Trump has no interest in collaboration or cooperation. He wants to lay down the law and have everyone obey.

6. Just last week, Trump betrayed that he didn't know the difference between Kim Jong Il (deceased) and his son, Kim Jong Un. He referred to both of them as if they were one person, and even worse, referred to them both as "gentlemen." It's likely he used the term "gentleman" because he either didn't know or couldn't remember the name of the North Korean dictator. (I am sure that Kim Jong Il and Frederick Douglass are both somewhere having a good laugh about Trump's stark stupidity.)

7. Of course, on an almost daily basis, Trump asserts that he is smart. So smart, in fact, that
    a. He doesn't need intelligence briefings. (Where is his crystal ball? The information gathered from intelligence briefings cannot be had via "common sense" regardless of what Trump might say.)
    b. He doesn't pay income taxes. (Are people who pay taxes stupid? Is it a good idea to NOT pay one's fair share for the operation and maintenance of the US Government?)
    c. He's used bankruptcy to avoid financial loss. (How does a casino—where the "house always wins"—go bankrupt?)

The list of Trump's stupid statements pre-dates his run for president and probably extends to this very moment. Let me consult my clock. It's 6:46 pm [PDT], and I wager that Trump has said something stupid or uninformed today. I only wish Vegas were taking bets.

A Trump Primer

Because we live in the Information Age, and because almost all processes have experienced incredible acceleration now that we live in the Digital Information Age, ignorance and stupidity—whether from genetics or carelessness—can prove dangerous, if not fatal. Put another way, if one ignores the DIA—Digital Information Age—one may end up DOA.

Trump thinks he knows.
Trump is wrong.
Trump thinks he is never wrong.
Trump is wrong without ever knowing that he is wrong.
Trump thinks he is right even when he is wrong.
Trump has no respect or appreciation for knowing.
Trump has no time for knowing.
Trump enjoys the "illusion of knowing," that is, Trump knows many things that are simply not so.
Trump believes that whatever he knows must be so, because he is never wrong.

BUT

Trump is an empty vessel.
Trump does not know.
Trump does not know that he does not know.
Trump doesn't care that he does not know that he does not know.
Trump's not knowing will end badly…for everyone…

Finally: A Brief Drama from the Trump Administration

I have reveled in the *Saturday Night Live* skits that open the program. I thought I'd like to write a skit that emphasizes Trump's rank ignorance—of policy, of history, of procedures.

The Donald Trump Turkey Shoot

Scene: *The Oval Office*
Time: *Now*
The president is putting a golf ball across the American emblem on the rug in the Oval Office when his National Security Advisor HR McMaster rushes in.

McMaster: Mr. President, Mr. President.
Trump: Quiet, Mick, this is a crucial putt. If I make it, I win The Masters.
McMaster: Sorry, Mr. President.
[The president putts and misses]
Trump: So what couldn't wait? I'm working hard for the American people here. And thanks to you, McMaster, I've lost the Masters.
[The president puts down the putter]
Trump: There's always next year, I suppose.
McMaster: Sorry, Mr. President. But North Korea has just successfully launched a ballistic missile.
Trump: Ballistic?
McMaster: Yes, sir. Ballistic.
Trump: Is that bad?
McMaster: Very bad, sir.
Trump: Bigly bad?
McMaster: Very bigly bad, sir.
Trump: You said it was North Korea?
McMaster: Yes, sir.
Trump: Are they the good guys or the bad guys?
McMaster: Sir, they're the ones run by the pudgy gentleman.
Trump: The one with the goofy haircut?
McMaster: Yes, sir.
Trump: You can always tell bad guys by their haircut.

McMaster: [McMaster looks dubious.] So what should we do, Mr. President?
Trump: Get him a better barber. I know the best barbers. [McMaster does a classic double-take]
McMaster: Good, sir. I can see that, sir. But what should we do about the ballistic missile launch?
Trump: Do we have to do something?
McMaster: I think so, sir. We have to show North Korea that we won't tolerate them threatening the United States or any of our Asian allies with a nuclear missile.
Trump: You mean like China?
McMaster: No, sir. China's not really one of our allies.
Trump: They're not?
McMaster: No, sir.
Trump: Then why do I have Trump ties made in China?
McMaster: Probably because it's cheaper, sir?
Trump: That's true. Very true. They make the best ties.
McMaster: Yes, sir. But about the missile…
Trump: Is it coming for the US right now?
McMaster: No sir, it's a test flight. But if it were armed, it could reach South Korea or Japan very easily.
Trump: I have an idea. I always have the best ideas. Tell those folks that they'll just have to move.
McMaster: But sir, the Koreans and Japanese live there.
Trump: So, they can't move?
McMaster: It's highly unlikely, sir. They need our protection.
Trump: Okay. Good. I have another very good idea. Tell them to join NATO.
McMaster: I'm afraid that isn't possible, Mr. President.
Trump: Nothing's impossible, Mick. By becoming president, I've shown the world that anything is possible, haven't I?

McMaster: Yes, you have Mr. President. But NATO is the North Atlantic Treaty Organization.
Trump: What are you saying?
McMaster: South Korea and Japan border on the Pacific Ocean.
Trump: It's all salt water, isn't it?
McMaster: That's true…
Trump: And it's the same salt water that's in the ocean next to Mar-a-Lago, isn't it?
McMaster: That's probably true, sir. All the oceans are connected…
Trump: So really it's all one big ocean, right?
McMaster: Sure. One big ocean.
Trump: See, I knew I was right. Being right is what I do best.
McMaster: But, sir, I need to know what your policy is regarding ballistic missile launches that threaten…
Trump: Excellent point. Excellent. I'd like to know what my excellent policy is, too.
McMaster: You do have a policy, don't you, Mr. President?
Trump: Absolutely. And it's the most excellent policy ever conceived in the world of excellent policy-making. Just tell me what it is.

[Sean Spicer enters and interrupts the president.]

Sean: Mr. President, the press wants to know what you plan to do about the North Korean missile launch.
Trump: Wouldn't they like to know.
Sean: Yes, sir, they would.
McMaster: Should we send the fleet, sir?
Trump: No. Not the fleet. Send the armada!
McMaster: The armada, sir?
Trump: Fleet sounds weak. Armada sounds strong.
McMaster: But the fleet—er…the armada—is three thousand miles away, sir. Near Australia.

Trump:	You just said it's all one big ocean, Mick. Right? I'm right. Right again. As always.
	[Sean Spicer interrupts again.]
Sean:	What should I tell the press, sir?
Trump:	Let me think, Seany. Let me think.
Sean:	That's not your style, sir.
Trump:	True, Seany. Very true. Thinking gives you wrinkles in your brow. And I hate wrinkles. So does Melania. We are doing our best to remain wrinkle-free.
Sean:	That's very nice, sir. Wrinkle-free.
Trump:	Okay, Spicey. Tell them I have a secret plan for defeating the North Koreans.
Sean:	A secret plan, sir. I don't think they'll believe me when I tell them that.
Trump:	Of course, they will. Everybody believed me when I said I had a secret plan to defeat ISIS, didn't they?
Sean:	Well, sir…
Trump:	What I never told them was that plan was so secret, even I didn't know what it was.
	[Kellyanne Conway enters out of breath…]
KC:	Mr. President, Ivanka wants to know if she can borrow Air Force One for the weekend.
Trump:	What does she want with my plane?
KC:	She's flying to China and Vietnam to visit the factories that manufacture her clothing.
	[McMaster interrupts]
McMaster:	Sir, we need to address this ballistic missile issue.
	[Sean Spicer interrupts]
Sean:	Sir, I need to know what to tell that nest of vipers we call the press. They'll want real answers.
	[Kellyanne Conway interrupts]
KC:	Just toss'em alternative facts and tell'em to shut up, Spicey.

Trump: I'd love to stay, I really would, but I think I have to go with Ivy to China. I bet I can get a better price for my ties. I'm a businessman, you know. Running the USA is just a sideline. I never wanted this job to begin with. But the people insisted. I got the majority, you know. Millions of illegal voters and I still won. Gotta run. Bigly.
[Trump leaves.]
[McMaster, Sean, and KC look at one another, and together they say:]
McMaster: Live from DC, it's White House Stupidity!
Sean: Live from DC, it's White House Stupidity!
KC: Live from DC, it's White House Stupidity!

Solum Optimis Verbis

One Hundred Days of B.S.

Week 14 / April 23 – April 29, 2017

The First One Hundred Daze…Only 1360 to Go
I believe I know why Trump's presidency has me in so much turmoil.

There are certain norms that most of us accept as citizens of the United States—and as responsible human beings. First, we keep our word and expect others to keep theirs. I'm not talking about the taking of oaths or vows here. Nor am I referencing the silly, "Cross my heart, hope to die, stick a needle in my eye" promises of childhood. I'm talking about human commerce, the business of daily life. Our daily lives consist of myriad minor transactions filled with small promises to do something. Consider:

> *I'll be home by five. I'll pick up the UPS package on the way home.*
> *I'll make sure that I get the 2% milk for you.*

Each of those statements appears to be a good-faith promise to let our loved one—husband, wife, significant other, child—know what they can expect on or around 5:00 pm. This is the way we conduct our lives. We tell people what we are going to do. Each day we make small promises. By doing what we say we'll do, we earn a reputation for reliability, and people learn to trust us. However, if that person stumbles in the door at 1:00 am, without the package and without the milk, then several promises have been broken. If this happens often enough, the person making the promises will not be believed, will be branded as unreliable, or worse, will be branded a liar.

The pharmacy calls to tell you your prescription is ready.
The dry cleaner assures you that your suit will be ready for pick-up tomorrow.

Small verbal agreements. Small promises that something will happen. We all rely on such promises. Bigly. Still, if your prescription is not ready when you get to the pharmacy or your suit not cleaned and pressed when you arrive at the cleaners, a promise has been broken. Such broken promises can be remedied: a different pharmacy, a new dry cleaner. Small promises, small consequences.

Broken promises are part of the human condition. In our interpersonal relationships, we can abandon unreliable or lying friends, divorce unreliable or lying spouses, or take our business to an establishment that can deliver goods and services on time and at cost.

For me, the key problem with the Trump presidency is this:

I cannot unfriend him, divorce him, or fire him. Leaving the country in not practical. My wife has explicitly told me that assassination is out of the question. As is creating a Crowd-Funding site for that particular purpose. There is little likelihood that he'd ever die from shame. So...I—dare I say "we?"—are trapped in a long-term toxic relationship which has no remedy that any of us can apply.

We are trapped in this relationship with a man who:

1. Is both stupid and arrogant beyond all belief. (Perhaps stupidity and arrogance are reciprocal attributes.) The breathtaking depth of his ignorance and stupidity defies the imagination.

2. Thinks people who are dead are still alive. (Frederick Douglass is also a personal friend of mine.)
3. Possesses neither the big picture, nor any of the details.
4. Pretends to know what he does not know.
5. Has no principles—beyond his own immediate self-interest—to guide him.
6. Prefers to live in secrecy so any underhanded, dictatorial, or deceitful practices or policies will be hard to detect. (We can't know his taxes nor who visits him at the White House.)
7. Is a con man from start to finish. (How else could the Christian Right abide him?)
8. Lies all the time, even about things that are provably false.
9. Cannot distinguish fantasy from reality.
10. Respects no one.
11. Craves attention and the spotlight. (See #6. The spotlight has to be on his terms. When asked questions by reporters, he frequently turns to stone.)
12. Can declare someone his friend after a ten-minute conversation.
13. Can actually ask, "Who knew health care was so complicated?" (How about everyone?)
14. Is proud of his bigotry. (Take your pick: Racism, sexism, anti-Semitism, anti-Muslim)
15. Cares only about himself. (He's not a "blue-collar billionaire." That's a manufactured fantasy. PR)
16. Refuses to believe the science of climate change.
17. Risks the health of our planet—and thus the health and safety of our children and grandchildren.
18. Appears to be a warmonger.
19. Thinks the US Military is his personal army.
20. Treats the presidency as a part-time job.
21. Has no idea what democracy is all about.

22. Has no knowledge of the Constitution. (See # 1)
23. Appoints unsuited, ill-qualified people to posts.
24. Has no idea how to do his job, i.e. to *be* president.
25. Appears to have no interest in finding out how to do his job.
26. Wants to rule—not lead. (That's why executive orders will always trump legislation. Trump would prefer dictator status with unbridled power to rule as he pleases.)
27. Reverses policy positions more quickly than a grand mal seizure.
28. Wants to have his cake and eat it, too.
29. Sees the presidency as his personal ATM.
30. Is in bed with the Russians.

Bluff, Bluster, and Bullshit

These are the *3 B's* of the Trump presidency. I'd call it "fake news" but while Trump appears to be opposed to "fake news," that's all a ruse. As I've said before, when he opposes something, look behind the curtain. He opposes fake news even as he generates huge amounts of it. Unfortunately, there are sufficient numbers of my fellow citizens who lack all discernment and possess the same intellectual acumen as Trump.

Yes, I'm calling them stupid. That's why so many people bought into Trump's barrage of "I'm gonnas."

"On the first day, I'm gonna..."
"In the first 100 days, I'm gonna..."

How should we characterize Trump's penchant for bragging what a terrific negotiator he is, his ridiculous inclination for superlatives, his delight in making reckless, impossible claims? Well, I place them in the category I call the *3 B's: Bluff, Bluster, and Bullshit*. On a more literary level, let me dip into my Shakespearian cache of quotations to explain that the story of Trump's first one hundred days is:

...a tale told by an idiot, full of sound and fury, signifying nothing.

Trump is full of meaningless sound and fury. Despite his personal claims of being intelligent and having the best words, the past one hundred days are filled with abundant evidence to the contrary. Let me reiterate what I said earlier. When I coached the Debate Team at Newport High School, my debaters laughingly adopted a slogan that seems particularly apt. These teenagers knew the power of language—that it could elucidate or obfuscate. That it could clarify or cloud an issue.

*If You Can't
Dazzle'm with Brilliance,
Baffle'm with Bullshit*

Which leads us to the word of the week:

Bullshit [ˈbo͝olˌSHit], *noun*
1. *stupid or untrue talk or writing; nonsense*
2. *almost everything Trump says*

Example: Trump saying, The first 100 days of my administration has been the most successful in history. Quoted April 28, 2017.
Synonyms: bull· crap · bunk · drivel · gibberish· *guff* · hogwash · nonsense · rubbish · baloney · bunkum · lies · flim-flam · hokum · hooey · malarkey · moonshine · poppycock

That catchphrase, particularly the "baffle'm with bullshit" phrase, is the centerpiece of Trump's entire administration. They clearly

The Donald Trump Turkey Shoot

prefer bullshit to brilliance just as they prefer ignorance to knowledge. Let me list a few of the issues which Trump has either failed *[F]* to move forward legislatively, or has switched *[S]* his position on—even if temporarily. For wins—which are few—I use a *[W]*.

1. Winning. *[Mostly F]* Trump said there would be so much winning, we'd grow tired of winning. Ah well.
2. Supreme Court Justice *[W]* If you listen to Republican commentary about why they never considered Obama's nominee, the word bullshit is plainly insufficient.
3. The Border Wall with Mexico. *[F]* With encouraging hints at switching from Congressional Republicans. Apparently, Mr. Dealmaker has been unpersuasive with Mexican authorities.
4. NATO *[S]* "NATO is relevant again." Trump has declared it so. Good to know.
5. Declaring China "a currency manipulator." *[S]* Trump has changed his mind because Xi Jinping is his personal friend. Another quickie, ten-minute relationship I suppose.
6. Going to war in Syria. *[S]* "Stay out, stay out, stay out" has become "Show me the missiles."
7. Repeal and replace Obamacare *[F]* Big item. Big failure. Remarkably, the Republicans are talking about "states' rights" when it comes to healthcare legislation. Shouldn't they be focused on "people's rights?"
8. Make sure everyone is covered (by healthcare). *[S] [F]*
9. Ban Muslims *[F]* Big failure, and rightly so. The federal courts interpreting the Constitution in light of Trump's own statements of intent said "No!" Trump doesn't know, understand, or appreciate the US Constitution. Nor does his Att. Gen. Jeff Sessions.
10. Jobs, jobs, jobs. *[F]* True, Trump lifted environmental regulations that make coal-mining more costly and difficult,

The Donald Trump Turkey Shoot

but coal has been on the way out for two decades now. He might as well tell people in Rochester that he's planning to bring back photographic film that needs developing, or tell America that we'll put people back to work manufacturing typewriter ribbons.

11. Infrastructure *[F?]* If Trump has made any real effort in this direction, it's a well-kept secret. His promised tax cuts would appear to undermine broad infrastructure projects. Reducing revenue while increasing spending by hundreds of billions seems to be a non-starter.
12. Hiring freeze on all federal employees. *[S]* The freeze has thawed. Remarkably, many high level positions still await his administration to appoint ~~qualified~~ people. (Sorry, I got carried away.)
13. Leaving the TPP—Trans-Pacific-Partnership. *[Huh?]* Since the US had never ratified the agreement, we could hardly leave it. Put this under the "Bluff and Bluster" column.
14. Leaving NAFTA—North American Free Trade Agreement *[S]* When Trump had a real chance to do exactly what he said he'd do, he didn't do it. All it took to dissuade him from not abandoning the NAFTA agreement were two recent phone calls from Canada and Mexico.
15. Release my taxes. *[S] [F]* (Actually this is just one big, fact lie.)
16. Tax plans to help the Middle Class. *[S] [F]* (Actually this is just one big, fact lie, too.)
17. Suing all those women who accused Trump of inappropriate behavior. *[S] or [F]*
18. Cancel funding to Sanctuary Cities *[F]* Federal judges said "No!" Again.

Finally, This Just In...

Just today,

> *President Trump touted the accomplishments of his first 100 days in office, calling his administration one of the "most successful" in history.*
>
> —*The Hill*, Nikita Vladimirov, April 28, 2017

Success must have a very low bar. Shall I call this sheer, unadulterated bullshit?

And so it goes. We are trapped in a toxic political relationship with an ignorant, unprincipled, rudderless, infantile man who wields incredible political and military power without the mental capacity to understand or consider consequences.

Trump is not an idiot. He is a dangerous idiot.

Solum Optimis Verbis

Saying Makes It So

Week 15 / April 30 – May 6, 2017

An Observation

In the days when I was teaching high school—back in the 70s & 80s—I taught a class called Basic Speech. The course required some public speaking, but I dedicated a significant part of the class to interpersonal communications. While I feel tempted to explore the death of interpersonal communications with the advent of the cellphone, and humanity's headlong rush into heads-down, cellphone-absorbed, solipsistic isolation, I will save that for another day. Let me return to my point.

Part of the Basic Speech class involved a video presentation by Leo Buscaglia, a professor at University of Southern California. One of Buscaglia's comments on the video invariably provoked laughter among my students. "No one gets out of this life alive," Buscaglia declared. "No one." While I still hold onto a slim hope that I'll be the exception, all the evidence proves him to be absolutely correct.

I thought of Buscaglia's declaration as I listened this week to the disheartening news describing the most recent craziness committed by the Republican Congress and their stand on pre-existing conditions. I can hear Buscaglia telling them, "Ladies and gentlemen, life is a pre-existing condition."

It's as if the Republicans associate infirmity and illness with a lack of personal responsibility. "If you're sick, it's your fault. That's why we expect sick people to pay more." It's the same argument that they've always used to compel higher premiums from women. After all, women are the people who get pregnant, who suffer from a multitude of women's issues. Why should men have to pay for situations and conditions that don't afflict them? Of course, erectile dysfunction is undoubtedly a "pre-existing condition," but I'll wager that there will be plenty of waivers for guys who can't wave.

Most disturbing, Trump told all Americans that his health care bill would "cover everyone," would provide "better coverage," and would "cost less than Obamacare." We have the video proof of Trump promising the best for less. What a deal! But once again, truth and reality are Trump's enemies. He doesn't appear to know the truth or how to ascertain the truth. Worse, he seems to have no intention of keeping this campaign promise to help people when they are the most vulnerable.

If our president were able to articulate his governing philosophy—something I am certain he is incapable of doing because he lacks both the vocabulary and the thinking skills necessary to articulate almost everything of consequence—he'd say, "The truth is what I say it is. If I say it, it must be the truth."

That is, if Trump asserts that the AHCA is better than the ACA, it must be true. QED. In Trump's world, saying makes it so. Not wishing.

Dramatic Sketch of the Week
On the Phone with Melania
Two scripts are provided below. The first provides Melania's speech using a Slavic accent. The second renders the scene in standard American English—something with which Trump is wholly unfamiliar.

Imagine a Split Screen:
Trump, clearly upset, is seated in the Oval Office in right-hand screen, dialing a phone number with great determination. In the left-hand screen, we see an old-style, gilt-edged phone ringing several times before anyone appears. As the phone rings, Trump impatiently switches the phone from one ear to the other. In the left-hand screen, we see Melania enter and answer the phone, seating herself, tossing her hair, and crossing her legs. Melania and Trump are a study in opposites. Melania relaxed. Trump harried.

SCRIPT # 1 with SLAVIC ACCENT

Melania:	Ah-loh.
Trump:	Mel?
Melania:	Dawnnie?
Trump:	I just passed my first milestone, Mel. It's a big deal, Mel. Very big. Everybody understands how big it is.
Melania:	Da? Vat milestone is dat?
Trump:	I've been president for 100 days. More than 100 days now.
Melania:	Veddy gud, Dawnnie, veddy gud. Venn you come home, I vill haff zumting for you—a geeft, no?
Trump:	Don't you understand what this means, Mel?
Melania:	Da. You haff not bin impeach-ed?
Trump:	Mel, I told you never to use the "I" word.
Melania:	[Whispering] But Dawnnie why not? I am immigrant, too.
Trump:	Not that "I" word, Mel. The other "I" word.
Melania:	Vich vun? Inventile? Imbeezile? Indeziziff?
Trump:	Impeach.
Melania:	Ah, Dawnnie. Da. Sawry. I vill nut use impeach-ed efer eh-gen.
Trump:	Mick Mulvaney said funding the government is a win for us. My first win.

Melania:	Gud. Gud. I vatch news. Senator Lindsay says dat you got clock repaired.
Trump:	No, Mel. Senator Graham said we got our clock cleaned.
Melania:	Is gud, no?
Trump:	Not exactly.
Melania:	You gawt money for vawl wit Mexico?
Trump:	No.
Melania:	So you keeled dat awfil Plan-ned Perrenhood?
Trump:	No.
Melania:	But Big Baird and Muppets and PBS get nutting, right?
Trump:	No.
Melania:	How about EPA?
Trump:	No.
Melania:	So vat ees deeferent?
Trump:	Everything, Mel. Everything. I found out I can lose and still win. All I have to do is say I won.
Melania:	Vuddent reelly vinning be better?
Trump:	Maybe. But really winning is hard work. I'm too old for hard work. Saying I won is so much easier.
	[Melania: pauses. She scratches her perfect scalp beneath her perfect hair with her perfect fingernails, wondering what to say next.]
Trump:	Mel, are you still there?
Melania:	I vill kawl Vladimir, no?
Trump:	What for?
Melania:	Ez Russian hendler, I moost meek serten you stay in aw-vice. Is why gud buddy Putin zend me to you. He gawt you elektid. He vill keep you elektid.
Trump:	Okay, Mel. But be careful. Talking to the Russians got Mikey Flynn in lots of trouble. If anyone finds out, Spicey will have to explain it to the fake news press.
Melania:	Don't vurry, Dawnnie. No buddy beleefs Russian stawry.

	Dey tink is liberal nunsense. Beside. I like Spicey. He make gud stend-up cohmidee effry day. He vill cunfy-use effryting and effrybuddy.
Trump:	True. He's really great at that. You know, Mel, the fake news folks make me sick.
Melania:	Oh, Dawnnie. Pleez. Pleez down't get sik.
Trump:	Don't worry, Mel. You're talking to the healthiest man on the planet. Just ask my doctor.
Melania:	Gud. Down't get sik. Pleez. You no vat vee must do ef you do get sik?
Trump:	Yeah. Move to Australia.

SCRIPT # 2 without SLAVIC ACCENT or THE TRANSLATION

Melania:	Hello.
Trump:	Mel?
Melania:	Donnie?
Trump:	I just passed my first milestone, Mel. It's a big deal, Mel. Very big. Everybody understands how big it is.
Melania:	Yes? What milestone is that?
Trump:	I've been president for 100 days. More than 100 days now.
Melania:	Very good, Donnie, very good. When you come home, I will have something for you—a gift, okay?
Trump:	Don't you understand what this means, Mel?
Melania:	Sure. It means you haven't been impeached.
Trump:	Mel, I told you never to use the "I" word.
Melania:	[Whispering] But Donnie, why not? I'm an immigrant, too.
Trump:	Not that "I" word, Mel. The other "I" word.
Melania:	Which one? Infantile? Imbecile? Indecisive?
Trump:	Impeach.

The Donald Trump Turkey Shoot

Melania: Oh, Donnie. Yes. Sorry. I won't use the word impeach ever again.
Trump: Mick Mulvaney said funding the government is a win for us. My first win.
Melania: Good. Good. I watched the news. Senator Lindsay said that you got your clock repaired.
Trump: No, Mel. Senator Graham said we got our clock cleaned.
Melania: That's good, isn't it?
Trump: Not exactly.
Melania: So, you got the money for the wall with Mexico?
Trump: No.
Melania: So you killed that awful Planned Parenthood?
Trump: No.
Melania: But Big Bird and the Muppets and PBS get nothing, right?
Trump: No.
Melania: How about the EPA?
Trump: No.
Melania: So what is different?
Trump: Everything, Mel. Everything. I found out I can lose and still win. All I have to do is say I won.
Melania: Wouldn't really winning be better?
Trump: Maybe. But really winning is hard work. I'm too old for hard work. Saying I won is so much easier.
[Melania: pauses. She scratches her perfect scalp beneath her perfect hair with her perfect fingernails, wondering what to say next.]
Trump: Mel, are you still there?
Melania: I will call Vladimir, okay?
Trump: What for?
Melania: As your Russian handler, I must make certain you stay in office. That's why your good buddy Putin sent me to you. He got you elected, and he will keep you elected.

Trump:	Okay, Mel. But be careful. Talking to the Russians got Mikey Flynn in lots of trouble. If anyone finds out, Spicey will have to explain it to the fake news press.
Melania:	Don't worry Donnie. Nobody believes the Russian story. They thinks it's liberal nonsense. Besides, I like Spicey. He makes good stand-up comedy every day. He will confuse everything and everybody.
Trump:	True. He's really great at that. You know, Mel, the fake news folks make me sick.
Melania:	Oh, Donnie. Please. Please don't get sick.
Trump:	Don't worry, Mel. You're talking to the healthiest man on the planet. Just ask my doctor.
Melania:	Good. Don't get sick. Please. You know what we must do if you do get sick?
Trump:	Yeah. Move to Australia.

NOTE: Truth is stranger than fiction—or drama. On May 5th, Trump described the U.S. health system as "failing," and pointed out during his conversation with the Australian Prime Minister, "I shouldn't say this to a great gentleman and my friend from Australia… because you have better health care than we do."

Solum Optimis Verbis
Liar, Liar, Pants on Fire
Week 16 / May 7 – May 13, 2017

So What's New?

You're all thinking, "Trump fired FBI director, Jim Comey. That's new."

Well, yes and no. Comey's firing is simply a new example of an old behavior. Behaving irresponsibly and recklessly has become a Trump hallmark—consider Michael Flynn, the Muslim ban, permitting mentally disabled people to buy guns, etc.—something we've come to expect from Trump. Then, trying "to shape the narrative about what really happened," i.e., lying about the whole damn thing, is hardly new. That "shaping the narrative" stuff—whether from the Oval Office, or from Sean Spicer (or now Sarah Suckabee Handers), or from Kellyanne Conjob—that's old news.

Trump is the Prevaricator-in-Chief, a liar extraordinaire—a man who is a veteran, practiced, skilled dissimulator. Please carefully note all the new and wonderful words that we've seldom had a chance to use in any context before his presidency. Thanks to Trump, we are given the opportunity to fortify our vocabulary. Perhaps we should all give thanks for that. This brings us to the word of the week:

> Liar [lī(ə)r] *noun*, plural, liars, *e.g. The Trump Administration*
> 1. *A person who tells lies or falsehoods.*
> 2. *President Pants-on-Fire.*

Synonyms: cheat · con artist · deceiver · deluder · dissimulator · equivocator · fabler · fibber · false witness · fabricator · fabulist · falsifier · maligner · misleader · perjurer · phony · promoter · storyteller · trickster

Trump embraces lies in all their synonymous manifestations—deception, legerdemain, and half-truths. Whether lying about the size of his inaugural crowd *[despite photographic evidence]*, or declaring that he'll proclaim China a "currency manipulator" *[which he declined to do when given the opportunity]*, or insisting that the unemployment rate was "as much as 35%" *[despite the statistical data provided by the Bureau of Labor Statistics]*, or bragging that he "never settles" lawsuits filed against him *[despite his most recent settlement in the Trump University class action]*, or…shall I continue?

This administration is not to be believed…about anything. That's why this week's journal is…

Peppered with Poetry ➔ "Trump on Fire" © 2017

*"Liar, Liar pants of fire."
So think you there's a chance
That President Trump's a falsifier
Who's wearing flaming pants?*

Everyone seems to have recently discovered that President Trump lies. Like a rug. (Old cliché) Like a Shakespearean strumpet. (Literary allusion) As if his presidency depended on it. (Reality) Wow! Who knew? Just everyone with half a brain—a fact that eliminates most Trump supporters.

*Our vaunted leader's a misleader
In all things great and small,
No one's finer as a maligner
He tells his tales so tall.*

He does that because he is uninformed, ignorant, and quite probably a sociopath.[1] He is a remarkable liar who appears to be able to surround himself with people who are prepared and willing to lie for him, as well. Let me quote briefly from the article I just footnoted:

> *He is a serial and compulsive (pathological) liar. PolitiFact named Trump the winner of its annual "Lie of the Year" Award in 2015 – a competition which PolitiFact said "was not even close," unquestionably in reference to the fact that it rated 72% of Trump's public remarks about factual circumstances as false. Any further doubt about Trump's capacity for truthfulness should be erased by even a cursory review of the website, Trumplies.us – a vast compendium of misstatements, inaccuracies and outright falsehoods.*
> —from *Profile of a Sociopath*

<u>*Trump, the Liar*</u>

*He fabulous as a fabulist
A legendary fabler.
When asked if he could tell a lie,
"I am the Great Enabler.
I am a cheat who can't be beat,
A perjurer supreme.
I just can't wait to fabricate,
(I really love to dissimulate,)
A fact-checker's horrible dream."*

---

[1] Read this link: Profile of a Sociopath
http://www.huffingtonpost.com/daniel-berger/trump-profile-of-a-sociopath_b_11318128.html

The Donald Trump Turkey Shoot

Let me quote the first sentence of a George Will editorial mailed to me by my friend, Floyd Murphy. George Will, you may remember was a pre-eminent Republican. Until recently. George Will found the current state of the Republican Party so untenable, so philosophically and ethically repugnant, that he left the party. George Will speaks so eloquently in the *Washington Post* about Trump's lack of knowledge and his communicative failings. Concerning the latter...

> *It is urgent for Americans to think and speak clearly about Donald Trump's inability to do either.*

And the former...

> *[Trump] lacks what T.S. Eliot called a sense "not only of the pastness of the past, but of its presence." His fathomless lack of interest in America's path to the present and his limitless gullibility leave him susceptible to being blown about by gusts of factoids that cling like lint to a disorderly mind.*

———◆———

Trump, the Liar, (continued)

> "The truth requires many facts
> Which is why I have to lie.
> And a grasp of facts is what I lacks
> I'm so stupid I could cry."
> That's what he said, I swear it's true,
> (Can we know just what he meant?)
> But because we do, what should we do
> While we wait for impeachment?

We must not trust a single word that this administration says. Let me finish with a biblical caution:

> *The one who says, "I have come to know Him," and does not keep His commandments, is a liar, and the truth is not in him...*
>
> *King James Bible* 1 John 2:4

Please listen to John—John the Apostle and John the Journalist. (We are both saints, you know.) The truth is not in him. 'Tis futile to expect it.

Solum Optimis Verbis

Trump Limericks

Week 17 / May 14 – May 20, 2017

White House Comedy

Well, well, well. Who would have thought we'd ever return to third grade jokes? The silly ones that your best friend told you as if they were brand new.

> *What do astronauts call athlete's foot?*
> *Missile-toe.*
>
> *When is a door not a door?*
> *When it is a jar.*
>
> *When is a crime not a crime?*
> *When the criminal is the president.*

But we grew up and we grew older. Anyway, most of us did. Sadly, we discovered that some adults never grow up, and such people become jokes all by themselves. Unlike most jokes, however, these jokes are not funny. And now we've reached the point when the saddest joke of all is the President of the United States. Late night hosts and various shows like John Oliver's *Last Week Tonight* and *Saturday Night Live* continue to have a field day with Trump in office. He's fertile comic material, an infinite source of incredible contradictions that the comedians can't resist. He's a walking, talking, comic bulls-eye.

What are the appropriate metaphors for satirizing Trump? For making Trump the target of a seemingly endless stream of jokes?

> *It's like shooting ducks on a pond?*
> *It's like shooting fish in a barrel?*

I won't pursue either metaphor any further because I am sure the NSA is monitoring my key strokes or sneaking a peek through my computer's camera, and I would be loathe for them to discover any discussion about shooting our president—whether he's on a pond or in a barrel. (Just kidding, NSA.)

For my part, I confess that Trump's presidency causes original limericks to spill out on the page like whiskey at an Irish picnic. (I still prefer the whiskey, but limericks *with* whiskey is not an unpleasant prospect.)

> *As a womanizing narcissist liar*
> *Trump's everything we don't admire.*
> *Double-dealing and fraudulent,*
> *It's perverse how his mind is bent.*
> *We can't wait for Trump to retire.*

> or

> *The Russians know Trump is a dupe.*
> *That's why he keeps them in the loop.*
> *"I give them our secrets*
> *And I ain't got no regrets,*
> *When I send them intelligence poop."*

or

Trump's in bed with old Vladimir
That explains why his thinking's never clear.
(Thinking's just not his game,
We've got Russians to blame.)
A sad truth we should all dread and fear.

As I said, comics don't need a high-power scope to hit a target that moves as slowly as Trump does. Trump, of course, claims he moves too fast, that people can't keep up with him. To quote a famous movie, "He's a legend in his own mind."

Conundrum of the Week

Apparently, FBI director James Comey was fired for being honest about his loyalty. And to whom he was loyal.

I pledge allegiance to the flag
Of the United States of America...

Revised and updated:

I pledge allegiance to the flag
~~Of the United States of America...~~
And to Donald Trump and his vision

Trump asked Comey for his loyalty and Comey promised him honesty. What more could the president ask for? What a stupid question. Promising honesty to such a blatant liar and perverted prevaricator could never be sufficient. Look no further than the phalanx of liars surrounding Trump. It's clear that he values loyalty far more than honesty. In fact, honesty doesn't exist in Trump's universe. It doesn't have to. The attribute we call Honesty conforms with facts, and in Trump's universe, there are no facts. In a universe devoid of facts, honesty is never expected, required, or rewarded. Lies—from sloppy and inept to cunning and clever—are the accepted currency in the Oval Office.

If you're willing to lie
Then you'll be my guy.

Just ask Sean Spicer, Kelleyanne Conway, Steve Bannon, Steve Miller, Mike Flynn, Mike Pence, Jeff Sessions, Scott Pruitt and so many more, who also live in that fact-free universe and are happily spending the Trumpian coin of the realm: Lies. But James Comey doesn't live in that universe. That's why Trump fired him. Any man who attempts to import facts into Trump's fact-free universe is clearly a miscreant, someone who can't be trusted with a lie.

The Last Word

Quote of the Week: [from *New York Times*, David Brooks, May 15, 2017]

> *[Trump] is...the all-time record-holder of the Dunning-Kruger effect, the phenomenon in which the incompetent person is too incompetent to understand his own incompetence. Trump thought he'd be celebrated for firing James Comey. He thought his press coverage would grow wildly positive once he won the nomination. He is perpetually surprised because reality does not comport with his fantasies.*

Solum Optimis Verbis

Will Rogers Never Knew Donald Trump

Week 18 / May 21 – May 27, 2017

The President's trip overseas this week reminded me of something Will Rogers once said. And once I looked up the exact quote, I found that Will Rogers' capacity for insight has not been diminished one bit by being dead.

> *The taxpayers are sending Congressmen on expensive trips abroad. It might be worth it, except they keep coming back.*
> –Will Rogers

> *I don't make jokes. I just watch the government and report the facts.* –Will Rogers

Happy Memorial Day
If you have any memories of someone in your family who went to war—Civil War? World War I? World War II? Vietnam War? Iraq/Afghan War?—to defend our freedom and our country, share them with everyone you can.

In my family, my great Uncle Bill Timmins fought in France in WWI with the United States Army Expeditionary Force. Other than seeing a black-and-white photograph of Uncle Bill in his army uniform, I know little else.

Twenty-five years later, my Dad and his brother, my Uncle Ed, went to war in Europe.

Uncle Ed was a sergeant in Patton's Third Army as they swept across France and southern Germany. His uproarious claim to fame: "I made more money playing the piano in Officer's Clubs than I ever made fighting the Germans." Apparently he was typically paid for his musical gigs with bottles of liquor, and liquor was in high demand and short supply—a great money-making opportunity. He once told me that when US troops reached Berchtesgaden—Hitler's famous Bavarian hideaway—it was immediately turned into an Officer's Club…and my Uncle Ed ended up playing Hitler's piano.

My Dad, Jack Scannell, was a B-24 bomber pilot in the United State Army Air Corps [USAAC] flying missions out of a base in Tibenham, a town in East Anglia. The actor, Jimmy Stewart, was stationed at Tibenham as well, although he commanded a different bomber group. He and Dad knew one another on the biggest stage available. Dad flew 35 missions—one of them on D-Day—earned the rank of captain, and was awarded the Distinguished Flying Cross—the highest award given to any member of the USAAC. When I asked him years later what he did to earn the medal, he modestly said, "I brought the airplane back every time." When one realizes that the USAAC had one of the highest per capita casualty rates of any of the American armed forces, surviving was medal-worthy.

William Anthony Scannell & Michael Dennis Scannell, my older and younger brothers, both served with the 1st Marine Division in Vietnam. Both returned safely home, unlike the 58,209 soldiers whose names are inscribed on The Wall in Washington, DC.

The trouble with practical jokes is that very often they get elected. –Will Rogers

Will Rogers was probably not referring to Montana Congressman Greg Gianforte, but he could have been. Gianforte is worse than a joke, he is a thug. His *bona fides* as a thug may be viewed in the video where he body slams Ben Jacobs, a reporter for *The Guardian*. Jacobs had the audacity to ask a question Gianforte didn't like.

Gianforte's got plenty of company. Trump thinks wealth and fancy suits shield him from the "thug" label—but they don't. Trump is a thug. His hostility toward the press has set the table for sanctioning violent behavior. Keep Maya Angelou's sage advice in mind: "When a person shows you who they are, believe them."

If Stupidity got us into this mess, then why can't it get us out?
—Will Rogers

It is disturbing to me that we have elected a man of monstrous stupidity and ignorance. Even more disturbing, several foreign journalists reported this week that Europeans, on the whole, believe that our president "is not intelligent." That's so true. I ache because his stupidity is so obvious, and he is completely unafraid to put it on display. The man's self-awareness is non-existent. He is not sufficiently intelligent to be self-aware. He cannot see himself as others see him. Poet Robert Burns once wrote:

O, wad some Power the giftie gie us
To see ourselves as others see us.

When we realize that Trump is on the trailing end of the Bell Curve—just slightly ahead of those we label "mentally challenged"—that's scary. Below are quotes that range from the baffling to the brazen, from the dishonest to the outright stupid. I was going to call these Donald Trump's Greatest Hits, but he has so many quotes and you prefer to spend your holiday out-of-doors rather than laughing (or crying) at what you're about to read.

"One of the key problems today is that politics is such a disgrace. Good people don't go into government."
—Donald Trump (We know.)

"An 'extremely credible source' has called my office and told me that Barack Obama's birth certificate is a fraud."
—Donald Trump (Right.)

"I will build a great wall – and nobody builds walls better than me, believe me – and I'll build them very inexpensively. I will build a great, great wall on our southern border, and I will make Mexico pay for that wall. Mark my words."
—Donald Trump (They've been marked.)

"All of the women on The Apprentice flirted with me – consciously or unconsciously. That's to be expected."
—Donald Trump (All stupid women?)

"The point is, you can never be too greedy."
—Donald Trump (Or too stupid.)

"I thought being President would be easier than my old life."
—Donald Trump

Finally...from The Having Your Cake and Eating It, Too Dept.

Trump stood in the new NATO facility in Brussels and scolded NATO members for not contributing sufficiently to the NATO alliance. Then he pulled the maneuver that we've all grown accustomed to. While talking about money, he digressed and said, "And I've never even asked how much it [the new facility] cost. And I won't."

But he just did, via the back door. He's always saying that he's not saying something when he's actually saying just that. "I'm not saying Obama's not a citizen."

Trump is a double-dealing fraud. The only thing he excels at is The Art of the Con—not the Art of the Deal.

His book should have been The Art of Doubletalk. He actually says he's not saying something even as he's saying it. Here is my Trump-style doubletalk approach:

"I'm not going to say anything nasty about Trump, okay?. Some people thinks he's a first class asshole. Some think he's the dumbest son-of-a-bitch to ever occupy the White House. But I'm not about to call him names."

Lest We Forget…
Happy Memorial Day

Solum Optimis Verbis

A Letter to OMB

Week 19 / May 28 – June 3, 2017

Some Thoughts: Can the President Be Indicted?

<u>Short Answer:</u>

Hell, yes.

<u>Long Answer:</u>

There are many things that are complicated these days. Truly complicated. But whether a sitting US president can be indicted should not be one of them. President Trump may be "first among equals," but the key words are "among equals." Occupying the highest job in the land shouldn't make him any more or less of a citizen than any other citizen.

Article II, Section 1, Clause 5 of the Constitution sets forth the requirements for the president. That person must:

- be a natural-born citizen of the United States;
- be at least thirty-five years old;
- be a resident in the United States for at least fourteen years.

President Trump is a US citizen, and a powerful one at that. But does that mean he is more powerful than the laws that bind us all as US citizens? Any man who possesses that kind of power ceases to be a president. He becomes some other species of ruler, akin to those kings, queens, and emperors that once ruled by divine right. They considered themselves to be above the law, and the framers of the Constitution called them "tyrants."

My Civic Responsibility: A Letter to the Director of OMB

Mick Mulvaney
Director, Office of Management and Budget
725 17th Street, NW
Washington, DC 20503

June 2, 2017

Dear Mick,

Regarding the most recent budget you've submitted for consideration, I conclude that you are:

1. Terribly deficient in your math skills—I am married to an accountant. (Don't they teach addition and subtraction at Georgetown?) OR
2. Just plain stupid. OR
3. A liar. Like your boss.

Perhaps you are all three. I'd like to know.

Or perhaps you are simply one of the many incredibly unqualified Trump appointees, ill-suited to the posts they've assumed. Just ask Betsy DeVos or Scott Pruitt or Jeff Sessions or Sean Spicer…or Donald Trump. In which case, perhaps you should be forgiven for being as royally inept as they are. After looking at your budget, I have only two questions:

1. Can you balance your checkbook?
2. Do you really believe your fellow countrymen are as stupid as this budget would suggest?

Or perhaps it's because you are a Catholic living in South Carolina. I completely understand that Catholics embrace the wildest fictions and call them the truth, but your budget is the wildest fiction of all. And what can I say about South Carolina, the state you represented in Congress? South Carolina's principal claim to fame is that it started the Civil War, America's bloodiest war. And less than a century later, South Carolina repeatedly elected Strom Thurmond, a racist who managed to father a daughter with a black woman, and then never publicly recognized his daughter because she had the audacity to be black. South Carolina has such a proud heritage, Mick. Might I suggest South Carolina's tourist bureau manufacture hats declaring, South Carolina: Make America Racist Again? Decorate the brim with the Stars and Bars?

And look at you, Mick Mulvaney, an obvious overachiever, the pride of racist South Carolina, and a Catholic, whose budget would deliberately screw over the poorest of the poor. Have you forgotten Matthew 25:45? Did they never open the bible at Charlotte Catholic HS or Georgetown?

> I tell you the truth, when you refused to help the least of these my brothers and sisters, you were refusing to help me.
> Matthew 25:45

Your behavior and budget make me wonder. Have you been to Church and confession lately? Or are you simply a Sunday Catholic—a Catholic of convenience—good for getting elected but anathema when governing?

I know it is 2017, but let me encourage you and all your fellow South Carolinians to once again stand for secession. I assure you, no one will protest. With South Carolina gone, the national average IQ might rise about ten points, perhaps more. And South Carolina would stop being a drain on the US economy. May I quote? "South Carolina receives $7.87 in federal funds for every dollar spent in income taxes, the highest ratio of any state." So, by all means, please secede. Then you could reside in the Republic of Independent South Carolina

[RISC] and ruin only the lives of those 4.9 million citizens who call it home, rather than the lives of the other 320 million United States citizens who know they're all better off without South Carolina...and the author of the current fiction-filled, bogus budget. That's you.

I make only two requests: Please resign, then secede. When you do, I promise to send you a gracious thank you note.

Respectfully, (Don't you love irony?)

from *The Making-It-Up-As-We-Go-Along* Department

After the last two weeks of jaw-dropping news coming from the nation's capital, here are maybe the most important questions to ask: Why did President Trump fire FBI Director James Comey? Did the firing have anything to do with the FBI's probe into Russia? Well, there have been changing answers coming from the Trump White House.

- *May 9:* In its announcement of the Comey firing, the White House said it was due to how Comey handled the Hillary Clinton email investigation — and it was based on the recommendation of Deputy Attorney General Rod Rosenstein. "President Trump acted based on the clear recommendations of both Deputy Attorney General Rod Rosenstein and Attorney General Jeff Sessions," White House Press Secretary Sean Spicer said in a statement. "I cannot defend the Director's handling of the conclusion of the investigation of Secretary Clinton's emails, and I do not understand his refusal to accept the nearly universal judgment that he was mistaken," Rosenstein wrote to Trump.
- *May 10:* The White House denies that Trump had already decided to fire Comey. Question: "Sarah, isn't it true that the President had already decided to fire James Comey, and he asked the Justice Department to put together the rationale for that firing?" Answer: "No."

- *May 11:* In his interview with NBC's Lester Holt, Trump said he was firing Comey regardless of what Rosenstein recommended. "I was going to fire regardless of recommendation," Trump said. And he suggested the Russia investigation was a reason behind the dismissal. "When I decided to [fire Comey], I said to myself, I said, you know, this Russia thing with Trump and Russia is a made up story."
- *May 19:* The New York Times reported that Trump, in the Oval Office on May 10, gave this account for his firing of Comey, according to a document summarizing the meeting. "I just fired the head of the F.B.I. He was crazy, a real nut job," Trump said. "I faced great pressure because of Russia. That's taken off."
- *May 19*: In a statement responding to that New York Times article (and not denying it), the White House said Comey was interfering in its foreign policy with Russia. "By grandstanding and politicizing the investigation into Russia's actions, James Comey created unnecessary pressure on our ability to engage and negotiate with Russia," White House Press Secretary Sean Spicer said.
- *May 21:* Speaking to ABC, National Security Adviser HR McMaster said he doesn't remember "exactly what the president said" to the Russians in that May 10 meeting, but that the gist of it was that Comey "hamstrung" Trump's ability to find areas of cooperation with the Russians.

Summary

1. The Trump White House first said it fired Comey due to Deputy Attorney General Rod Rosenstein's complaints about how Comey handled the Hillary email investigation.
2. Then Trump told Lester Holt that the Russia investigation was the reason.

3. Then Trump told the Russians, "I faced great pressure because of Russia. That's taken off."
4. Then the White House explained that Trump was talking about Comey impeding its foreign policy with Russia.

Got all of that? And by the way, former FBI Director Comey is scheduled to testify before Congress on Thursday, June 8th.

Solum Optimis Verbis

Only You Can Prevent Global Climate Change

Week 20 / June 4 – June 7, 2017

With Trump as our president, I sometimes feel as if we need an International Smokey the Bear:

**Remember
Only You Can Prevent
Global Climate Change**

We should be so lucky. With Trump, the hits—like jabs, crosses, and uppercuts—just keep on coming. Trump tells the world that the United States will abandon the Paris Accord, and Trump acts as if environmental science is trying to dupe the world's population. Well, by gosh and by golly, he won't stand for it. Only he, Trump, is wise enough to see that the Paris Accords are a clever attempt to subvert the United States' industries. (That's why all the world's nations, except two, signed onto the accord. So they could laugh at us and avenge themselves on a hapless US economy.) Trump is truly a man of insight. I bet he was a big Buffalo Springfield fan.

*Paranoia strikes deep
Into your life it will creep.
It starts when you're always afraid...*
Buffalo Springfield [1967]

Let's discuss human extinction. True, at the moment it is a hypothetical. Movies depict asteroids or comets fire-balling to earth and threatening the human species, or giant calderas erupting—like the one beneath Yellowstone National Park—and our planet self-immolating, but the likelihood of such events is considered to be extremely low. More likely the cause will be anthropogenic—that is, the result of human action. As my father was always fond of saying, "You did this to yourself." The probability of anthropogenic human extinction within the next hundred years is the topic of an active debate. Unfortunately, Trump doesn't debate, or think, or contemplate. He tweets...no thought required.

What are the things we might "do to ourselves?" How about a global nuclear exchange, or a biological war causing an irreversible pandemic, or an ecological collapse from climate change?

The good news is that we could act with political circumspection and stop all saber-rattling—thereby lowering the likelihood of precipitating a nuclear or biological war—or we could behave with environmental wisdom and join the whole world by enrolling in a cooperative effort to lower carbon emissions (like the Paris Accords?)—and thereby save our planet for future generations. As science and scientists have pointed out, [C]arbon is the culprit responsible for raising planetary temperatures.

The bad news is that the United States as a nation—and, in particular, the Republicans as a party—have abandoned both circumspection and wisdom by electing Trump president. In this case, the bad news outweighs the good news.

If you'd like to explore this scary and depressing topic even further, let me suggest you read *The Sixth Extinction: An Unnatural History* by Elizabeth Kolbert [2014]. It won the Pulitzer Prize for General Nonfiction in 2015. I read it when it first came out, and although I am tempted, I won't give away the surprise ending.

Or you could come to my home here in Washington State and

get thoroughly drunk on some really fine wines—reds and whites. Getting drunk doesn't change presidents; doesn't solve political, psychological, or personal problems; doesn't save the earth. But for a few brief hours, you'll find pleasant diversion from the unrelenting madness of Trump. We offer a variety of fruits, cheeses, and breads, too. Consider this your invitation. Travel is on you. The wine is on us…and then in us…or in you if you choose to drop by. Things could be worse. We could have Trump and no wine. A brief poem might help.

Political ~~Whine~~ Wine

Everything's easy-uh
With anesthesia.
When your mind is so numb,
Midst the champagne's fine fizz,
You'll forget just how dumb
Donald Trump truly is.*

*Your seven choices are (in alphabetical order):
Trump is as dumb as

1) *a bag of hammers*
2) *a box of rocks*
3) *a doorknob*
4) *a fossilized dinosaur turd*
5) *a post*
6) *an ox*
7) *a stump*

Time for a Sidebar

A certain Trump supporter and climate change denier told me recently that the millions of Americans who deny climate change (and who elected Trump) can't all be wrong, as if sheer numbers actually prove the correctness of their position. But I remember something my Uncle Ed once said about being right and wrong. "It doesn't matter what everyone else thinks. Each of us is right or wrong, one at a time."

I can hear the climate deniers screaming that people like me believe in climate change because more than 98% of scientists engaged in studying the phenomenon believe that we are experiencing a man-caused problem. Yes, that's true. Unlike the climate deniers, however, climate change believers have more than empty words and hot air; they have extensive data to support their position. I believe it's called "proof." Climate deniers have only their assertions and accusations. These are people who are not only wrong, they are wrong at the top of their voices. What they lack are facts and a reasonable hypothesis on which to hang their alternative facts.

Let me simplify: We have facts; they have noise. I just don't want the extinction of mankind to be the fact that finally stops the noise.

𝔖𝔬𝔩𝔲𝔪 𝔒𝔭𝔱𝔦𝔪𝔦𝔰 𝔙𝔢𝔯𝔟𝔦𝔰

Not Feeling the Love

Week 22 / June 19 – June 25, 2017

Theater of the Absurd

The Trump Administration *is* Theater of the Absurd incarnate. In that spirit, I thought it appropriate to open his week's journal with a brief, absurd, dramatic sketch.

[We find Trump pacing around the Oval Office with Mike Pence standing center stage.]

Trump: Why do they all hate me so much?

Pence: Mr. President, they don't *all* hate you. According to the latest CBS poll, the patriotic 36 per cent think you're doing a fine job, sir. Really, really fine. Probably the finest job ever done by any American president. And if they were here, they would tell you what an honor it is to be a subject…er…citizen of the United States.

Trump: Thanks, Mikey. Good to know. Is that the same 36 per cent who wouldn't mind if I shot someone on Fifth Avenue?
[Looking out the window while pretending to aim a rifle.]

Pence: Yes, sir. The very same brave, supportive patriotic 36 per cent, sir.

Trump: Do you think they'd jump off a skyscraper for me, Mikey.

Pence: No question, sir. Of course they'd jump. They'd do anything you want. They wouldn't even have to think about it.

Trump: I wish all Americans were like that, don't you?

Pence: I completely agree, sir. Everyone would be better off if they didn't think…

[Interrupting]

Trump: That's right, Mikey. Damn it. Why do they always have to think about everything? I don't. I get all kinds of things done and never have to think.

Pence: That's because you're you, Mr. President.

Trump: That's right. I am me. Maybe I'll put that in my next Twitter.

[Takes out cellphone and tweets]

"I am me."

Pence: People will be impressed, sir. Impressed. The wealth of your thoughtless insights is astounding. You shoot from the hip, sir. Tell it like it is. Thinking is for sissies.

Trump: That's true. Not like the fake news folks. I read something in the Washington Post—fake news, right? fake news!—that when I gathered my cabinet here, and I asked everyone to say a few words, that we had—let me get this right—

[Takes a ragged newspaper article from his inside coat pocket]

"an avalanche of obsequiousness." Fake news! I didn't see an avalanche. Did you?

Pence: No avalanche, sir. None whatsoever. Who ever heard of an avalanche in June, sir?

Trump: That's what I mean, Mikey. I hate it when those vipers make up untrue things—some things are even false!—about me.

Pence:	Vipers, Mr. President?
Trump:	The fake news crowd.
Pence:	Oh, *those* vipers. They think our administration is not sufficiently transparent, sir.
Trump:	That's crap. My life is an open book. What do they want from me?
Pence:	They'd like to see your income tax filings.
Trump:	That book is closed.
Pence:	Or know what happened to your secret plan to defeat ISIS.
Trump:	That book's closed, too.
Pence:	Or know how you plan to create the best healthcare system in the world for all Americans while cutting Medicaid.
Trump:	How would I know that? They'll have to ask Turtle McConnell and Ryan, the Cowardly Lion. That's not my job. Creating bills that benefit all Americans while lowering taxes on the incredibly rich is not my job. It's their job.
Pence:	That's very true, sir. You have enough on your plate just campaigning for re-election.
Trump:	You're right, Mikey. There's only three-and-a-half years to go until the next election. As I see it, I have two major jobs: As president, my job is to fly off to places like Cedar Rapids and make people believe we are actually doing the impossible—like lowering taxes and improving healthcare at the same time.
Pence:	And those impossible things can actually seem possible if you don't think about them, Mr. President.
Trump:	There's that thinking thing again. Thinking about the healthcare bills in the House and Senate will only make you miserable. So if you don't think about them, you won't be miserable.

Pence: I'd like to say, sir, you certainly know how to solve those sticky problems.

Trump: That's why I'm universally loved by that unwavering, do-what-you-damn-well-please 36 percent. They understand that thinking equals misery. And it's why I love the second part of my job—going to rallies so I can cheer up the poor folks and in return they can adore me and shout things that make me feel good.

[Stands center as if receiving the adulation of his adoring mob]

Pence: Don't forget, sir, you are also our Commander-in-Chief.

Trump: I know, I know. But I'm probably giving that job to the people in the Pentagon. You know? I've already handed over control of Afghanistan, and nobody seems to mind. I think the generals like being in charge of wars and stuff. Besides, when North Korea blows up, I want that to be someone else's problem.

Pence: Excellent point, Mr. President. Even if you give away your Commander-in-Chief job, you still must deal with important legislation.

[Clearly exasperated]

Trump: Not true, Mikey, not true. My job is to sign bills, not write them. But just because I sign legislation doesn't mean I have to take responsibility for it. Besides, I like signing stuff. I sign stuff good. It's what I do best.

Pence: That's true, Mr. President. We all love it when we gather around your desk in the Oval Office and watch your delicate little hands scrawl that big, bold, beautiful signature.

Trump: Nicer than the pope's too, isn't it.

Pence: Quite a bit nicer, sir.

Trump: The pope wanted me to kiss his ring. Do you think I should get a ring so everyone can kiss it?

[Holds out his hand to MP. MP genuflects and kisses the ring]

Pence: Probably too soon, sir. Maybe during your second term.

Trump: Right. So, why else do the fake news folks detest me?

Pence: Sir, if I may, they make up stories because they think you lack experience.

Trump: Me? Inexperienced?

Pence: But I know that's not true. The 36 percent of brave, patriotic, unthinking Americans know it's not true, too.

Trump: I'm loaded with experience. I've got three wives.

[Very deferential]

Pence: Pardon me, Mr. President. You have only one wife and two ex-wives.

Trump: But that's experience, isn't it? I built a university…

Pence: Mr. President, I think you better steer clear of that subject a bit longer…

Trump: And I got Mexico to pay for the wall…

Pence: Mr. President, Mexico is still being a bit stand-offish about that.

Trump: They'll come around. They can't say no to me forever, can they?

Pence: The Mexicans?

Trump: We've got the most powerful military the world has ever seen. How can they say "no" to me?

Pence: Good question, sir. I don't know what you have in mind, but it would probably be unwise to attack or invade Mexico…

Trump: As always, Mikey, you're right. Absolutely right. It's probably too risky even if I am still the Commander-in-Chief. It would look bad to build a wall *and* go to war. It looks petty. Makes me look small. Hmmmmm. I'll get the Russians to do it.

Pence: Great idea, Mr. President. I'll get Ambassador Kislyak on the phone. I've got him on speed dial.
[Takes out cellphone and dials. Trump takes cellphone from Pence]
Trump: Sergey, how are you? It's Donnie. That's right.
[Laughing]
The Trumpster. Right! Hey, I was wondering. What's your military doing next week?

𝔖olum 𝔒ptimis 𝔙erbis

Letters, We Get Letters

Week 23 / June 25 – July 1, 2017

NOTE: This week I've written three letters. I've directed the first letter at the Trump Voter, the second to the American people, and the third to Speaker Paul Ryan (a letter I actually sent).

LETTER ONE:

This letter is to all the folks who continue to support Trump, who got him elected, and who still invest their hopes in him. In my estimation, there are two kinds of Trump voters:

1. *Trump voters who have finally been screwed by Donald Trump despite his promises. (That's what Letter One is all about.)*
2. *Trump voters who haven't been screwed by Donald Trump... yet.*

Dear Trump Voter,

I know you are tired and even more than a little annoyed that I have characterized you as profoundly stupid, incredibly misinformed, thoroughly gullible, or just plain greedy. Perhaps all four. But as I watch the man you so proudly promoted to the presidency, I need to ask several questions:

1. How many lies does a person have to tell before you consider him a liar and shun him?

2. How often does a person have to scam or bilk other people before you consider him a bad risk—a con man with whom you can no longer do business?
3. How many secrets does a man have to have before you suspect his secrecy masks a nefarious purpose? How many second chances does a public figure deserve? One second chance? Five? Ten? As many as he needs as long as he is "your guy?"

There are other questions, but they can wait. In a CBS News article dated June 25, 2017:

> In December, then-President-elect Trump told hundreds of workers at the Carrier manufacturing plant that he had worked out a deal to save their jobs.
> But it's not working out that way. A steady downpour today did little to wash away the fact that the jobs of 600 union employees are going south.
> "They're going to Monterrey, Mexico," said Robert James, president of the local union.
> [James] said he felt betrayed, since Mr. Trump told workers during his December visit to the plant that 1,100 jobs would be saved.
> "That is what he said was going to happen," James said. "That's what he told all of us."
> "And a lot of these people voted for Mr. Trump" with the understanding that he would save their jobs, James added.

Imagine that! Trump voters getting screwed by Donald Trump. I ask you: Does the loss of *Carrier Corporation* jobs go under the heading of *Lies Told,* or do we put that in the *Successful Scams* category? Maybe the displaced workers can get retrained by signing up for courses at *Trump University*? Oh, sorry. That was a scam, too. Ah, well.

Sincerely yours…and sincerely sorry,

LETTER TWO:

Dear American People,

Memory is a funny thing. When memory fades, some people act as if the event(s) remembered never really occurred. My mother [b.1919] and father [b.1916] lived through The Great Depression—that dreadful period in American history that spanned the years 1929 to 1941, the year America went to war. Naturally my grandmother and grandfather lived through The Great Depression as well, but they both died in the early 1970s, and whenever we'd gather for holidays or other celebrations, they seldom dwelled on the dreary days past. The Great Depression was something they'd survived, not something they wanted to discuss.

Sadly, those who remember The Great Depression—those with direct, first-hand knowledge—grow fewer by the minute. In another decade all those who struggled through hardship and privation, all those who pulled together collectively so that the United States could recover from an unthinkable financial catastrophe, they will all have joined the cadre of lost loved ones.

What then? What happens when no memory of The Great Depression exists, when no one remains to testify, "I was there?" What then? Will our government decide there is no need for the Social Safety Net born in the midst of The Great Depression? That's what is suggested by 2017's as-yet-unsuccessful legislation called The American Health Care Act [AHCA]. The AHCA would gut Medicaid, and financially cripple millions of American citizens.

Why would anyone vote for such legislation?

Since the hard days of The Great Depression, America has developed a Social Safety Net—Social Security [1935], Medicare [1966], and Medicaid [1982]—because the United States is a community. The word "community" rings hollow until members of that community act with *other-interest* rather than *self-interest*. What the Social Safety Net declares—for all the world to see—is that the United States is a community.

We are interested in others. We take care of our own. We don't abandon the weak, the infirm, the old, or anyone in need. A collection of self-interested people can never call itself a community.

Additionally, a day seldom passes without a congressman or senator bragging that the USA is the greatest country on Earth, the richest country God has ever endowed, or the moral leader of the known universe. Do they really mean what they say, or is it all just scripted for the cameras? Can we be moral if we abandon those who so desperately need Medicaid? What does it mean to be "the richest country in the world" if we defund programs that feed children? How can we be great when we elect a president who is a womanizing bully with no impulse control?

It's time. Time to live up to our vaunted reputation—"greatest," "richest," "most moral"—and act and legislate that way, or admit to ourselves and to the world that we are a small, selfish, petty nation, and that greatness has passed us by.

Respectfully,

LETTER THREE:

June 28, 2017

To: Congressman Paul Ryan

From: John Scannell

Dear Congressman Ryan,

You make me sad. I once thought you had the intellectual capacity to look at issues and decide how to best proceed, but I see I was wrong. You have neither the intellectual acumen, the wisdom, nor the moral courage to hold the position, Speaker of the House. I remember you demurred when first asked to become the Speaker. At that time, I was convinced that you would be an excellent Speaker of the House, but as events have unfolded, I've come to realize why you initially declined the Speakership. You understood something about yourself that the rest of us now realize. You're neither wise nor courageous. I am sad because the poorest, the oldest, and the most infirm Americans will suffer at your hands precisely because you lack wisdom and courage. Worse, you're neither generous, nor kind, nor Christian, despite your avowed Catholicism.

As a former Catholic, I thought that you would certainly see the unsuitability of Donald Trump—a chronic liar and deceiver—as president. Catholics profess a certain ethos, a certain sense of right and wrong, a certain expectation that those who would lead us ought to lead by example. Trump cannot be that person because his entire history demonstrates he is incapable of it. However, taking a stand opposing Trump would require courage—and apparently you have none.

Your first decision, to decline becoming Speaker of the House, exhibited a level of self-knowledge—and in self-knowledge we find the seeds of wisdom. Unfortunately you were seduced by ambition, forsaking wisdom for position; self-aggrandizement over service. You do realize that occupying a position of leadership doesn't make you a leader, don't you? Being a leader requires so much more. It requires wisdom and courage.

As I said, you make me sad. You could have been—and could possibly be—so much more. I wish I could convince you to act wisely and to be courageous; but I fear you have made peace with your cowardice.

Regretfully sent,

Solum Optimis Verbis

Twitter-Pated

Week 25 / July 9 – July 15, 2017

The Trump Countdown

It's Saturday July 15th, 2017. This is the 176th day of Trump's administration. Each presidential term lasts 1461 days which means Trump has 1285 days remaining. Unless he is impeached. Or some awful fate should befall him. Last week I hoped that a wandering asteroid might provide relief; this week I'm widening my appeal to include mosquitoes and tsetse flies.

Get Smart

Donald Trump and his administration are liars. Lying has been a regular theme in my journal, but there are things worse than being liars…like being bad liars, amazingly bad liars. You'd think with all the practice the various Trumps, Trump in-laws, and Trump surrogates have had at lying, bending the truth, or creating imaginative fiction out of thin air, they'd seldom get caught in their lies, but they get caught in their lies all the time. It's as if Trump and Company have all used the sitcom *Get Smart* as their template for effective prevarication. For those of you who don't remember *Get Smart*, it was a TV situation comedy created by Mel Brooks, airing first in 1965. It starred Don Adams as the inept secret agent, Maxwell Smart. Maxwell Smart was given to bragging [lying] and then revising his brag when the listener decided that the original brag was unbelievable. Maxwell Smart, always surprised by his listener's lack of belief, inevitably asked, "Would you believe…?" as if the new lie would somehow be believed, the old one having been clearly rejected. As an example, I offer a few lines from one of the *Get Smart* scripts:

Smart: I remember being captured in Burma during the war. I never told the enemy anything except my name, rank, and serial number despite being subjected to the most fiendish torture ever devised by man: water torture. A drop of water on the forehead every minute for three hundred gallons. Three hundred gallons, would you believe it?
Brown: That's pretty hard to believe.
Smart: Would you believe a quart?
Brown: No, I wouldn't.
Smart: What if I told you they came by every day with a glass of water and an eye dropper?

Isn't this what Donald Junior is doing? After every lie is proven demonstrably false, he asks, "Would you believe…?" So the theme of LYING is augmented this week by the theme of STUPIDITY. The motto of this White House appears to be "Lie First." The corollary of that policy is: "Lie until you are caught, and then lie again." In case you haven't noticed, we are in the midst of "government by chaos."

The Donald Trump Turkey Shoot

Twitter-Pated

I don't twitter and I don't tweet
I like my mind in the driver's seat.
But Mr. Trump, that guy's all thumbs,
That's why his twitters are oh so dumbs.

He rants and raves, his thumbs are hot,
His words are short 'cause his mind is shot.
He thinks he's right when he's oh so wrong.
Leave the White House, man, you don't belong.

The Trump Administration…in the Service of Stupidity

If I twittered…here are some tweets I'd send the president. Perhaps I could help educate him? Nah. Think of the following as wisdom in a small space…as opposed to Trump's stupidity in the same space.

We live in an era of smart phones and stupid people.
    Unknown   [60 characters]

Better to remain silent and be thought a fool than to open your mouth and remove all doubt.
    Abraham Lincoln from *Proverbs*   [121 characters]

We are all born ignorant, but one must work hard to remain stupid.
    Benjamin Franklin   [84 characters]

Stupidity is a force unto itself.
    Latin Proverb   [47 characters]

The Donald Trump Turkey Shoot

I'm allergic to stupidity. I break out in sarcasm.
    Unknown   [58 characters]

Never argue with stupid people, they will drag you down to their level and then beat you with experience.
    Mark Twain   [116 characters]

Stupidity is not the lack of knowledge, but the illusion of having it.
    Grigore Iulian   [89 characters]

It's too bad that stupidity isn't painful.
    Anton Lavey   [54 characters]

A Sign that Should Be Posted at the White House

Stupidity Is Not A Handicap

―――――――

Please Park Elsewhere

Solum Optimis Verbis

A Family Affair

Week 26 / July 16 – July 22, 2017

LOCATION: The Oval Office.
DRAMATIS PERSONAE:
President Trump [Trump]
Donald Junior [Junior]
Jared Kushner [Kushner]
Melania Trump [Melania]
Ivanka Trump [Ivanka]

Family members are scattered around the Oval Office. Trump is at the desk. Melania and Ivanka are downstage right putting on make-up.

Trump: Glad you all could make this special meeting of the intellectual elite here in the White House. We are the smartest of the smart. The goodest of the good. We all have the biggest words and the bestest ideas. We are all high-quality people.
[President preens, looking at all his in-laws and pointing at them.]
That's why I agreed to let you and you marry one of my off-spring.
All: Thanks, Dad.
[President holds up his hands. Clearly frustrated.]

Trump: Last year I thought that six months into my reign…
Ivanka: *[Interrupts]*
Administration, Dad. Don't use that word "reign." We've haven't had a king since 1776.
Trump: That long? Well, then we are way overdue, Ivy Divy. Am I right? Huh? Of course, I'm right.
Ivanka: Dad…
Trump: Why not? It's the truth. I'm in charge. The emperor. Besides, I'm among friends. They can't arrest me. I'm bulletproof. I got rid of Comey. Sessions is a kiss-ass. Who's gonna stop me? Betsy deVos assured me that she'll do her best to keep everyone stupid…
Junior: She's doing a wonderful job.
[General agreement among all.]
Trump: Before I begin, I want to summarize what I've accomplished since I've become president. Somebody tell me what I've done and what a wonderful job I'm doing.
[Long silence. A loooooooooog silence. Everyone looking at one another. Finally…]
Kushner: You were inaugurated.
All: That's right. Good job, Dad. I remember that day.
Trump: Got that right. Biggest crowd ever. Ever.
[Everyone hushes everyone else, not wanting to contradict.]
Melania: Da. And you appointed best ever member of Supreme Court.
Trump: Damn right, I did. *Roe v Wade* is toast.
[Another long silence. Trump grows impatient.]
Trump: What else?
Junior: You pushed aside the leader of Montenegro.
Trump: He got in my way. Don't ever get in my way.
[Everyone laughs and applauds.]

Melania: You het goot meeting vit our good friend, Vlad, at G20.
Trump: True. True. I shook Putin's hand longer than he shook mine. I think I won that handshake.
Melania: Da, darlink.
Ivanka: You gave guns to crazies.
Trump: I almost forgot. Everybody needs a gun, right?
[Silence]
What else? Come on. What else?
Junior: You told people that Andrew Jackson opposed the Civil War?
Trump: Damn right, he did. Thanks, Junior, thanks for remembering that. You are a high quality person. *[Pause]* How about the wall? I'm building the wall with Mexico, right?
Ivanka: Not really, Dad.
Trump: Well, we're about to repeal Obamacare, right?
Melania: Dat's a longshot, darlink. Nobody likes da bill. Is mean bill, no? Even you don't like bill.
Trump: So, I don't like the bill…so what? That bill won't ever affect me. I need a win. Being president is all about winning…for me. I promised lots of wins. I need wins.
[Silence]
Kushner: May I suggest you just "manufacture" a story about your accomplishments?
Trump: "Manufacture?"
Kushner: You're a salesman, Dad. Salesmen tell stories.
Trump: What kind of stories? What kind of stories should I be telling?
Junior Didn't you create 45,000 new coal jobs since January? *[Wink, wink.]*
Trump: Did I? Did I really create 45,000 new jobs?
[Kushner shrugs.]

Kushner:	That's the story, Dad.
Ivanka:	And haven't you passed more legislation than any president in history in your first six months?
	[Wink, wink.]
Trump:	Have I?
	[Ivanka shrugs and smiles]
Ivanka:	That's the story, Dad.
Kushner:	Look, Dad. North Korea's Kim Jong Un's dad shot a 38-under-par round of golf his first time on the course. That included five holes-in-one. If Kim Jong Il can do that, 45,000 coal jobs and the best legislative record ever is child's play.
	[The light bulb goes on over Trump's head]
Trump:	Good point. So I should manufacture a better golf score?
All:	No, Dad. Just stick to the issues.
	[Silence]
Trump:	Okay. Stick to the issues.
All:	And make America great again.
Trump:	Hey, hey. Maybe we should have a "Buy American Week."
Ivanka:	Whoa, Dad. That's a great idea in theory, but my entire line—all the clothing, all my shoes, and my purses—they're all manufactured in India, Vietnam, China, and Malaysia. Just like most of your stuff. If people buy American, they won't be buying Ivanka.
Kushner:	Okay. We can argue overseas manufacturing some other time. Why did you call this meeting, Dad?
	[Trump looks troubled.]
Trump:	I'm worried. I don't want to say that, but I'm worried. Every news channel I turn to says that this whole Russian thing isn't going away. I watch them all. For hours every day—on the big screen TV. Even FOX says we're in

The Donald Trump Turkey Shoot

	trouble. I knew I could expect bad news from ABC, CBS, NBC, MSNBC, CNN. But FOX?! All day long I'm watching and getting more and more depressed.
Junior	Maybe you should watch Law and Order.
Trump:	Can't. I can't watch bad guys going to prison.
Kushner:	Like my dad, Dad.
Trump:	Right. Like your Dad. *[Looks at everyone.]* We have to be more transparent.
Ivanka:	No, Dad. We simply want everyone to believe we are being more transparent.
Kushner:	We've just redefined transparent. Trans means "to go beyond" and parent, well, that's you Dad. I want "to go beyond the parent." My story was transparent. Well beyond any crazy story you ever made up.
Trump:	I'm proud of you, son. Proud of you.
Kushner:	That's a private definition, of course.
Trump:	That's fine. I'm glad you're me. Wanna watch some television together?
Junior:	We can't, Dad. We have work to do. Promises to keep.
Trump:	Promises to who?
Junior:	We have to meet with the Russians.
Trump:	No. No. Everyone has to stop meeting with the Russians.
Junior:	We can't.
Trump:	What do you mean, "we can't?"
Kushner:	They got you elected.
All:	Shhhhhhhhh.
Trump:	No, they didn't.
Junior:	Yes, they did.
	[Trump is emphatic]
Trump:	No, they didn't.
All:	Yes, they did.

Trump:	Oh.
All:	Sorry.
Trump:	I thought I got me elected.
All:	Nope.
Melania:	Aren't you gled? My goot friend Vlady put me here in America to be your hendler?
Trump:	He did that? My handler? I thought you loved me. *[Melanie shrugs and steps away.]*
Melania:	Nyet. Luff you? Talk about fake news.
Trump:	But what about my campaign. My wild promises. The wall. No Muslims. No Obamacare.
Melania:	Oh, Dawnnie, grow up. Paul Manafort, Jeff Sessions, and Jared and Junior all met wit Russians to make sure you get to live in White House. Vuz on your bucket list, no?
Trump:	*[Trump is confused and depressed.]* What's next on my agenda?
All:	Impeachment? Retirement? A world golf tour?
Ivanka:	They can't arrest you, Dad. Not as long as your president.
Trump:	So I either have to remain president for life, or die in office?
Ivanka:	Pretty much.
Trump:	*[Trump shakes head.]* Gotta get my TV viewing and golf in. *[Opens door. Peeks out. Returns.]*
Trump:	There's a dozen guys out here in the hallway. They're not Secret Service.
All:	They're lawyers. We all have lawyers.
Kushner:	Even some of our lawyers have lawyers.
Trump:	Do you think they'd like to watch Law and Order with me? What are you all going to do?
Kushner:	Practice saying, "I forgot." *[Moving up the musical scale while singing "I forgot.]*

The Donald Trump Turkey Shoot

Junior: I forgot.
Kushner: I forgot.
Melania: I forgot.
Ivanka: I forgot.
Trump: I love the Trump Family singers.
All: We forgot.

𝔖olum 𝔒ptimis 𝔙erbis

Savior McCain

Week 27 / July 22 – July 29, 2017

Metaphors: Trump, The Two-Year-Old

Lately, pundits and commentators on the various television news programs report how exhausting following and reporting on the current Trump administration is. It is, indeed, Government by Chaos. One metaphor seems most apt: our country has been tasked with watching over a two-year-old. Remember how tiring watching a two-year-old could be? Because he's been spawned by Republicans, Trump's parents need to exercise some parental authority over him even as their two-year-old runs recklessly over every norm, ounce of truth, and sense of decency. If the Republicans could find the strength to act as responsible parents, they'd keep their two-year-old in his playpen or in a locked room or harnessed and tethered to a pole in the White House's backyard. But truth and responsibility have been abandoned simultaneously, so their two-year-old goes wherever he wants to go, does whatever he wants to do, while we all watch in horror knowing he hasn't the sense or intelligence to avoid causing harm or being harmed. His Republican parents ought to be willing to take charge of their truculent, terrorist, tweet-happy-but-illiterate tyke. Instead, they shrug and ask, "Isn't he cute?" The answer is: NO.

The Phone Call

I don't know how many watched the final healthcare vote—the one taken on the "Skinny" Healthcare bill which had been unveiled only a few hours earlier—that occurred on the Senate floor around 1:30 AM [EDT] or 10:30 PM [PDT]. Wendy and I were returning from The Paramount Theater where we'd just watched *The Curious Incident of the Dog in the Night-Time,* and we were listening to the vote tally in real time on the radio. Spoiler alert: the Skinny Healthcare bill failed 49-51.

I expected the "No" votes from Lisa Murkowski and Susan Collins, but I found myself pleasantly surprised by John McCain's "No" vote—the one that essentially sealed the fate of the bill. Just prior to voting, VP Mike Pence had taken John McCain off the Senate floor "to discuss his vote." I have no idea what was said. However, in the interest of encouraging dramatic imaginations everywhere, I've scripted what transpired in the hallowed halls of Congress just before John McCain re-entered the Senate chamber to pull the rug out from beneath his Republican colleagues.

PLACE: Senate Floor. We discover John McCain standing and surveying the gallery [CS centerstage] when VP Mike Pence joins him.

Mike P: How are you feeling, John?
John M: I'm feeling alright. As well as could be expected. It was just brain surgery, you know.
Mike P: *[Looks a bit perplexed, he hesitates]* Oh, that's a joke?
John M: *[Smiles tolerantly]* Yes, Mike, that's a joke.
Mike P: Very funny. Very funny. *[Fake Laugh]* Glad to see that your healthcare crisis hasn't affected your sense of humor.
John M: No, it hasn't.

Mike P: We're all praying for you, John. All of Indiana and the whole country is praying. We prayed hard that your surgery would go well and here you are. You're here because of our prayers. You know that, don't you?

John M: That's nice to know, Mike. *[Smiles]* And here I am. Why are you here tonight? It's past midnight.

Mike P: I'm here to talk with you, John.

John M: Really?

Mike P: Yes, John. Could we step out into the hallway and talk for a moment?

[John McCain and Mike Pence walk down left in front of the grand curtain.]

John M: So what's up, Mike?

Mike P: Big vote tonight, John. Certainly the biggest ever for this administration. Donald needs a win and he's hoping that you'll carry the day for him.

[John McCain remains silent. Nodding and listening.]

It's no mystery that Murkowski and Collins are going to disappoint the president again, and Donald is tired of women "ruling the roost." He just told me this morning that "Those damn women should understand their place. But they don't." Then he said, "They think they're equal. But we'll deliver a message of equality into their fat female faces tonight when we get the vote." You gotta love his passion, don't you?

John M: I happen to like Lisa and Susan, Mike.

Mike P: *[Surprised by McCain's response]* Of course, of course, we all like them, John. They're good people. But they're women, that's all. The Bible makes women's roles explicitly clear. I bet they don't read their Bible like my wife. My wife knows her place. I wish we could help the women in the Senate understand the Divine pecking

	order. The "Big D" pecking order. *[Mike chuckles to himself.]*
John M:	Divine pecking order…? Big D?
Mike P:	Sorry, John. Sorry. I'm getting off topic here. I came out here so the president could have a word with you before the vote.
John M:	Is the president here?
Mike P:	No. He's back in the White House watching *FOX News* and *Law and Order* re-runs. Melania got him the complete *Law and Order* 20-year collection on DVD. *[Mike begins dialing his cellphone as he continues talking]* She's a real sweetheart. Never says much in public and a woman who really knows her place. He's on season six. He'd be here if he wasn't so attached to Lennie Briscoe—Jerry Orbach. *[Laughs]* Sometimes we watch together. *[McCain and Pence stand as we hear the phone ringing. President appears downstage right in his pajamas, sitting in a recliner with the footrest elevated, and with a TV remote in his hand. President picks up phone.]*
Trump:	Mikey, is that you?
Mike P:	Yes, Mr. President. I'm here with John McCain. Are you available to talk?
Trump:	Let me mute *Law and Order*. *[Clicks on the remote]* Okay. Can't talk long. Good episode here.
Mike P:	Mr. President, I'm handing the phone over to John McCain. *[Hands phone to McCain.]*
John M:	Mr. President…
Trump:	Senator McCain. Glad you're back from Arizona. Gonna need your help tonight. Bigly. Very bigly. No question. Need you to show the world that you are a high quality person.

John M:	I understand, Mr. President. So why do you like this particular bill, sir?
Trump:	What? This particular bill? I don't know anything about this particular bill except it's our last chance. All I know is what I see on FOX News. It's the "Skinny Repeal Bill," right? *[Laughs]* Just glad it wasn't named the Fatty Repeal Bill. Besides, it's my job to sign bills, not to know what's in them.
John M:	But why would you want any of us to vote for a bill when none of us knows anything about it, sir?
Trump:	Why the hell else? It's a win. You want a win, don't you, John? It's all about winning. That's why I love *Law and Order*, John. Lenny Briscoe always wins. We have to win big tonight or look foolish. You don't want to look foolish, do you?
John M:	No, sir. I don't want to look foolish.
Trump:	Good. Good. Tonight you have a chance to become a hero.
John M:	A hero, sir? Tonight? A hero for you?
Trump:	Damn right, McCain. A hero for me.
John M:	I thought I was already a hero, Mr. President. Remember Vietnam?
Trump:	Sure, I remember…
John M:	And your personal war on bone spurs?
Trump:	*[Voice growing tense]* Now, don't take us down that road, Senator.
John M:	How can I possibly be a hero, Mr. President? Wasn't I captured? Isn't that what you said? You didn't consider me to be a war hero because I was captured?
Trump:	But that was more than forty years ago.
John M:	No, that was only two years ago, on July 19th, 2015. That's what you said on July 19th, 2015.

Trump:	I thought you'd be over all that by now.
John M:	Oh, I'm over all that Mr. President.
Trump:	So what's this all about?
John M:	I'm afraid I've been captured again.
Trump:	What? By who?
John M:	Conscience, sir. And by common sense. Turn to your favorite news channel, Mr. President, because I'm heading back into chamber to vote. *[Turns to Pence]* Mike, you can go home. There won't be any tie votes tonight. *[Turns back to cellphone]* Mr. President, I plan to be a national hero tonight. Just not yours.

What have I (we) learned during six months of Trump?

I don't like Trump.
This is not a recent revelation. I never liked Trump even during his presidential campaign. But, if it is possible for something to become truer than it once was, that statement is truer now. So many ordinary citizens—like my own sister—have said "You should give the man a chance, John"—and I was thought to be contrarian when I said, "Absolutely not. The man is who he is. His behavior is not suddenly going to change. Why would you expect him to be suddenly 'presidential,' when his entire life has been so 'un-presidential,' so uncouth, so driven by selfishness?" I blanch at the tameness of my own language, for in truth, I loathe, abhor, detest, and despise the Donald. He is repugnant for a whole host of reasons. Perhaps because he is an execration and an abomination. A man devoid of beliefs. Cruel and petty. (There. That should do it.)

Trump is a liar.
This is not a debatable statement. It is eminently provable, and Trump daily provides additional proof. Less than two weeks ago

[July 18], he actually said that the US had increased mining jobs by 45,000 since he took office. He was only off by 44,200 since the real number is about 800 jobs according to the *Bureau of Labor and Statistics*. Ah, well. Is this a big lie, or just a "little white one?" And can any coal-mining lie ever be "white?"

Trump surrounds himself with liars.
Trump can spot a liar a mile off…probably further, since he's had lots of practice. Once Trump has spotted a liar, he hires him… or her. Consider all the people we've heard tell lies—both monstrous and miniscule—during the past six months. The Presidential Prevaricator sent Sean Spicer into the public eye on Day 1 of his presidency to boldly lie as no man has lied before. Spicer had plenty of company, until he was replaced by liar and *vulgarian extraordinaire* Tony "The Mooch" Scaramucci.

Trump is delusional.
This is related to, but different from, lies. Howard Gardner, Harvard professor has called Trump "a textbook narcissist" and said that he suffers from a severe "narcissistic personality disorder." According to the Mayo Clinic, narcissistic personality disorder is "a mental disorder in which people have an inflated sense of their own importance, a deep need for admiration, and a lack of empathy for others." If that definition needed a single image to accompany and sum up the text, it would be a picture of Donald Trump. If one needs a demonstration of a "lack of empathy," consider his remark on July 28th, "Let Obamacare implode." "What of the people?" we might ask. "Who cares?" says Trump.

Trump is both lazy and stupid.
"Lazy and stupid" pairs well with being a liar or being delusional. If you make it up as you go along, you don't have to know anything. If

the truth and facts don't matter, information is only an impediment likely to trip you up.

Trump has only one speech.
Six months into his presidency, Trump is still stuck on the "Hey, I Won the Electoral College" Speech which he delivers to any and every audience—whether to members of the CIA at Langley or at a Boy Scout Jamboree. I often wonder what happened to all his big words—you remember?—the best words?

Trump wants to rule, not govern.
Issuing an anti-transgender edict via tweet this week might normally be considered, in times past, "the royal prerogative." Tweeting his will, as is his wont, Trump believes he can simply change carefully crafted policy on the strength of his silly say-so. This worked very well in the 16th century, just ask anyone who lived under the reign of Henry VIII or his daughter, Elizabeth I. But Trump needs to update his calendar.

Trump believes in Government by Thuggery.
I don't think this needs additional explanation. Let me refer you to Jeff Sessions, our soon-to-be-gone Attorney General. Trump is angered that Sessions isn't acting as his personal lawyer and advocate rather than as America's chief law enforcement officer. I expect Trump is mobbed up in a variety of places—perhaps not unusual for someone in the building and construction trade. And the thuggish style suits him to a tee. He's not interested in the rule of law—only the Rule of Trump.

Trump has no concept of constitutional democracy, the separation of powers, and the meaning of civil service.
Trump's been annoyed that he cannot have Government by Fiat. His authoritarian instincts have been thwarted at every turn. His Muslim

ban was immediately overturned, and the United States still has crime despite Trump's assurances that our dark days of crime are behind us—because he would simply not permit it. Oddly, he's now talking about pardoning himself—something even past royalty were unable to do. Ask England's King Charles I. He got his head handed to him in 1649…literally.

Trump is disloyal.
Except to Vladimir Putin. For Trump, loyalty is a strictly one-way street. Ask James Comey. Ask Sean Spicer. Ask Reince Priebus. Ask his first two wives.

Solum Optimis Verbis

Ode to Trump

Week 28 / July 31 – August 5, 2017

Ode to Trump © 2017

The president we have is just a photo op, you see?
A heinous ignoramus without maturity.
He rails against America's hardworking immigrants
Alerting the whole world that he's devoid of any sense.
Yes, the president of all is just a fulminating bigot,
Spouting nonsense through his tweets like a sadly broken spigot.

The other day he tweeted 'gainst trans-genders in the service
Without consulting or discussing—his bad judgement makes me nervous.
Our leader makes pronouncements, says he uses "the best words,"
But they're usually one syllabic ones that drop like herds of turds.
Then making things so much the worse—with ignorance immense—
He selects a bigot for VP who's not worth a half-a-Pence.

The Donald Trump Turkey Shoot

He hires sycophants galore to kiss his flabby bottom.
Think of a man's pernicious traits—our president has got 'em.
He lies and scams like breathing air, so unapologetic,
When he is called into account, his thumbs become frenetic.
He tweets "Fake News" as if that term absolves him of all blame
Diverting all attention with a tweet-storm hurricane.

One tweet I'd like to see him write—'cause he thinks he's royalty—
"I live upon a one-way street, I've named it Loyalty."
Ask Spicer or ask Priebus—the ones who were let go—
Is loyalty a two-way street? The answer's surely, "No."
If plagued by doubt, feel free to ask Miss Marla or Ivana
They'll tell it straight, "He's such a putz! You can even ask Madonna."

We live in fear his ignorance will likely lead to strife
With North Korea, Syria—he wants to bet your life.
He's imbecilic, dangerous, he thinks he knows it all
The truth is he's a nothing-head—no memory, no recall.
Holds no beliefs, no policies, that define him as a person,
For when he opens up his mouth, our problems only worsen.

We're all exhausted, day by day, with Trump's inanity,
Clinicians everywhere agree, he suffers from insanity.
So there you go, that's Donald Trump, the Village Nincompoop.
I'm hoping by the end of year, some saneness I'll recoup.

The News with Critical Commentary
August 1, 2017
Associated Press
Kushner Says Trump Campaign
Too Dysfunctional to Collude

Critical Commentary

Here is what they are saying: "We are too dumb to collude. We want the world to believe we are incredibly smart—except when we get in trouble—and then we play stupid."

And it's exceptionally easy to play stupid when you really are stupid. Besides, the word collude is way too big for Donald Trump to understand. Collude is probably an SAT word—maybe even an AP word. Trump prefers words like "cheat" and "scam" because they're easy, one-syllable words.

The New York Times
White House Defends
President's Effort to Help
Write Trump Jr. Statement

Critical Commentary

What an admission! This is the "I'm a better liar than my son" excuse…er…explanation. "So they ought to let me write the lie because I have so much more experience at bending the truth than my son. I can bend the truth so far it's really a circle. Amazing, right?" The article went on to basically assert that any father would lie for his son…especially when the FBI or a special prosecutor is involved. After all, the truth is likely to look bad and cause trouble. Why tell the truth when a lie works as well?

NBC News
What Really Happened
To Anthony Scaramucci?

Critical Commentary
What happened to Tony "The Mooch" Scaramucci is what ought to happen to an arrogant bloviator who decides he can bad-mouth colleagues because "that's my style." Pundits used words like colorful to describe The Mooch when they should have used words like "vile" or "obscene." There is a difference—you can look it up. Please feel free to borrow my dictionary.

Vox
GOP Sen. Jeff Flake:
Donald Trump Is Like
The Biblical Flood, &
We Need to Build an Ark

Critical Commentary
I think the headline says it all. Finally, a Republican who is willing to call Donald Trump a dangerous, irresponsible president. I just want to be sure that Trump is not aboard the ark when the waters begin to rise.

Remember when all the commentators incessantly wondered when Trump would act "presidential?" As if a 70-year-old billionaire—a childish adult who has never heard a "No" he couldn't and wouldn't snidely ignore—could ever be expected to change behavior, especially when being an irresponsible bully had worked so well for so long. Trump is the "dent" in "presidential" and can reliably be expected to trample over every norm of decency and thoughtfulness that governs the behavior of good people.

Trump is not "good people."

August 2, 2017
The Hill
Chelsea Clinton Thanks
White House Staff After
Trump Calls It a "Dump"

Critical Commentary
Perhaps Donald Trump has grown so used to the "gilded bordello" look that typifies his Trump Tower residence that he's forgotten how the other 99.9% live. Thank goodness we have former residents like Chelsea Clinton to gently correct the President's inaccurate observation. So...to ignorance and stupidity, please add insipidness, rudeness, crudeness, and ingratitude to Trump's list of winning personality traits.

The New York Times
Trump Administration Sets Up
Inquiry Into Discrimination
Of White College Students

Critical Commentary
From the "Can't Leave Well Enough Alone" Department, we find the Justice Department—led by "disappointing" Jeff Sessions—looking to disenfranchise students who have benefitted from Affirmative Action policies in our universities. I'd find that strange if I didn't know that Jeff Sessions—a bedrock Alabamian—is still fighting the War of Northern Aggression and this is simply a way to carry on the fight by different means. I'm sure Jeff Sessions would say, "I never met a black man I couldn't dislike...same for immigrants...and Muslims...hell, mah list grows longeh eveh year. There just ain't nuff people 'round heah to hate no mo."

Perhaps Jeff Sessions will make the cover of TIME magazine as America's *Bigot of the Year.* Do you think he's familiar with the 14th and 15th Amendments of the US Constitution?

Solum Optimis Verbis

The Sock Song

Week 29 / August 6 – August 12, 2017

The Countdown, An Update:

It's Saturday, August 12th, 2017. This is the 204th day of Trump's administration. Each presidential term lasts 1461 days which means Trump has 1257 days remaining. Unless he is impeached. Or some awful fate should befall him. During the first week of *The Countdown*, I hoped that some wandering asteroid—or meteorite—might provide relief by burning through our atmosphere and surprisingly coming to rest inside Trump's empty skull. One burnt cinder crashing into another. When the heavens failed to respond, I appealed to nature in the form of deadly mosquitoes and tsetse flies—giving a whole new meaning to "biting satire." Insects apparently have better things to do. Alas, there are no venomous snakes indigenous to New Jersey—people like the Trumps may be venomous, but they are not indigenous. Then I prayed to the God of Manufactured-Goods hoping a faulty golf cart might carry our fearless leader to that Great 19th-Hole-in-the-Sky. Nope. Now that Trump's on vacation at his New Jersey golf resort, my hopes have turned to an errant golf shot striking him in the temple and nullifying his presidency.

Hey, Let's Have a War…or My Missile's Bigger than Your Missile

I've have tried (mostly) to avoid blunt, scatological language when I speak of our president, but it seems that such language is the easiest way to describe Trump's latest stupidity:

The Donald Trump Turkey Shoot

Our president and the president of North Korea are in a pissing contest.

It really is that simple…and that crass. One wonders: What passes as diplomacy in the mind of Trump? I'll admit that using a phrase like "the mind of Trump" strikes me as oxymoronic largely because the threat of "fire and fury" that he leveled at North Korea on Tuesday, August 8, is moronic in the extreme. An American president who is willing to risk the safety and well-being of two of our closest allies—South Korea and Japan—is no friend. Why should South Korea or Japan trust the United States? And Secretary of State Rex Tillerson aided and abetted Trump's reckless, thoughtless show of bravado by saying that United States citizens should sleep well when they think of North Korea. I wonder if he has the same vacuous advice for South Korea and Japan. Do you think they're sleeping well at night with Trump making his macho-chest-thumping remarks?

So, let me ask once again: What is a bridge too far? What presidential misbehavior, which words and actions, will his Republican supporters see as just too much to abide? Are Republicans truly satisfied having a man as grossly ignorant—intellectually and personally—as Trump?

So, in the interests of engaging my crasser, angrier core, I offer you *The Sock Song* with an apology. I used the f-word. Sorry. It just fit the song so well. If you are offended…I apologize. But ask yourself: Is it more offensive that Trump's presidency?

The Sock Song © 2017

Some people they really like nylon
Some others they just prefer wool
Some like the really long tube types
The sort worn at a posh private school.

But socks serve more than one purpose.
They do more than keep tootsies warm.
They help when the president's spouting
Such nonsense that's way past the norm.

CHORUS

So stick a f**king sock in it
Your ignorance is showing.
And stick those tweeting thumbs of yours
Where the sunshine's never going.

Yes, stick a f**king sock in it
Stupidity's contagious.
And stop those tweeting thumbs of yours
Both foolish and outrageous.

𝔖olum 𝔒ptimis 𝔙erbis

A Child's Bedtime Tale

Week 34 / Sept. 10 – Sept. 16, 2017

Once upon a time, in a city far too close to home, there lived a child named Little Donnie Trump. Little Donnie was very old for his age but most people simply thought of him as a huge child with bad hair and a bad complexion. Little Donnie was also hugely rude and ill-mannered, so much so that anyone who knew him called him a brat. But he didn't mind being called a brat because he was rich.

"I'm really rich," Little Donnie said, whenever anyone accused him of anything. "You can be a brat when you're really rich like I am."

The thing that Little Donnie loved most of all was conning people.

"I love conning people," he would say. "I can con people all the time because people are stupid." Then he would laugh an evil laugh. "But I'm really smart. Everyone knows how really smart I am. I think a philosopher once said 'I'm really rich therefore I'm really smart'…or something like that."

"Stupid people believe anything you tell them. Can you believe that? How stupid do you have to be to believe Mexico'll pay for a wall that I want to build? Bigly stupid. But bigly stupid people vote too, and I wanted them to vote for me—and they did! And can you believe it? They still think Mexico's going to pay for the wall. They're pretty dumb…but then they're not really rich either. Not like me. I'm really rich."

The Donald Trump Turkey Shoot

Little Donnie had a big plan. He said, "I want to make America great again." He didn't know exactly what "Make America Great Again" meant, but it sure sounded great, and he meant every word of it. "My slogan is on hats and t-shirts, so it's got to be true."

When someone told Little Donnie that all he had was a slogan—and that a slogan is not a plan—he scoffed. "Plans, slogans. What's the difference? Doesn't matter. What matters is getting elected. Besides, when you're really rich—you know I'm really rich, right?—you don't really need plans. That's the best thing about being really rich, believe me. Besides, people are really stupid, and the people who'll vote for me are too stupid to understand plans that even someone as really rich as I am can't understand."

No one else knew what Little Donnie meant by "Make America Great Again" either, but some people are better at believing than at thinking. "I tell them the truth: all politicians are liars. Then I tell 'em that I'm not a politician. I tell 'em I'm a really rich, really smart guy, and they fall for it. Can you believe it? That's why I love really stupid people. They're my kinda people. And I get away with it because I'm really rich. That's the best thing about being really rich: the bigly stupid masses want to be really rich like me. They're too stupid to know I'm just conning them."

Yes, Little Donnie conned people for months and months during his campaign. He said he'd build a wall and that Mexico would pay for it. He always thought that was really funny, and it made Little Donnie laugh his evil laugh whenever he thought about it. "I can say anything I want because I'm really rich," Donnie said again and again. "That's the best thing about being really rich."

Along the way, he figured that "his kinda people" didn't like Muslims, so he told them that when he was elected *Little Donnie the First, President of the United States of America,* he would ban Muslims.

Little Donnie also figured he'd scrap free trade, repeal and replace Obamacare, roll back environmental standards, get thousands more coal jobs, and get rid of that annoying global warming Paris agreement. And his really stupid bigots were with him every step of the way.

But Little Donnie worried he couldn't count on really stupid people to get him into office—they are *really stupid*, after all—Duh!!! So Little Donnie did what he always did to win. He cheated. He asked his bestest friend in the world, Shirtless Vlady Putin, to help him get into office.

"I can cheat because I'm really rich," Little Donnie said. "That's the best thing about being really rich. It's not cheating when a really rich person does it."

And Shirtless Vlady Putin delivered. Little Donnie got elected.

But Little Donnie didn't know what he was doing. Oh, no, Little Donnie didn't know at all. Worse, Little Donnie didn't know what he didn't know, and Little Donnie wasn't interested in knowing what he didn't know. Instead, Little Donnie just started spewing executive orders willy-nilly. One of his first executive orders banned Muslims. "So America will be safe again," Little Donnie said.

But the courts said, "Hold up there, Little Donnie. You can't do that. This is the United States, and we have a Constitution."

But Little Donnie didn't know that he couldn't do that. *Constitution, schmonstitution*, Little Donnie thought. *I don't care about all that. Didn't I just get elected Little Donnie the First, King of the United States of America?*

Why should Little Donnie care about things he didn't know about? And Little Donnie figured it didn't matter that he didn't know that he couldn't do that, so he figured he could do it anyway. After all, he said, "That's the best thing about being really rich. You can do whatever you want—even when people say you can't—and you get away with it."

His predecessor tried to give him some tips about how to be

president, but Little Donnie was too much of a brat to take the advice of anyone who thought they were smarter than him. (Which, sadly, is almost everyone.) Besides, Little Donnie knew his predecessor was a man of color, and *that* kind of man certainly couldn't be smarter than him, could he? After all, Little Donnie was really rich and a good white Caucasian boy. Little Donnie believed that's an unbeatable one-two punch.

By and by, Little Donnie was often overheard mumbling in the Oval Office, "I'm really rich. I should be able to do anything I want. I should. I should. I should. I don't understand. Maybe I should ask Nerdy Bill Gates or Show-off Jeff Bezos for some advice. They're two really rich white guys, right?" And presto, Little Donnie figured he should make nice not just with the really rich people, but also with the really white people. And a small todo in Charlottesville gave Little Donnie just the chance he needed.

Little Donnie made sure that the *really* white people knew Little Donnie loved *them* most of all. Little Donnie knew that really white people accomplished everything good in the known universe. Little Donnie knew that really white people were God's chosen, weren't they?

"I'm really rich and so I'm really smart, so maybe that's why everyone else can't see things that like I can," Little Donnie figured.

But *Little Donnie the First, Emperor of the United States of America* eventually figured out that not everybody loved him, and, unbelievably, not everybody agreed with him. Not Mexicans. Not Muslims. Not Blacks. Not Democrats. And now, not even Republicans. Gasp! Sure, the stupidest of the stupid agreed with him, but then he was *Little Donnie the First, Emperor of the United States of America, The Boy Who Could Do No Wrong*. (It was an honorary title.)

There was one thing that almost everybody agreed on: Little Donnie had put his foot in his mouth, but Little Donnie said he didn't care. "I'm really rich," Little Donnie said. "I can get the most bestest podiatrist in the country to get that foot out of my mouth. That's the best thing about being really rich."

And, remarkably, Little Donnie surprised the media folk—the media folk who should have long ago ceased being surprised—when Little Donnie spoke the day after he made his tiny, racist, white-supremacist *faux pas*. Of course, Little Donnie used a teleprompter to read someone else's words that were manufactured to be heartfelt—words that were not in Little Donnie's vocabulary, speaking a sentiment that was not in Little Donnie's heart.

"I'm really rich," he said afterwards. "I can pay people to put heartfelt words in my mouth. That's the best thing about being really rich."

But Little Donnie was unhappy. Too many days passed with the spotlight on something other than him.

"When you're really rich," Little Donnie said with pride, "it's all about you. And I'm really rich. So it's really all about me. That is, after all, the best thing about being really rich."

Others said, "No, Little Donnie, it isn't all about you. It's all about the 320,000,000 citizens of these great United States. They need reliable, affordable healthcare. They need a living wage. They need reasonable tax rates. They need infrastructure."

"What about me? What about my needs?" Little Donnie whined. "I need a win. I need Congress to bring me a bill to sign so I can say, 'I did that. Ain't I somethin'?'" So he threatened the House and the Senate to get a healthcare bill passed.

"What kind of healthcare bill would you like?" asked members of Congress.

"Don't ask me," shouted Little Donnie in frustration. "That's your job. My job is to sit behind my desk and sign the bill once you have done all the hard work."

And Little Donnie knew he was right. "That's the best thing

about being really rich. You pay someone else to do all the hard work, the tough thinking."

And everything was going just as planned—the Stupid House of Representatives had passed an awful healthcare bill—but he was happy.

"When you're really rich, you can afford all the best kinds of healthcare. That's the best thing about being really rich. You don't have to worry about things like a bunch of poor people?"

But then a few upstart Republican Senators voted "No."

Little Donnie hardly knew what to say. Little Donnie wasn't sure what "No" meant, since he almost never heard it. Not from his parents. Not from his nanny. Not from his ex-wives. Not from his employees. Hearing "No" was something unexpected. Something new. Worse, he heard "No" from a stupid ex-prisoner-of-war who Little Donnie had denigrated during the presidential campaign. The Tortured "Really-Not-A-Hero" John McCain had said "No."

"He can't do that to me," Little Donnie fumed. But Tortured John McCain could and he did, and the healthcare bill flamed down to ignominious defeat. Or so they said on the television news that Little Donnie loved watching. Little Donnie asked his advisors, "What's ignominious mean? Is that good?"

That's when he heard "No" again. For a second time. It was tantrum time.

"What am I supposed to sign if Congress doesn't send me a healthcare bill?" Little Donnie wailed. And then it hit him. "Those Republicans in the Senate— the Mick brothers, McConnell and McCain—they're losers. I'm not a loser; they're the losers. I didn't lose this contest, they did. I can't be a loser. I'm really rich. That's the best thing about being really rich. Really rich people never lose. Really rich people always win. I always win."

And Little Donnie vowed to get back at those losers…somehow…sometime. Little Donnie was a champion pouter, and he could out-pout almost anyone, just ask his ex-wives. So when the chance to bigly snub the Republicans arrived—along with two hurricanes and a debt ceiling—Little Donnie told the Democrats how much he loved them, and that they were his newest and bestest friends—except for Shirtless Vlady Putin (but he never really mentioned Shirtless Vlady Putin because that was a really touchy subject).

But Little Donnie decided he wanted to do something big. Something everyone would notice. Doing something big was an itch he just had to scratch.

"I can scratch whenever I want to," Little Donnie said, "because I'm really rich. In fact, I can pay someone else to scratch any itch for me—like I once did in Russia with some ladies. That's the best thing about being really rich."

But what could that something big be? What could he do on his own without anyone standing in his way? What could he do that the stupid federal judges couldn't stop, that the stupid House of Representatives and the stupid Senate couldn't interfere with?

And then, Little Donnie knew. So Little Donnie ordered all his fleets and all his submarines and all his bombers and all his jet fighters to get ready to blow up North Korea if Crazy Kim Jong-Un even farted without permission.

Crazy Kim Jong-Un was incensed by Little Donnie's ultimatum. "I fahht if I want," said Fatty Kim Jong-Un, his plump cheeks quivering. "I no listen to man with bad hair. Stupid Little Donnie can no tell me if I can fahht." And then out of sheer spite, Crazy Kim Jong-Un farted. Several times. On television. His plump cheeks quivering.

Pandemonium reigned.

"When you're really rich, you can run for president and say any outrageous thing you want," Little Donnie told the nation. And everyone knew it was true.

"You can lie, you can make stuff up, and bunches of stupid people will believe you." And all the really stupid people nodded in energetic agreement.

"And when you're elected president, you can launch nuclear missiles when someone like Crazy Kim Jong-Un farts disrespectfully at you. That's the best thing about being really rich."

"I'm tired of that piss-ant Crazy Kim Jong-Un," Little Donnie told the general who sat beside him. "Besides I'm *Little Donnie the First, God Emperor of the United States*. So, go get me the launch codes. We gonna have us some fun."

The End
(Sweet Dreams)

Solum Optimis Verbis
Trump's Letters to Losers
Week 36 / Sept. 24 – Sept. 30, 2017

The Countdown

It's Saturday, September 30th, 2017. This is the 252nd day of Trump's administration. Each presidential term lasts 1461 days which means Trump has 1209 days remaining. Unless he is impeached. Or some awful fate should befall him. Now that he's alienated the NFL as well as the wealthy owners who contributed to his campaign coffers, perhaps he'll get tackled as he walks along Pennsylvania Avenue. While I await that event, I present a series of Trump's private letters written this week after he read (or saw) a news article. These letters were purloined from the Oval Office and faxed to yours truly by Mr. Anonymous.

Monday, September 25, 2017
GOP Effort to
Repeal Obamacare
Falls Short Again

~~Dear Mitch~~ Loser,

I ask you to do one thing—just one ~~damn~~ thing—and what do you do? Nothing. Where's the great deal-maker everyone said you were? Cause I'm not feeling him. Sure, they never said you were anywhere near as good as me—not even close—but who is? I am the #1 best ~~damn~~ deal-maker ever. That's what everyone says, so you know it's true. I'm the best. At everything. But everyone said you were the guy. They said you make things happen. But did you? Did you? No. Not even close. You're just a big stupid loser! McConnell and McCain, sitting in a tree—two big fat McLosers.

Thanks to you—no, wait—NO thanks to you—I don't have any big bills to sign. Not one. No wall. No repeal and replace. I don't like looking like a loser. I don't even hang around losers. When I see a loser, they're fired. Fired. Ask Spicey. Ask Flynn. Ask the Mooch. All losers. I gotta have winners like me cause I'm a winner. Everyone knows I'm a winner. A big winner. I won the November election by the most votes ever. Everyone knows it. That's why I've been signing tons of those executive orders cutting stupid environmental and financial and government regulations, and keeping ~~Muslims~~...terrorists out. Signing stuff makes me a winner. Everyone knows that. So that Strange guy in Alabama better win. He's your guy, right? He better be a winner. Not like you. I went down there on Friday to help him and you out. Where were you? I bet you were too busy losing to come.

Do I have to do everything myself? Do I? I'm always working really hard even when I'm golfing or visiting new places or staying at one of my resorts or going to campaign rallies in Alabama. Let me tell you, those rallies are almost as much fun as making threats to Little Rocket Man. What an idiot! Talk about losers. Just you wait. We're gonna light up that tubby little pudgepot and he's gonna wonder what kicked him in the nuts. Everyone says I should bomb him back to Hell, and I have the codes so I can do it.

You're a real disappointment, Mitch. I'd fire you if I could. Government rules suck bigtime.

DJT

Wednesday, September 27, 2017
Trump Infuriated
After Backing
Alabama Loser

Dear Vlady,

That Strange guy lost. You remember that Strange guy, right? I know you do. That Strange guy from Alabama who I told you I wanted to win for the Senate? He lost last night. I figured you'd get your monster hackers to help me like last year, but you didn't. Why not Vlady? Strange losing is huge. Huge. I can't be backing losers, you know that. Or I thought you did. Cause I'm not a loser. Its bad Vlady. Very bad. Standing next to a loser is the worst thing that can ever happen to me, especially since I'm never a loser. It's even worse than being hit by a hurricane like all those people in Puerto Rico.

Just try being me standing next to a loser. Its way worse. Way, way worse.

That's the other thing, Vlady. You know those Mexican Puerto Ricans? They want big money from me—billions of dollars for food and water and infrastructure and ~~crap~~ other stuff—you should see the list! And they already owe those Wall Street guys buckets of dough and they want even more now? Those are some big balls, Vlady, if you ask me! Really big balls. Like I should treat some Mexicans as if they were honest to god American citizens. Why should I give them anything? They're just lucky I'm not building a wall yet. Hey, that's a great idea. We need to build a floating wall. That'd be really cool. Nobody else has one. And I bet everyone would want one when they see how cool mine is.

But it would have to float cause Puerto Rico is in an ocean—a really big ocean. You knew that, didn't you? Most people don't know that. I bet those PRers think I should help them just like I helped those folks in Texas and Florida…you know…the Real Americans who voted for me. But its way harder and way more expensive to get stuff to the middle of a big ocean than it is than to get stuff to Texas or Florida. Maybe Puerto Rico should move back to Mexico. And why isn't Mexico paying for all this help anyway?

Sorry Vlady but I'm really P.O.'d. I really am. I should have guessed that stupid Mitch McConnell couldn't come through for Mr. Strange in Alabama—they're both losers, you know. McConnell is a real loser. Big loser. Pass a healthcare bill? I bet he couldn't pass gas after eating a ton of beans. And now there's this Roy Moore guy. Now I know this Roy Moore guy is a winner. Those idiot judges keep trying to kick him around, but he's a winner just like me. I need more guys like this Roy Moore guy. This job is way harder than anyone knows, but I'm winning it. Anyone can see I'm the most popular president of all time. Way better than Obama. Did you see how high my approval ratings are? Best approval ratings of a president ever!

Listen. I can count on you in 2018 and 2020 right? I know I can. You scratch my back and I'll scratch yours. Nuff said.

Your best buddy,

Donnie (Almost Emperor) Trump

The Donald Trump Turkey Shoot

Wednesday, September 27, 2017
Sean Spicer Lawyers Up
As Russia Probe Heats Up

Hi Spicey,

    We're still friends right? Sorry about that Mooch business…but I know we're still friends, right? And we don't want to go to jail, am I right? Jail's for losers, so I can't go to jail. I mean you can, 'cause you're a loser, but I can't cause I'm a winner. You understand that, right? Just imagine someone like me in prison with all those big dudes asking me for money. Like I'm a charity or something.

    Here's the deal. That Mueller guy is gonna ask you alot of questions. You know him, he's all questions. Just say, "I can't remember." Got that? "I can't remember" or "I don't remember" or "It's really hard to remember." You'll say that 'cause we're still friends, right? I'm counting on you to help me be a winner. Act like you never heard of Russia. Okay?

    Hey, I'll pay your lawyers, Spicey. Okay? You just have to ask. You scratch my back and I'll scratch yours, right? You trust me, right? We're still friends, right? I wouldn't lie to you, would I? Only a loser would lie to you and you know I'm a winner.

    Just say, "I can't remember." That's it. "I can't remember."

Your BFF,

DJT

The Donald Trump Turkey Shoot

Thursday, September 28, 2017
Secretary Price Says He
Has Trump's 'Confidence'
Amid Jet Controversy

Hi Tommy,

You flying the friendly skies? Just joking. Looks like you got yourself in a pickle flying on private airplanes. Acting like a billionaire. Acting like me. But you aren't me, are you Tommy? See Tommy I don't have to act like a rich guy. I am a rich guy. A really rich guy. Everyone knows that. Even Melania. Especially Melania. Not only am I the richest president ever, I'm Mr. President in Charge of Everything including your life. I'm such a good president that they gave me my own huge plane. It's a seven-forty-something-or-other. Really huge. Huger than any other plane of any other president in any other country on any other planet. Even huger than Putin's. (But don't tell him 'cause he'll probably want mine and I don't want to give it to him. Its mine.)

Here's the thing, Tommy. You ain't rich. Not at all. You'd have to do way more insider trading than you used to do when you were in Congress to get really rich like me. Besides, you don't look like you're smart enough to be rich. Rich people look like me… or Melania…or Ivanka. Rich people are beautiful. We are the most beautiful people you'll ever meet. And you ain't beautiful, Tommy, believe me.

Not rich. Not beautiful. Sorry to have to break it to you Tommy, but I always tell the truth.

Now, I'm not saying you're a loser like the McTwins, Tommy. No. You're a schmuck—not a loser really—but a schmuck. And the Fake News people are asking me all kinds of questions about your schmucky behavior— flying private planes like you were me.

Throwing money around like you were me. And I think we know, you ain't me. Not rich. Not beautiful. And I don't want all your flying and spending making me look bad. The Fake News folks are all over this, and they're trying to make me look bad, and that's pushin' you closer and closer to being a loser. You don't want to be a loser like the McLosers, do you? I fire losers. You don't want to become a loser and make me fire you, do you?

So, from now on Tommy, when you think about flying on a private airplane, just say you're Ben Carson. He's a black guy, and people expect him to break the law and screw the taxpayers, right? Hell, he says he's a surgeon but his favorite story is about some stupid knife fight he had when he was a kid. It's okay if you make him look bad. He already looks bad. I know I'll end up firing him and I'll look like a winner. You'll still be a schmuck, but you won't be making me look like a loser. See? Just like that. Problem solved.

Don't forget to be someone else—probably Ben Carson.

DJT

Mr. President in Charge of Your Life

September 30, 2017
Trump Calls San Juan's
Mayor a Weak Leader

Dear Madame Mayor,

Should I even start with Dear? Like I really mean "Dear Mayor?" 'Cause I don't. You know that, right? Women shouldn't be mayors. That's a guy job, believe me.

If you had power in that god-forsaken country of yours, you'd know I've been tweeting about you all morning long. Especially after you decided you could say nasty things about me. Don't deny it. I saw you. Last night on network TV. Melania ran in and turned the channel from FOX to MSNBC and there you were, bad-mouthing The President of the United States of America. That's me.

Saying things like I haven't been doing a really, really good job for Puerto Rico. You're wrong, Miss Cruz. Wrong. Wrong. Wrong. You're just like that lyin' cousin of yours, Lyin' Ted. All you Cruzez are alike. He doesn't know squat and neither do you. Nobody with a name like Cruz ever knows anything. Let me tell you, the reviews are in lady. And I'm a hit. Ask anybody still alive in Puerto Rico.

Besides, how would you know if I haven't been doing a really, really, great job? You couldn't know that unless you have power. Hey, that's it, isn't it? You do have power. I bet you've been watching those all those awful pictures on TV? I just bet you have. Don't believe 'em. Nothing ever looks that bad. The Fake News folks and their special effects teams are making it all up, and you've been watching too much TV instead of being out there in the town taking care of your folks, haven't you?

You know you've been talking to the wrong people, right? If you'd been talking to any of the great people I've been talking to, you'd know what a really, really great job I'm doing for that Mexican-speaking country of yours. Everyone I talk to is telling me what a truly, over-the-top, really, really superb job I'm doing. Ivanka said so not ten minutes ago. Now, they're not just saying great, they're saying greater than great. Super-great. The greatest job any president has ever done for anybody after an ~~earthquake~~… er…hurricane. Yeah. That's right. And by the way, Seen-your-uh Cruz, I don't know how to spell Mexican words but you get what I mean—when I tell you in English. Great English.

Gotta get the rest of my tweets in before I hit the links, lady, but I started with you 'cause you really pissed me off. I don't know.

Why should I care about Puerto Rico? You're an island. Islands are in the middle of the ocean, in case you haven't noticed. And oceans are big. What's it mean when you are surrounded by water? It means you're just looking for trouble when hurricanes come. And then you guys want us to do everything for you. Get your power back up, send food, send water. Would you like some fries with that, too?

I'd care lots more if you didn't already owe Wall Street a load of cash. Or if you had even one electoral vote. But you don't. Not one. *Nada.* (Barron just left and he told me how to spell *nada* so I could give this letter some Mexican flair.)

So, I hope you realize how wrong you are. Take that from a guy who's never wrong. That's the best thing about being rich…and being me.

North American USA president

Solum Optimis Verbis

The Doctor Is In

Week 63 / April 1 – April 7, 2018

The Countdown
It's Saturday, April 7th, 2018. This is the 442nd day of Trump's administration. Each presidential term lasts 1461 days which means Trump has 1019 days remaining. Unless he is impeached. Or Mueller indicts him and finds him a suitable new residence: perhaps Guantanamo or the Mariana Trench. Or Stormy Daniels releases the full video—probably a "short-short" movie. Or Hope Hicks writes a tell-all, *"My Life Under Trump."* Or FOX News decides to abandon him. Or something even more awful than being abandoned by FOX News should befall him.

Take Two Aspirin…and Maybe a Xanax
I worry that our democracy is dying and those charged with keeping it healthy are too clueless or craven to do what is necessary.

Having Donald Trump as President feels a great deal like being diagnosed with a terminal disease. No matter how much you'd like to get back to your life, or return to your daily routine and enjoy your friends and family, almost every minute is hijacked by dark thoughts. The life you had is gone. The happiness that you so easily took for granted has flown.

While certain voices vainly attempt to offer hope, a growing despair seizes you as you watch previously reliable systems—The

State Department, the EPA, the Department of Justice, Immigration and Customs Enforcement, and others—collapse. Systems that have always contributed to the health of the body politic are failing because the Trumpian Disorder has spread.

Which of us can assert that our current government is reliable and truthful? None of us. It's as if the Trumpian Disorder has a dementia component which compels the President to speak and tweet without any reference to reality, truth, or facts.

Would any of us let a relative suffering from dementia—a loved one who no longer connects with our shared reality—make decisions for us? Or would we be solicitous but firm in saying, "Perhaps you mean well, but your mind isn't working to your benefit or the benefit of anyone around you." Would any of us simply allow that person to hold sway over us? No. We would not.

Even now I try to understand how we got here. I try to comprehend what makes President Trump tick. So much has gone wrong in this administration that it's easy to get lost in the morass of everyday details. The lies, the firings, the absurd or hurtful policy positions, all divert our attention from the simple truth: President Trump is clearly unfit for the office of the presidency.

As an average United States citizen with no ties to Washington, I have read the papers and watched the news—carefully, with great trepidation—and drawn conclusions distilled from those observations. I can state my conclusions about Trump in four words: ignorant, stupid, and mean...but wealthy.

It would be difficult to find someone in high office who is more obviously ignorant and stupid than Donald Trump. Now ignorance and stupidity are not criminal qualities—but they don't qualify as virtues either. Plenty of people are stupid and/or ignorant. Let me offer the 61,201,031 voters who voted for Trump. But as long as people realize where their gifts lie, and realize how they can positively contribute to society, then neither ignorance nor stupidity have to be problems. However, a president both ignorant **and** stupid could prove fatal to our democracy.

As for stupidity, it's not so much that Trump doesn't know or understand important things, it's that

1. He doesn't know that he doesn't know.
2. He doesn't know but he thinks he knows…but he doesn't.
3. He doesn't know but he doesn't care that he doesn't know.
4. He's both unwilling and incapable of learning what he doesn't know.

Astonishingly, even the Republicans in Congress seem to understand what a dolt we all have in the Oval Office. What I find most amazing is this: They don't feel the threat—posed by an ignorant and stupid president—more keenly than they do.

Trump may "have the best words" and "gone to best schools," but he cannot disguise just how feeble his intellect is.

———◆———

Let's move on to mean.

For starters, President Trump has given the term "bully pulpit" a whole new meaning. He truly has become "The Bully-in-Chief." In true elementary school fashion—dare I say infantile fashion?—he stoops to name-calling when anyone opposes him. When people talk about "the grown-up in the room," they are never speaking of Donald Trump. Never. He is, in every respect, a child. A mean child.

He coins insulting, dismissive nicknames for people he does not like: Little Marco, Lyin' Hillary, Pocahontas, and Rocket Man. He has disparaged individuals like Meryl Streep—"one of the most over-rated actresses in Hollywood"—and taken aim at Alec Baldwin, tweeting,

The Donald Trump Turkey Shoot

Just tried watching Saturday Night Live *- unwatchable! Totally biased, not funny and the Baldwin impersonation just can't get any worse. Sad.*

Yet, a year later, Trump was still watching the unwatchable Baldwin—Hmmmm??—"whose dying mediocre career was saved by his terrible impersonation of me on SNL." All evidence to the contrary.

Stupid/ignorant people…aka Donald Trump…have no use for, nor interest in, facts. Nevertheless, for those of us who do value facts, here are a few. Meryl Streep has twenty-one Oscar nominations [3 wins] and thirty-one Golden Globe nominations [8 wins]. Baldwin's two Emmys, three Golden Globes, and seven Screen Actors Guild Awards may have been given in error but his impersonation of Trump, lauded by audiences across America, would indicate they were well deserved.

The sweep of Trump's meanness goes well beyond individuals, embracing whole continents with caustic epithets. Remember when he characterized Africa as full of "shithole countries?"

Such remarks are the confluence of ignorance, stupidity, and meanness, traits that also explain his racist and misogynistic tendencies. Combining stupidity and meanness yields intolerant, dangerous people—the Donald Trumps of the world.

He may be mean and be a bully, but he is also a coward. Despite his reality television persona—the boss declaring, "You're fired!"—he seldom fires any of the people himself and certainly not face-to-face. He dismisses employees via Tweet or has one of his subordinates do it for him. Call it firing by proxy.

Finally, his antipathy to ever making apologies reinforces both his meanness and stupidity. The brightest people know when they've overstepped an acceptable line, and apologize. Fortunately for Trump, he is never wrong.

Then, of course, there is Trump's wealth.

Most of us have successfully navigated a world populated by stupid/ignorant people. And one would have to be an ascetic living without newspapers, television news, movies, or novels to avoid any encounter with the surfeit of meanies in the world. Mean people are mean because they think it gets them what they want or need. They bully and use threats because they have no idea that kindness or thoughtfulness can be persuasive.

It's only when one adds extraordinary wealth to the dubious mixture of ignorance and meanness, that things become truly dangerous—dangerous because Trump is a man immune to consequence. Wealth has done that. Trump believes—and no one has truly stepped up to contradict this belief—that his wealth will shield him from genuine consequences. Wealth is his shield.

Lie to people about the real effects of the new tax plan? No problem. Wealth protects Trump.

Dispense with EPA regulations or ignore global climate change? No problem. Wealth protects Trump.

Foolishly apply tariffs that most of his advisors opposed? No problem. Wealth protects Trump.

Revoke DACA and then lie to everyone about your true position? No problem. Wealth protects Trump.

Demand non-disclosure agreements from everyone who has ever worked for you? No problem. Wealth protects Trump.

Create a bogus university? And get caught doing it? No problem. Wealth protects Trump.

It's truly that simple. Trump is an amazingly ignorant simpleton, who has never learned to share and takes whatever he wants. He is instinctively mean and selfish. And his wealth has always rescued him because he surrounds himself with sycophants whose livelihoods require feeding at the Trump trough.

That's my diagnosis. Please send in the next patient, please. I believe it's a Mr. Pence? Oh, yes. I'm treating him for homophobia.

Solum Optimis Verbis

Trumpian Truthiness

Week 64 / April 8 – April 14, 2018

Trump and Ivanka Discover the Truthiness of Truth

Ivanka: Daddy, they say nasty things about you and these other women.

Trump: What do they say?
[Ivanka whispers in his ear then steps back]
Sounds like fun.

Ivanka: They say you're incapable of telling the truth.

Trump: What is truth, Ivy? The truth is just a relative of a lie that nobody talks about. You know, like you sister, Tiffany. Lies are just the flip-side of the truth. So it's all the same. Remember my motto, "The truth is a lie." Or flip that over and "A lie is the truth."

Ivanka: I'm not sure I understand, Daddy.

Trump: *[Takes a quarter from his pocket]*
See this, Ivy? What is this?

Ivanka: Don't be silly, Daddy. It's a quarter.

Trump: That's my girl. You've always known your currency.
[Pats Ivanka on the head like a dog]
Daddy has lots of quarters. Big lots. Huge lots. Daddy loves rolling around in rooms of quarters. Daddy rolled around on a bed of quarters once…in Russia, I think… coulda' been rubles
[Realizes he's daydreaming]

	Well, this quarter has two sides.
Ivanka:	Yes, Daddy. Heads and tails.
Trump:	Wow, you really do know your money. And if you flip this coin...
	[He looks intently at the quarter]
	Hey, who's the guy on this coin? Anybody important?
Ivanka:	That's George Washington, Daddy. Our country's first president. He's also on the dollar bill.
Trump:	Not much of a president if they only put him on a quarter. Or a buck! What can ya buy for a buck? Musta' been a cheap guy—that George whatever-his-last-name-is. Everybody says I'm a much better president, don't they? Lots better. I want my picture on the millions dollar bill, Ivy. Then everyone will know just how valuable I really am.
Ivanka:	I don't think there is a million dollar bill, Daddy.
Trump:	Not yet. But I'm president now. I can do anything I want. Anything.
Ivanka:	You were going to flip the coin, Daddy.
Trump:	Oh, yeah. Yeah. Now, let me flip this coin and you tell me if it's heads or tails.
	[Flips coin and has difficulty catching it. Shows the result to Ivanka]
Ivanka:	That's a head.
Trump:	Now I'll do it again.
	[Flips coin again and shows the new result to Ivanka]
Ivanka:	That's a tail.
Trump:	That's right. And this quarter is like the truth. It has two sides but it is still the same quarter. Am I right? Am I right? One side is not worth more than the other side, is it?
Ivanka:	*[Unsure]* No...
Trump:	Both sides are of equal value, right?

Ivanka: Yes...*[Still unsure]*
Trump: So lies and the truth are of equal value. They both spend the same. You just have to know where to spend them. If you ever need any more information about the truth, just ask me. Those awful reporters—like the ones from the Failing New York Times or that Amazonian Washington Post. They actually think there's a difference between the truth and a lie. But we know different, right?
Ivanka: I always thought there was a difference, too, Daddy.
Trump: That's because you believe in facts, Ivy. And we all know that the facts are what I say they are, not what they appear to be. Just like the truth.

Solum Optimis Verbis

New Word: Kakistocracy

Week 71 / May 27 – June 2, 2018

It's New Word Time!
<u>NOTE:</u> This week my friend AJ sent me a very interesting e-mail about a word she'd discovered while doing research. She felt she "just had to pass it on." I want her to know how grateful I am for this new "old" word.

Kakistocracy, [kakə'stäkrəsē] *noun*
    A system of government which is run by the worst, least qualified, most unscrupulous citizens.
    Examples: Italy under Mussolini. The USA after the election of Donald Trump. [See Fascism]
    Sentence: Mr. Scott Pruitt, Ms. Betsy DeVos, and Mr. Ben Carson were all pleased as punch to join the Trump Kakistocracy.

One final comment on this word: we probably derive the slang term "kaka" from it. It's been around since the 17th century, but it is "oh so very relevant now." Yes, indeed.

Don't we all love the malleability of language? Despite how much I loathe Trump, I'm fascinated by his verbal prestidigitation. He implements bad policy and…SHAZAM!…the Democrats get the blame. At some time or other, he takes *every* side of *every* issue and… SHAZAM!…he's always right. It's like a man playing darts without a dartboard…he cannot miss. Just throw it and see where it lands.

Since we are clearly now living in the *Trumpian Kakistocracy*, I'm still attempting to sort out what his official title might be. Is one the *President* of a *Kakistocracy*? *Premier*? *Prime Minister*? *Emperor*? *Czar*? Perhaps we can dispense with the traditional titles and invent something completely new. Of course, any new title should also come with a host of appended titles all reduced to their initials—something like placing PhD after someone's name. And now for something completely different, I give you…

His Imperial Kaka, Donald Trump,
OAH – Order of the Asshole; EES – Emir of Endless Stupidity;
SPP – Sultan of Perverse Prevarication

Naturally, we'll have to enlist a designer to create the proper medallions and pendants suitable for each title. *His Imperial Kaka* would undoubtedly be proud to wear them at all official functions. (I'm dying to see what the OAH medallion might look like.) While he'd probably feel naked without these medallions of honor, I'm sure he'd much prefer to be naked with them. Wouldn't that impress all the girls?!?! Wouldn't that be something?!?!

By the Sea, By the Sea, By the C--t!

Do remember the movie, *Casablanca*? I hope you do, because I'd like to make reference to a scene that appears to be relevant to the Trump-supporter's outrage concerning Samantha Bee's comment on her show *Full Frontal* earlier this week.

Samantha Bee called Ivanka Trump, Donald Trump's daughter,

a "feckless c-nt." The "C" word was bleeped by the network, of course, but it landed like a hornets' nest amidst Trump's mind-numbingly stupid apostles. And here's the *Casablanca* moment: They are shocked! Shocked I tell you!

Of course, the right-wingers are saying that there is a double standard here. *Roseanne Barr was exiled from network television, her show cancelled because of her vile, racist tweet earlier this week. But has Samantha suffered the same punishment? No. Ooooh. Double standard! For shame! Hang your heads, you left-wingers! Hang your heads!*

Here's the important difference: Roseanne Barr's tweet was both racist and wrong. Samantha Bee's observation—using a word that even I feel is beyond vulgar—is completely true. But we all know that "true" doesn't fly in this administration. And when it tries, we have a whole cadre of Trump acolytes willing to shoot it down. People like: Rudy "Which-Lie-Should-I-Tell-Today" Giuliani, or Kellyanne "I-Can-Fold-Staple-and-Mutilate-Any-Known-Fact-Anywhere-in-the-Known-Universe" Conway, or Miss Sarah Huckabee "I'm-Primetime-and-This-Is-My-Fifteen-Minutes-of-Fame" Sanders.

Perhaps Samantha should have hedged her bets and used the word "bitch" instead of the infamous "C" word. Better yet, she should have gotten creative and called her Ivanka a "Feckless Can't," because that word is equally true. Ivanka *can't* or won't answer questions concerning her father's endless philandering. Ivanka *can't* or won't answer questions about his habitual lying.

Ivanka Trump is a Feckless Can't.

The real problem is that Ivanka—truly a member of the Trump kakistocracy—can't make up her mind if she's the president's daughter, a *bona fide* member of the administration, or just a business woman attempting to make a billion-dollar killing in China because her Daddy's in the Oval Office. She's unqualified, self-serving, insensitive, and greedy.

The apple doesn't fall far from the tree.

Trump's Interior Monologue

It's scary. I believe Trump ran for president on a lark—his own brand of reality television—never believing he could win, and now that he's become president, he doesn't care. Even the ex-speaker of the House, John Boehner, said the two most surprised people on election night were Hillary Clinton and Donald Trump.

So Trump doesn't have to care. He got a job he never really wanted. And now that he has it, no one can make him really care about having it. Besides, nowhere in the Constitution does it say that the president has to care—about anyone but himself. Perhaps we should introduce the 28th Amendment to the Constitution of the United States. It would be simple and straightforward:

The President must care about ALL the people in the United States.

If we'd had an amendment like that back in 2015, Trump would never have run. He couldn't have run. He'd be disqualified just on the basis of Trump University alone. Please notice, the amendment reads: ALL the people *in* the United States. That means folks who are here. Not just citizens.

I can just imagine the dialogue Trump hears when he's talking to his best friend in the mirror, or when he's eating his Happy Meal in the morning while flipping the channel to FOX News:

If those people out there were stupid enough to vote for me, that's their problem.

They voted for me—and they're stuck with me. With me! I never wanted this job, anyway. Anyone with half a brain could see that during my campaign. I kept saying the most *outrageous, hurtful, spiteful, even vicious things, and they still voted for me. Hell, I said I could shoot someone on 5th Avenue, that Mexicans were rapists, and that I loved grabbing women by...well...I know where I love to grab'em, right? I'm just that kinda guy. Guys understand that, right?*

I told my audiences to punch out the hecklers at my rallies, I told Russia to hack the DNC. I've done all kinds of shit. And I never released any of my tax returns. If I did, everybody in the world would know that I'm all mobbed-up and a cheapskate to boot. So...who the hell did they think I was? I'm me. I'm not gonna be some version of me that the liberals—or even the conservatives—think I ought to be. I'm not changing the way I've lived my life for that last 71 years. I don't give a shit about rules or norms or traditions or asking anyone else how to run things. I'll run things the way I goddamn please. I'm only interested in me. I take care of me.

The rest of you should learn to take care of yourselves. Taking care of you is not my job. Please don't tell me that it is my job, because I don't want it. Okay?

When does The Price Is Right start? Can I get another Happy Meal?

Solum Optimis Verbis

G.U.I.L.T
Genuine, Unscripted, Impromptu, Legislative Theater

Week 72 / June 3 – June 9, 2018

Reality Television Meets Immigration
My great-grandparents stepped off the boat from Ireland onto American soil sometime in 1888. They were unwelcome. Sneering signs declaring, "Irish Need Not Apply," were everywhere. Well, those days are gone, and now all the descendants from Ireland, Germany, Poland, Italy, England, Denmark, Norway, Sweden, Greece, Russia, Yugoslavia, Lithuania, South Africa, Nigeria, Kenya, India, Pakistan, Korea, China, Vietnam, Japan—and virtually every other country in the known world—are saying enough is enough. Well, we're not actually saying it, but our marvelous president and his incredibly adroit administration have made one thing quite clear.

"The 'Welcome' mat is no longer out. We don't want 'Your tired, your poor, your huddled masses yearning to breathe free...' Go somewhere else to be tired, poor, and huddled.

The Donald Trump Turkey Shoot

And don't breathe here. You can't have our oxygen. God bless America."

Best of all, it's no longer just idle chatter. And that makes me happy. Those like me who are members of the "LGB community"—the *Lucky Go Befores*—want everyone to know we are Americans. We are true-blue, rock-ribbed, flag-waving sons and daughters of immigrants past, and we don't want any more immigrants. Am I right?

However, I feel we must do something symbolic, something of consequence, to demonstrate just how serious our "No More Immigrants" stance is. Here is what I suggest. Rather than building a costly wall at our southern border, why not just dismantle the Statue of Liberty? After all, isn't it her siren call that has attracted immigrants to our shores since 1886? If we silence her now, perhaps the immigrants who have sought freedom and opportunity here for the past 132 years will just stop coming. When the lamp of freedom is extinguished, they'll get the idea. Once dismantled, we'll send her back to France, C.O.D. They can have her.

But wait, I've got an even better idea. Why not blow up the Statue of Liberty? Yeah! Lady Liberty's demolition could be a televised spectacular, sponsored by *Ivanka Trump Chinese Apparel for American Women.* Imagine the possibilities for slogans as the old green dame splashes to bits in New York harbor. "Get rid of that old, tired look. Stop saying howdy to dowdy. Blast into something new."

Wait! Wait! Why not hold a raffle to see who gets to push the demolition button? Ten dollars per chance with free airfare and hotel accommodations for the winner. Could reality television ever get any better? We might get enough money to reduce the national debt.

There is simply no point in half measures when you've decided to ban immigration in the "one nation, under God, indivisible, with liberty and justice for all." Except for immigrants. So what if immigrants built this country. We don't want 'em. Not now.

I just hope the demolition is televised on network TV, not HBO.

And finally this week, I offer you another thrilling SNL-style sketch:

G.U.I.L.T.

Genuine, Unscripted, Impromptu Legislative Theater
Episode: The Lie's the Thing

[Trump and his Chief of Staff, John Kelly, are looking out the window of the Oval Office. Trump is in a bad mood because he's now stuck working when he'd rather be entertaining crowds or playing golf.]

Trump: I liked it better when I was a candidate.

John Kelly: I understand that, but you are the president now, Mr. President. You stopped being a candidate more than 18 months ago.

Trump: Eighteen months? *[Mulling the amount of time]* Eighteen months. That's almost a year.

John Kelly: *[Pauses. Then with resignation.]* Yes, Mr. President.

Trump: It was more fun when I could wow the crowds with "Build that wall! Build that wall!" Or Mikey Flynn would get the crowd revved up with "Lock her up! Lock her up." I miss that, don't you?

John Kelly: I wasn't with you then, Mr. President.

Trump: That's right. Nobody was with me. Running for president was something I did all by myself. Everything I've ever done, I've done all by myself. I'm a self-made man. You know that, don't you, general? I don't like to brag, but nobody helped me. I got here all by myself.

John Kelly: That's impressive, Mr. President.

Trump: So why didn't you help me back in 2015?

John Kelly: Mr. President, I was the general in charge of the US Southern Command until you asked me to be your Secretary of Homeland Security.

Trump: So you were once the new Robert E Lee?

John Kelly: *[Quizzical look]* I'm not sure I understand, sir.

Trump: Come on, general. General Robert E. Lee, the man in charge of the US Southern Command.

John Kelly: I believe you've confused the US Southern Command with the Southern forces during the Civil War. Back then, the Southern forces were Confederate forces, not US forces.

Trump: Really, general? Really? I'm smart. Really smart. Went to the best schools. Got the best grades. And I know my history. When I hear Southern Command, I know you're talking Robert E. Lee, the man who fought like crazy to keep all those blacks happy and peaceful in those lovely cotton fields. The Civil War was a damn shame, general. Blacks haven't been happy since they left the plantation.

John Kelly: That was over a hundred and fifty years ago, Mr. President.

Trump: Wow. That long ago. *[Looks around the Oval Office]* I bet whoever was president back then didn't have to live in this dump.

John Kelly: That was President Lincoln, Mr. President. And he lived right here in the White House.

Trump: Well, it's a dump. It's white. Who likes white? I love it when everything glitters. That's how I decorated Trump Tower. Gold everywhere. Golden archways—kind of a McDonald's touch—golden chairs. Everything gold. You know why I do that, right? When you see everything

	gold-encrusted, what's the first thing that pops into your mind general?
John Kelly:	Uh…uh…a brothel? Mr. President.
Trump:	No, general! No! Think rich. Think wealthy. Think loaded. That's what I think when I see myself surrounded by gold.
John Kelly:	Yes, sir. *[Shakes head vigorously]* Rich. That's the second thing that occurred to me.
Trump:	I'm rich because no one is smarter than me. No one is a better businessman that me. I win, win, win. I win all the time. You've seen The Apprentice, right? You know I hate losers. Hate'em. Fire'em. Losers are…well… they're losers.
John Kelly:	And you're a winner, sir.
Trump:	Yes, I am. Not like those losers in the Senate and the House of Representatives. Even Republicans. My own party! Flaky Flake, Little Marco, and Loser POW McCain. They're supposed to do what I tell them to do. Am I right? They're losers. I need loyal winners around me, general. Loyal winners like you.
John Kelly:	I try to be loyal to you, sir.
Trump:	Don't worry, general, you are. You proved that when you dissed that goofball Congresswoman from Florida with your best ever lie.
John Kelly:	You mean the woman who wears that cowboy hat all the time? Frederica Wilson?
Trump:	Was that her name? Yeah, she's the one. What was it you called her?
John Kelly:	An empty-barrel, sir.
Trump:	*[Smirks]* An empty-barrel. Yeah, that was great. And then you said she improperly took credit for getting the funding for her local FBI Building. That really pinned her cowboy-hat ears back, didn't it?

John Kelly: I was just trying to fight for our team, Mr. President.
Trump: Don't think I haven't appreciated it, general. Being able to lie in a pinch, to come up with a fake story on the spur of the moment—one that sounds really true—that's a real gift. That's why I'm president. I'm the best liar the world has ever seen. And having you by my side—my own personal goodie-two-shoes—makes my lies look more truthful.
John Kelly: The military has taught me to improvise, to think on my feet, Mr. President.
Trump: You do it so well. That's also what I love about Ivanka and Jared. They're not as good as you or me, but they can lie on a dime and give you nine cents change. What's that quote you always use about lying?
John Kelly: You mean the Mark Twain quote? "A lie can travel half way around the world while the truth is putting on its shoes."
Trump: That's it. That's it. I love it. Don't you love sending those fake news folks, and their radical, left-wing fact checkers, on another snipe hunt?
John Kelly: Happy to help, Mr. President.
Trump: I'm glad you're not that stand-up guy everyone thought you were when I brought you aboard. I fired Priebus—what a wuss he was—and hired you, and the fake news folks went on a John Kelly love fest. Boy, they loved you. You were gonna tame me. Get me to stop tweeting. Make me to be more presidential.

[Both Trump and Kelly laugh. They both mouth the word, "bullshit."]

John Kelly: We really fooled them, didn't we?
Trump: So...we're off to the G7 summit in Canada, right?
John Kelly: That's right, sir, we leave today.
Trump: I plan to surprise the hell out of them.

John Kelly: How's that, sir?
Trump: I'm not gonna lie to them or kiss their asses either.
John Kelly: That should surprise the hell out of them, Mr. President.
Trump: Damn right! I'm just going to be rude. First, I'll arrive late. That'll get 'em steamed. Then I'll leave early before we get to talk about Global Warming or sign any agreements.
John Kelly: That sounds like very boorish behavior, sir. Don't be so boorish that they vote you out and then it's only the G6.
Trump: Hell, Kelly, I can be the G1. Me. Who's on the front page every day? Me. Who do the Fake News folk look for on Twitter every day? Me. Who needs G two, three, four, five, six and seven? Not me! I can meet with myself anytime I want, and I don't have to suck up to anybody but me. I like me. I agree with me—all the time—even when I change my mind.
John Kelly: You're very skilled at that sir. But they will want to talk about tariffs.
Trump: Well, I don't. They don't like my tariffs? Screw 'em. That Trudeau fellow thinks he can win a trade war with me, but he'll see. And that Macron guy from…from… uh, where's he from?
John Kelly: France, sir.
Trump: Yeah, that French sissy. You saw how I let him kiss up to me when he came here.
John Kelly: Was that whole act a lie, sir?
Trump: Damn right. I could'a got him in bed, but that's where Melania draws the line.
John Kelly: I can understand that, sir.
Trump: Besides, I got bigger fish to fry. Yep, in a few days I'm gonna shake hands with Kim Jong-Un, the world's worst dictator. He's a major league shit, for sure. But he hasn't met me yet. I'm a bigger shit than he is.

The Donald Trump Turkey Shoot

John Kelly: That's true, sir. You're the biggest shit I know. What do you think you'll get done at the Singapore meeting?

Trump: Nothing. Some people go in with low expectations. But I got'em beat. I go in with no expectations. I just want him to look me in the eye and say, "You're a bigger shit than I am." That'll boost my reputation for sure with my base.

John Kelly: Is that what your base wants, Mr. President?

Trump: Nah. My base wants me to light'em up with a few nuclear warheads. Matter of fact, that's what I want, too. But a nuclear war might look bad at the mid-terms, and Mueller would probably figure how to investigate that, too. I was hopin' for a Nobel and a mushroom cloud, but either one would cut into my golf game. Whatta' ya say?

John Kelly: Sound like you've got everything carefully planned, sir.

Trump: You got it, Kelly. I worry whenever I overthink things. You don't want to over plan.

Solum Optimis Verbis

Layperson's Guide to the Madness of Donald Trump

Week 73 / June 10 – June 16, 2018

Trump Fatigue is everywhere. No sooner does Trump lie about what he's done, or level another false accusation against an agency, institution, or media outlet that he feels has betrayed him by not doing his bidding, (After all, he is The President and everyone works for him, right?) than he stirs the pot all over again with a new problem or issue. Day after day after day after day. Those of us who lead our ordinary lives—going to work, loving our families, engaging the world—generally attempt to resolve conflicts, not create them. But Trump seems to thrive on chaos and conflict. And it is soooo tiring.

But it is always useful to simplify everything that you see or hear reported because, in fact, nothing is new. Nothing. It's just a new wrinkle on the four-point paradigm that has guided Trump in all his ventures for decades. When you find yourself scratching your head and saying, "What the hell is it this time?" here is all you have to remember:

1. **The Trump presidency is all theater.**

   All of it. Yes, it has real consequences, but Donald Trump doesn't really care about that. The presidency simply allows him to be the center of attention. He doesn't care about the presidency *per se*—that is, looking after the concerns of the United States and its people. He cares only that the presidency gives him the biggest stage he could ever have. He feels absolutely no duty toward his country and those of us who live here. His presidency is reality TV on steroids. Nothing else he could ever have done will ever equal having the spotlight continually on him.

You'll notice that whenever the center of attention is likely to shift, he does something brash, chaotic, or unsettling to bring the focus back to him.

He's interested in calling the shots—that's why he can say he supports DACA one day and reject it the next…or call Kim Jong Un names one day and shake hands with him the next. We are all tuned in to The Trump Show.

2. **Theater thrives on conflict.**

Imagine a TV show where everyone gets along and no one ever gets hurt physically, psychologically, or emotionally. It would be cancelled in a heartbeat. That's Theater 101. Without conflict, attention wanes and people get on with their lives—hoping that the government they elected will keep things calm and orderly. But calm and orderly is dull, and people ignore dull. Drama demands conflict, and Trump loves drama.

As long as Trump is in office, we will experience turmoil because it is baked into Trump's political cake. He cannot NOT have conflict. No one would watch him, and above all, he wants to be watched.

Trump espouses conflicting policy positions—being pro-choice and then being pro-life; supporting immigration legislation, and then backing out—not because he has changed his mind, not because he cares about either side of the issue, but because the conflict turns the spotlight back on him. Anyone looking for a thoughtful, intelligent policy discussion with Trump simply doesn't understand the man.

We, the people, are interested in policy, but Donald Trump is not. Policy positions are simply props for his on-going, conflict-ridden, political theater.

3. **Facts and Truth are not required for theater.**

Most of us are truly invested in the real world. We understand there are certain facts that guide our lives. The sun rises in the east and sets in the west. We subscribe to proverbs like "You can catch more flies with honey than you can with vinegar." We believe global climate change is negatively affecting significant parts of the world. Facts are, as we like to say, facts.

But if you deny a fact—call it false, call it fake, offer an alternative fact—you create conflict. And with conflict you have theater.

You can see where this is going, can't you? There is a pattern here.

Trump lies because it serves his agenda of keeping everyone stirred up. Opposing a fact gets people riled up, while agreeing with a fact only promotes a big yawn.

4. **Trump is interested only in his own interests, both financial and psychological. He is not interested in you or me.**

It's ironic that reality TV is not real. It is scripted. Trump's background in reality television should tell us everything we need to know. People who live in a scripted world don't need to know what reality is. They don't need to know facts just like the TV doctor doesn't need to know anything about surgery. If it isn't in the script, it doesn't exist. And even if it is

IN the script, it isn't real.

Caring about the American people, worrying about the future of all Americans, none of that is in Trump's current script. Advancing his own financial interests (or those of his daughter or son-in-law) or being continually in the spotlight are his only concerns. There is always some chance that Trump's interests and the interests of the 320,000,000 Americans he was chosen to lead might intersect, but if they do, it will be by sheerest chance. The merest accident.

Conclusion:

I truly believe that those of us seeking to understand why the President does or does not do something, why he formulates or rejects various policies, why he spurns our friends and embraces our enemies, need look no further than this four-point paradigm. The Trump presidency is all theater. Theater requires conflict. And lies and diametrically-opposed policy positions—along with insulting tweets and a barrage of conspiracy theories—supply the conflict. All of this keeps the camera on Trump giving him the psychological boost he wants…as I said, it's Theater 101.

I've been calling Trump stupid—when perhaps I should have been calling him simple. Yes, he is ignorant. Yes, he has a limited vocabulary and seems incapable of talking intelligently about politics, history, or any topic requiring study. But he doesn't care about knowledge and information. They would only serve him if he wanted to solve a problem—or reduce tension—and Trump has NO interest in doing that. He's not about solutions. He's about conflict.

Solutions bad. Conflict good.

When a television show's conflict is resolved, the program is over. Trump knows this…and he aims to keep The Trump Program going…and going…and going.

Solum Optimis Verbis

Trump Theater at the Border

Week 74 / June 17 – June 23, 2018

Some Dark Thoughts

The problem we've been observing for more than a week—the heartless, inhumane separation of parents and children at our southern border—continues. Don't take any comfort in the newest presidential edict apparently allowing children to remain with their families. Like all the presidential signing orders before it, it was done without thinking anything through. Done on the spur of the moment. Done without any thought to feasibility or consequences.

Never forget that it was a presidential policy created by Donald "Heart of Stone" Trump and implemented by Jeff "The Racist" Sessions. There is nothing ironic that the people who execute the policy wear the letters ICE on their vests.

The Presidential Order that the separations be stopped doesn't ameliorate the separations that have already occurred.

Let's look at what has happened through a different lens. If I had separated you from your child—regardless of my reasons—that would be called kidnapping. A Class A felony. So, now the United States government has decided they can commit more than 2,400 Class A felonies—kidnapping in the first degree—in our name. It's all been done in the name of *We, the People.*

The groundswell of opposition to this despicable policy—by

both secular and religious voices—has been heartening, but I wonder why religious leaders haven't been more outspoken well before this. Isn't lying—perpetual, endless, boundless lying—a sin anymore? Isn't running an educational scam like Trump University a violation of *Thou Shalt Not Steal*? Have we missed something? Don't Stormy Daniels and Karen McDougal come under one of the *"Thou Shalt Not"* categories? And why aren't Scott Pruitt's attempts to roll-back environmental regulations like clean air and clean water filed under the biggest one of all: *Thou Shalt Not Kill*?

I'm big on breathing and I like my water non-toxic. I bet you feel the same.

Some Dark Questions

1. Why have so many of these "separated children" been spirited away from the border in the dead of night—sometimes to destinations thousands of miles away? Does that make sense? Is the federal government involved in human trafficking? (This last point was made for the benefit of conspiracy theorists only. If you have questions, please contact Alex Jones at *InfoWars*. He always been interested in such lies.)
2. If Trump is so interested in "the rule of law," how can he violate the emoluments clause without consequence? How can he overthrow agreements made by predecessors—the Paris Climate Accord, The Iran Nuclear Agreement—and still say he is a man of his word when he so blithely undercuts previously made promises? How can he support Scott Pruitt's ever-growing folio of ethical violations?
3. Does anyone in the Trump Administration ever tell the truth? Are they ever tempted to tell the truth…even a little, harmless white truth once in a while?

4. Where are the vehement objections from the Republicans? Not the retiring ones, but the ones that plan to run again in the fall. The ones who are parents. The ones who feel that we are a Christian nation and bound by The Ten Commandments. What do they tell their children?

Letter # 1:
Published, June 19, 2018
The Seattle Times

Dear Times Editor,

America has become a cruel nation. Since Donald Trump's ascendency, we knew we'd become a crude nation, bullying and verbally abusing whenever it felt convenient, but now we've taken the next step. We've become a cruel nation.

Anyone who has listened to news broadcasts describing the separation of children from parents will also have heard the lament from horrified Americans, "This is not who we are." I, myself, have echoed that same sentiment. "This is not who we are. America is better than this."

But I was wrong. America is not better than this. What I want us to be—what I hoped we'd be—is not who we are. Gun violence flourishes without legislative remedy. Blacks die at the hands of police, and justice looks away. The residents of Puerto Rico—as much a part of America as Seattle—suffer a devastating hurricane and their struggle is largely ignored. And now this—children ripped from parents seeking asylum.

Any objective observer would have arrived at the devastatingly sad conclusion: America has become a cruel nation. But America is not only cruel, it is weak as well. As Leo Buscaglia once observed, "Only the weak are cruel. Gentleness can only be expected from the strong."

Letter # 2:
Mailed to the White House on June 22, 2018.
Written in reaction to Melania's fashion choice while visiting ICE border facilities.

June 21, 2018

Mrs. Melania Trump
President Trump's Wife Pro Tem
1600 Pennsylvania Ave
Washington, D.C. 20500

Dear Melania,

Until recently, I was willing to give you the benefit of the doubt. It's universally understood you married for money—why else would you have agreed to get in bed (literally and figuratively) with someone like Donald Trump? When money is your number one priority, you learn to put up with ugly, with clownish, with a charming-but-amazingly-ignorant buffoon. That's a given.

After all, until you met Donald Trump, you were a just a Slovenian immigrant model (I won't bring up the Green Card issue.) who got paid for wearing beautiful clothes or for taking her beautiful clothes off. Completely. Something that Donald Trump has always been attracted to—just ask Stormy Daniels or Karen McDougal. However, after those stories broke, it became clear that you prefer dollars to fidelity, and who am I to judge your choice? After all, US currency bears the inscription, "In God We Trust." In contrast, your husband only believes in himself...and we both know how much you can trust him.

But many Americans—Americans like me—always suspected that you were a better person than your dumber-than-a-box-of-rocks husband. However, when you wore that jacket that said, "I really don't care, do you?" as you went to visit those Mexican border facilities where asylum seekers and their children kidnapped by ICE agents were being detained, I sadly decided that you were not a better person. That's too bad. It's clear that you, like your imbecilic husband, have no moral code, no moral compass. As long as his money supports you, you will obediently do whatever Little Donnie Trump wants of you.

I pray daily that somehow a loving God—or a thoughtful universe—will deliver the United States from your husband. An alien abduction? A heart attack? A fatal hemorrhagic stroke? A lightning strike? A falling gargoyle? A stray bullet? An unfortunate tumble down the steps of Air Force One? Perhaps the Russians will decide to poison him, who knows? I once believed you said the same prayer.

Alas, I fear you are as idiotic and as compromised as he is. After all, who else would have gone on national television to ask all Americans to "Be Best?" You do understand most of us speak English, yes? (Did your husband approve the "Be Best" slogan? Why listen to him? His very limited grasp of English should have made you cautious. Michelle Obama could have helped you, and you've borrowed successfully from her before.)

Beware, Melania, your immigrant status is showing…and we both know how Little Donnie feels about immigrants…and how loyal he has been to those who loved him.

Sincerely,

Letter # 3:
Apparently the Republican Party believes my departed father-in-law Verne Kelling lives on. He does, of course, but only in our hearts. Recently, Mary McMorris Rogers, Republican representative from Washington's 5th Congressional District asked him for a campaign contribution. Let me let Verne tell you what's going on.

Hi Everyone,

This is Verne Kelling. If I'd lived, I'd be 89-years-old—ninety next month. But I died last year. If I were alive, there is always the possibility that I'd still be a Republican—but maybe not. When I use terms like "Eisenhower Republican," the current GOP looks at me as if I had two heads. The current GOP is cold and callous. They represent a selfishness I've seldom seen in America.

Mary McMorris Rogers, who represents Washington's 5th Congressional District, recently mailed me a request for campaign funds, and while I have traditionally donated to Republican coffers, I no longer can. What I want Ms. Rogers to know is this: I may be dead, but I am not heartless. They may be alive, but they are heartless. They might as well be dead. Don't they remember the America teeming with immigrants? How can they be so blind? Here is the letter I asked my son-in-law to send to Ms. Rogers on my behalf.

The Donald Trump Turkey Shoot

June 21, 2018

To: Cathy McMorris Rodgers
Representative
5th Congressional District
Washington State

From: Verne T. Kelling

Ms. Rogers,

Do you send all 89-year-old lifelong Republicans solicitations to fill your political coffers?

After receiving your letter of solicitation, a few comments and/or questions are in order.

1. The subtle, red bumper sticker you sent is very nice, but it would serve no good purpose in this congressional district. No one here can vote for you. I certainly can't.
2. Are you not at all concerned about the daily lying coming from this White House? Have you or any of the Republicans who represent the interests of Washington State ever criticized or denounced the President for his well-documented, unceasing barrage of lies? You always appear in photos and media releases behind the president. Is that so the lies don't hit you in the head? Or should people like me assume that you are fine with his torrent of lies?
3. Recently, the few remaining World War II veterans watched a United States president praise a vile, murderous dictator and shower him with compliments on the same week that he snubbed, ignored, and pilloried reliable European and Canadian friends. Are you or any of the Republicans who represent the interests of Washington State at all concerned?

4. Finally, this week may be the straw that broke the camel's back. This may be the week when my Washington Republican neighbors decided to vote Democratic this fall. Trump heartlessly and callously separated children from their families, and what have you said? Out loud…in the press? Have you or any of the Republicans who represent the interests of Washington State opposed him?

It is shameful today to be a Republican or affiliated with Republicans. Republicans have become the party of dishonesty, disloyalty, and cruelty. Your silence in these matters—the president's lying, his currying favor with murderous dictators, and his callous disregard for the family values Republicans have always stood for—is upsetting beyond words.

What have you to say for yourself?

Political contributions ought to only go to honest representatives who believe in American democracy—representatives who stand for American values. Is that you?

It certainly isn't Mr. Trump.

Sincerely,

Solum Optimis Verbis

Loyalty is the Thing

Week 75 / June 24 – June 30, 2018

The All-New, Very Short, & Extensively Revised Trump Annotated Dictionary

Loyalty ['loi-əl-tee] *noun*
   Definition: the quality of being loyal.
   Synonyms: ~~faithfulness~~ (sorta), devotedness, commitment, ~~honesty~~, ~~trustworthiness~~, ~~reliability~~

That's Merriam-Webster. But this is how the current White House has re-defined LOYALTY.

1. *LOYALTY* means never having to say anything but "Yes, ma'am" or "Yes, sir."
2. *LOYALTY* means NO disagreements. When the president answers "yes," he means "absolutely, positively yes," and everyone must also say "yes" until the president reworks his position and changes his answer to "absolutely, positively no." Then "no" is required from all loyalists. The same is true when the president's answer shifts once again to "absolutely, positively maybe."
3. *LOYALTY* means never having to worry about thinking about anything. All anyone needs to know is what the president is thinking—and that may require tarot cards, crystal balls, a Nostradamus, or watching FOX News.

4. *LOYALTY* means abandoning all sense of reason and decency. Those loyal must know how to lie—or learn how to lie—while keeping a straight face. They must abandon whatever moral code they ever had and become as amoral or immoral as the White House requires.
5. *LOYALTY* is NOT reciprocal. It is strictly a one-way street.

Indecency [in 'dee sen see] *noun*
Definition: indecent behavior.
Synonyms: ~~pornography · obscenity · rudeness · coarseness · dirtiness · smuttiness · vulgarity · grossness · crudity · crudeness~~ normal behavior

NOTE: Of course, since Trump began campaigning, indecency has become the norm. Although President Trump has sought to redefine the word—and to obliterate many of its synonyms—I offer the following as proof that he may have been premature:

Pornography:
- A date with Stormy Daniels while his wife, Melania, was having a baby.

Coarseness:
- Trump encouraging his followers to "beat up" anyone in his audience that disagrees. *[See Loyalty]*
- Trump calling his opponents names. Lyin' Hillary, Little Rocket Man, etc. The list is long.

Obscenity:
- Trump willfully and deliberately enacting a policy separating children from their parents at the southern border.

Rudeness:
- Trump's failure to pay workers for work performed.

- Trump accusing *bona fide* journalists of being peddlers of Fake News.

Smuttiness:
- Trump claiming to be able to grab women by the "pussy"... especially if one is sufficiently rich or famous.

Vulgarity:
- Trump calling Africa a collection of "shithole countries," even as his apartment is decorated like a bordello.

Grossness:
- Trump in golfing shorts.

Crudeness:
- Trump rejecting the friends of the United States—Canada, Europe, and Mexico—and praising our enemies—Russia and North Korea.

There's more. With Trump, there is always more.

The Maxine Waters Controversy

Trump calls Maxine Waters "Low IQ." Amazing. Has he ever looked in the mirror or listened to the things he says? My father had a favorite expression to describe people like Trump who had proven themselves particularly inept. He'd say, "That fellow couldn't pour piss out of a boot even if the directions were on the heel." I've used my father's colorful phrase from time to time, but I was curious to find out what other quaint expressions people use to describe the monumental stupidity on daily display from the White House.

Here is what I found. The following seven sentences could all easily describe Donald Trump.

1. Trump couldn't spell CAT if you spotted him the "C" and the "T."
2. Trump couldn't sell a dollar for fifty cents.

3. If Trump's brains were dynamite, he wouldn't have enough to blow his nose.
4. Trump fell out of the stupid tree and hit every branch on the way down.
5. Trump couldn't hit the water if he fell out of a fishing boat at sea.
6. If Trump's brains were shoes, he'd be barefoot all the way up to his knees. [Pogo]
7. Trump is as bright as a 2-watt bulb.

Talk about "Low IQ." Trump is the Simple Simon of the political world. Last year, in the spirit of nursery rhymes, I set out to see if my view of an infantile Trump might be transferable to rhyme. It was. Here are my contemporary nursery rhymes.

BAA, BAA, BLACK SHEEP

Baa, baa, Mr. Trump
Have you any truth?
"No, sir, no sir,
I'm just too uncouth."

"I lie to the liberal press
I lie to the world
For I am a little boy
Whose hair can't be curled.'

"I lie to the liberal press,
I say things untrue,
And I tell giant whoppers,
'Cause I haven't got a clue."

THE DONALD TRUMP TURKEY SHOOT

HUMPTY DUMPTY

Donnie Trumpie wanted a wall
Donnie Trumpie's wall couldn't fall.
Never went up and never was paid for.
None ever knew what his non-wall was made for.

Donnie Trumpie failed at his fence
Stubborn Mexico thought he was dense.
"He's dumb as a stump, and stupider still".
Our Mexican neighbors said, "No" to the bill.

Donnie thought all immigrants "Bad."
Donnie's pet phrase was "Sad, oh, so sad."
No one could tell him he ought to take care.
You stomp on your neighbors, you better beware.

𝔖olum 𝔒ptimis 𝔙erbis

The Scott Pruitt Edition

Week 76 / July 1 – July 7, 2018

Scottie Pruitt Nursery Rhyme

Pruitt, Pruitt, why did you do it?
Did we not pay you enough?
If it's moola you needed
We might have conceded
And given you more of the stuff.

But you just couldn't do it
(That's why you're Scott Pruitt)
You'd rather run scams like your boss.
Take vacations for free,
Wreck 'vironmental policy,
And all at the taxpayers' cost.

The Environmental Plundering Agency

The following transcript is of a conversation recorded on the day that Scott Pruitt was fired…er, quit on his own…er, was told to clear out his desk and take that "damn phone booth with you." Until the publication of this very secret and quasi-semi-maybe-almost-legal wiretap, no one truly knew whether Pruitt was fired or resigned. Or why he was fired. No aspect of Pruitt's departure was known…until now. From the Absolutely-true! Would-we-lie-to-you? files of the corporate leader in ferreting out the facts:

AT&T
Almost the Truth

[The telephone in Scott Pruitt's ultra-secure, James Bondian, cone-of-silence phone booth rings. The call goes to voicemail.]

Recorded Voice:	The number you have reached is no longer in service. If you have reached this number in error…
John Kelly:	Hey, Prune-Face, it's me, John Kelly. Chief of Staff to the biggest, bestest, healthiest president the world has ever seen. The Drainer of Swamps. The Lover of Little Guys. Pick up the damn phone. I know you're there. *[To himself]* Jesus, I hate reading from this damn script Trump gave me. The guy's a real… *[B-E-E-P! The phone call ends.]*
Marlyn Pruitt:	Don't you think you should have picked up, Scottie. That was John Kelly for goodness sakes. I bet the president wants to talk to you.
Scott Pruitt:	If the president wants to talk to me, he can call me. I don't answer to just any second fiddle.
Marlyn Pruitt:	Second fiddle? Should you be saying things like that? Especially about Kelly? This whole town is bugged, Scottie. What if someone hears you or records what you're sayin'?
Scott Pruitt:	Marlyn, why'd you think I got me this wing-ding, super-secret-secure phone booth installed right here in my office at taxpayer expense?
Marlyn Pruitt:	Cause you like land lines?
Scott Pruitt:	No, darlin'. I want to be able to say what I want about anybody and nobody will ever know.

	Besides, I didn't take Kelly's call 'cause I'm waitin' on the call from Dan Cathy, CEO of Chick-fil-A.
Marlyn Pruitt:	You still waitin' on that call? He hasn't called you back in almost a year. I'm tired of waitin.' Couldn't you just ask Donnie Trump to make me special assistant to somebody or other? Heck, you're doing everything he's asked—overturning clean air and water policies, helpin' our friends drill for oil in national parks and the arctic. He owes you. Maybe you could ask.
Scott Pruitt:	I'm a patient man, Marlyn. Besides, it's the job of the US Government to help me get my wife a Chick-fil-A franchise so we can Make America Great Again. What the USA needs—what Oklahoma needs—are more fast-food, cholesterol-inducing eateries so the poor people in this country will die of something before they die from filthy air and tainted water. I've got my legacy to look out for.
Marlyn Pruitt:	I know dear. You're so good at what you do. Hey, do you think we could take another vacation like the one to Morocco? I love flyin' for free. The president goes golfing almost every week—flies wherever he wants, whenever he wants. Maybe we could go to World Cup finals in Moscow. Wouldn't that be fun? We could fly first class...
Scott Pruitt:	We always fly first class, Marlyn. Coach is for losers. I wish the American people understood why I have to fly first class. Have to. Whenever I fly, my skin dries out somethin' terrible. That's why Kelly calls me Prune-Face.

Marlyn Pruitt:	I know, dear. Don't listen to Mr. Meanie. I'm so happy you finally have a job that allows you to send one of your staff to get that skin moisturizer from the Ritz-Carlton. It makes your hands and face so soft.
Scott Pruitt:	I know. World Cup or not, I'm not sure we should go to Russia right now.
Marlyn Pruitt:	Why not? Didn't you say you have some lobbyist friends who could lend us their Moscow apartment while we stay there? They practically let us stay for free here in D.C.
Scott Pruitt:	It might look bad, is all. We've got to keep up appearances. We can be as unethical as we want as long as we appear to be ethical. Or as long as we act as if it's all ethical and that everything is okay. That's Trump Rule # 1.
Marlyn Pruitt:	I thought Rule # 1 was "Never admit a mistake."
Scott Pruitt:	You're right. Truth is, the president doesn't have any rules at all that I can see.
	[The telephone in Scott Pruitt's office rings again. The call goes to voicemail.]
Recorded Voice:	The number you have reached is no longer in service. If you have reached this number in error…
John Kelly:	Hey, Secretary Pruitt, pick up…please, sir. Pretty please with sugar on it, sir.
Marlyn Pruitt:	He's being nice, Scottie. He put sugar on it.
Scott Pruitt:	I must be in a lot of trouble.
	[Picks up the phone]
	Secretary Pruitt speaking.
John Kelly:	I'm afraid I've got some bad news, Mr. Secretary.
Scott Pruitt:	Has the Ritz-Carlton run out of lotion?
John Kelly:	I'm afraid it's worse than that.

Scott Pruitt: Don't tell me I have to fly coach?

John Kelly: Nope. The Donald wants you to pack your bags and get out'a Dodge.

Scott Pruitt: But why? I keep hearing he thinks I'm doin' a good job.

John Kelly: You are. He does. But here's the thing, Scott. You look like a bigger shyster than the president. He's The Shyster-in-Chief. You lookin' snarkier, sneakier, and more corrupt than he does—well, that just makes him look bad. Can't have that, can we?

Scott Pruitt: Can't you just tell the president that I modeled myself after him? Tell him I'm sorry that I'm more unethical than he is? I didn't mean to be. I can tone it down.

John Kelly: No can do, Mr. Secretary. Just heard him say, "Who does Pruitt think he is? The President?" Oh, yeah. The President says thanks.

Scott Pruitt: But I was just about to lift the ban on lead in the nation's drinking water.

John Kelly: I know, Mr. Secretary, but appears the fun is over. Someone else is gonna have to take credit for poisoning the nation. Sorry. Between you and me, he's upset because you have more investigations looking into you than he has. You've got the EPA Inspector General, the House Oversight Committee, the Government Accountability Office, and a bunch more looking at you. You're always in the news and the president really doesn't like the competition. Looks like you're leaving.

Scott Pruitt: So is he firing me or am I resigning?

John Kelly:	I'm not sure. Let's just say you're gone, okay? We'll just leave it to the Fake Media folks to sort out whether you resigned or got fired. Whatever they say, we'll say the opposite. Don't you love it?!?! This is just one more chance for us to stir up confusion. The Donald loves that. Don't forget to tell Andy Wheeler he's in charge now.
Scott Pruitt:	Anything else?
John Kelly:	Get that damn phone booth out of Wheeler's office.
	[Phone hangs up]
Marlyn Pruitt:	What does all this mean, Scottie?
Scott Pruitt:	Well, looks like we won't be gettin' to meet Putin this year, darlin'. No World Cup either. But don't forget, I got you that real nice second-hand mattress from one of Trump's hotels, didn't I? The one you said you wanted. Say, you think any hookers have ever done anything on it? With the President? I get all excited just thinkin' about sleepin' on that mattress with you darlin'.
Marlyn Pruitt:	Me, too, Scottie. I got goosebumps.

𝔖olum 𝔒ptimis 𝔙erbis

Trump Overseas Edition

Week 77 / July 8 – July 14, 2018

A Conversation on Air Force One

Pompeo: When you go on TV, Mr. President, please try to tell the truth. You upset our allies with that 90% remark.

Trump: Come on, Mikey. When you deal in the truth, you have to have your facts straight. Not only that, you have to have facts. I don't like facts. Most real facts are dull. Most facts don't make any impression at all. Like yesterday. I said the US pays 90% of NATO expenses because it's a gigunda number. Big! Bigly big! 90% gets people's attention. I don't know if it's true or not, and I don't care. I got everyone's attention.

Pompeo: We only pay 22% of the NATO budget, Mr. President.

Trump: See. Dull, dull, dull. 22% is a dull number. Really dull. Sad, even. Who jumps up at 22% and says, "Jesus Christ! We're paying 22%? That's robbery!" Nobody. That's who. When you say, "The US pays 90% and we're getting' screwed," people jump up. Besides, I was only off by about 50%.

Pompeo: You were off by 68%, Mr. President.

Trump: Yeah, yeah, yeah. I was never good at math. But I've got great words…the best words.

Pompeo: These NATO countries are our allies, Mr. President. Our friends. You understand that, don't you?

Trump: You better grow up, Mikey. There's no such thing as friendship. They're only our friends because we provide them protection. I've been building buildings forever, and if there's one thing I know, it's protection. If people want protection, they have to pay for it. Besides, I'm looking for newer, better friends.

Pompeo: Better friends? Who could be better friends over the past half century than the UK, or Canada, or France?

Trump: How about Russia? How about North Korea? I like the way they operate. Did you know their leaders are practically presidents for life? For life. I like the way that sounds, don't you? I'd like to have them as friends. I know they'd love to have us as friends.

Pompeo: They're not our friends. They're our enemies, Mr. President. They don't believe in democracy or individual human rights.

Trump: Nobody does, Mikey. Not me. Not the Republican Party. Democracy? Really? That's a laugh. A democracy elected me. Does anyone believe in democracy anymore? Any democracy that can elect me isn't much of a democracy.

Pompeo: You've got a point there, Mr. President.

Trump: And all that civil rights crap—all that stuff about the people having the power—that's all crap. Money is power. The military is power. I've got lotsa money. I've got the world's best Army, Navy, Air Force, Marine Corps, and Coast Guard in my pocket. I'm the Commander-in-Chief. Pretty soon I'll have NASA straightened around and then I'll have the US Space Command. I've seen Star Wars. I'm gonna boldly go and kick some ass. When that happens, everyone will want to pay us for protection.

Pompeo: That "boldly go" line is from Star Trek, Mr. President. Not Star Wars.

Trump: Same difference. That's just another useless fact. Another fact I don't need.

Pompeo: We all need facts. The world operates on facts, Mr. President.

Trump: Your world, maybe. Not mine. When you're president, you get to make your own facts.

𝔖olum 𝔒ptimis 𝔙erbis

Scary Trumpins

Week 78 / July 15 – July 21, 2018

This week proves that Trump has no interest in any of us. (The same for most Republicans!) Incredibly, his self-interest doesn't even embrace the United States. That's scary. So… with that in mind, I offer two new and improved songs from the all-new musical entitled:

Scary Trumpins
The Musical © 2018 (with apologies to *Mary Poppins*)
Lyrics by John Scannell & Wendy Kelling

SuperCallousFragileRacistSexistNazi POTUS

SuperCallousFragileRacistSexistNazi POTUS
Trump's fact-free reality is something quite atrocious.
When he speaks he makes no sense, he's always out of focus.
SuperCallousFragileRacistSexistNazi POTUS.

Trump-did-a-little-piddle, Trump-told-a-lie
Trump-did-a-little-piddle, Trump-told-a-lie

When we met this Donald Trump our hopes for him were high
But it turns out he's ignorant—those hopes will never fly.
Our only hope's this healthy man will just eat shit and die,
Then we'll have our nation back and we won't have to cry—oh—

The Donald Trump Turkey Shoot

Trump-did-a-little-piddle, Trump-told-a-lie
Trump-did-a-little-piddle, Trump-told-a-lie

We want our NATO to be strong 'cause Russia's mean and low
But Trump he wants autocracy and Putin-love, you know.
He wants to be a dictator—he's such a dick—and so,
We may have to ~~kill~~ pay him off if we want him to go.

Trump-did-a-little-piddle, Trump-told-a-lie
Trump-did-a-little-piddle, Trump-told-a-lie

SuperCallousFragileRacistSexistNazi POTUS
We women know his empty brain is something un-precocious.
His wand'ring hands are everywhere, 'cause he just wants to grope us.
SuperCallousFragileRacistSexistNazi POTUS.

NOTE: There's a humorous photograph of Vladimir Putin with a Donald Trump puppet seated on his knee. The dummies mouth is wide open, and he is apparently saying something. What could that be? Let me offer one possibility is light verse:

When his hand is up my sphincter
I could not be succincter
'Bout the way my buddy Putin
Could hardly be colludin'.

Just Go Fly A Kite
From Scary Trumpins, the Musical © 2018
(with apologies to *Mary Poppins*)
Lyrics by John Scannell & Wendy Kelling

Just go fly a kite,
Somethin' 'bout Trump's not right,
Just go fly a kite
'Cause he's gone whoring
With girls around the world
His banner is unfurled.
Oh, just go fly a kite.

With Trumpie as leader and stuff
He don't know enough is enough.
When you scream to the sky
And wonder just why…
You can yell this for spite,
"Wish you'd go fly a kite."

Oh…oh…oh…oh

Wish he'd fly a kite!
Our leader is a fright.
Wish he'd fly a kite
Before we're warring
With North Korea's folk.
Trump is a stupid bloke,
Wish he'd go fly a kite.

Feel free to make t-shirts saying you wish to—
Make Mary Poppins Great Again
Currently, no hats are available.

Solum Optimis Verbis

Scary Trumpins, Part 2

Week 79 / July 22 – July 28, 2018

Ridiculous Lyrics for a Ridiculous Presidency
Scary Trumpins, the Musical © 2018
Lyrics by Wendy Kelling & John Scannell

I Don't Know How to Leave Him [Melania's Song]
To the tune of *I Don't Know How to Love Him* with apologies to *Jesus Christ, Superstar*

I don't know how to leave him.
To deceive or to cleave him.
Vlad and me, we had a plan
But in these past long months, he's exposed us all,
A doltish, orangish thug, he's got to fall.

Should I bring him down? Tell Vlad I've had enough?
Will he end me first? Have I tougher stuff?
I thought those porn stars would do the trick.
I gave them orange handcuffs.

I know you think it's rather funny
I should be in this position
From immigrant to refugee
Give me a nom de guerre, let's pinky swear

I'll give you everything to make them sing
… set up the sting … I'll keep the bling … I must take wing

President [Putin's Song]
To the tune of *Popular* with apologies to *Wicked*

President,
You're gonna be President,
I'll teach you to meet and greet
On Collusion Street
Threats and blackmail as your tools
With my crew's great hacks
For your crass attacks
Lies and spies that you can use
To be President,
You're gonna be President,
And when the world's in despair
Watch our bro' affair
It'll give them such a fright
So let's start
'Cause Mueller's getting ready to indict.

Don Trumpins Is a Fool
To the tune of *My Country Tis of Thee* with apologies to *All Revered American Melodies*

Don Trumpins is a fool
He's Putin's useful tool,
He's got to go.
We Secret Service guys
Can't serve a man who lies,
A president who never tries,
Trumpins is our foe.

We've got to end his reign,
All here are in such pain,
He's too insane.
'Cause he's a Russian pawn,
Don is an evil spawn,
A traitorous liaison
Causing great strain.

We're thinking, just for fun
Throw him off Air Force One
Into the night.
He'd fly away somewhere
Through the black, cold night air,

His ass lit by a flare,

Providing some light.

How to Handle a Traitor

To the tune of *How to Handle a Woman* with apologies to *Camelot*

How to handle a traitor?
Conduct all in strict secrecy,
Send subpoenas to every villain
Who will worry they may not go free.

Do I question them in private meetings?
Do I threaten them with jail terms long?
Do I frustrate them with mental beatings?
Yes, indeed, if I stay strong.

How to handle a traitor?
When indictments are in the air,
The way to handle a traitor,
Is to Mueller…simply Mueller…
Merely Mueller…Mueller…Mueller.

Before We Begin This Week
In Memory of
John Sidney McCain III, Aug 29, 1936 - Aug 25, 2018
He Saved Obamacare
May He Rest in Peace

****

𝔖olum 𝔒ptimis 𝔙erbis

Duncan Hunter, The Swamp Thing

Week 83 / August 19 – August 25, 2018

This past week, those Americans who were still unsure if Trump had really "drained the swamp" got a front row seat, complete with snorkel. Representative Duncan Hunter, Republican from San Diego, was indicted for violating campaign fund rules. He allegedly spent more than $250,000 of campaign funds for his own personal use. Perhaps it would help if I listed a few of the more egregious expenditures that caused him to be brought up on charges.

$1,008.72 on a ski trip to Lake Tahoe
$2,570.00 on books for family and friends
$1,912.00 for Pittsburgh Steeler tickets
$1,528.00 for video games
$3,724.00 for a trip to a family wedding in Boise via Las Vegas
$6,289.00 for a trip to Hawaii
$14,261.00 for a trip to Italy
$38,000.00 in bank overdraft fees

All of these personal expenses were "renamed" and submitted as legitimate campaign expenditures, which they clearly were not. Now I know that our judicial system declares that people are considered innocent until proven guilty, but this guy is a Republican, which means I no longer need to suspend my judgement. Republicans are guilty.

Duncan Hunter is part of Trump's primordial swamp, currently undrained and teeming with many more creatures just like him. Some swamp creatures like Scott Pruitt and Hope Hicks have already been captured in the Net of Stupidity, or the Jaws of Overindulgence. Unfortunately for all of us, each will probably live to slime again. ***NOTE:*** If Duncan Hunter is found innocent in the coming days, I shall write a sincere, heartfelt apology for having said he was guilty before the verdict was in. But he's guilty.

Disclaimer: The following script is a phone conversation that I captured on my highly classified *Imaginary Device Instantly Overhearing Trump. [I.D.I.O.T]* a device informally referred to as "the Idiot." It works really well. The following is an *I.D.I.O.T.* intercept I thought I'd share with my readers.

            [Duncan Hunter's cellphone rings. Hunter answers.]
Hunter: Hello.
Trump: Hey, Hunter. This is Donnie Trump. Senior. You know, the President?
Hunter: *[Clearly unsure if he is being spoofed.]* Okay.
Trump: I'm calling to give you a hand with the bit of trouble you've got yourself into.
Hunter: Can't be worse for me than it has been for you this past week, Mr. President.

Trump: You talking about Mikey "The Rat" Cohen? You talkin' about Mr. I'll-Say-Anything-the-Prosecutor-Wants-Me-to-Say? Is that who you're talkin' about?

Hunter: Yeah. His testimony made you an unindicted co-conspirator this week. Aren't you worried?

Trump: Worried? Why should I be worried? Come on, Hunter, who are people gonna believe? Him or me?

Hunter: *[Long pause]* So…what kind of help are you talking about getting for me, Mr. President? 'Cause I'm not guilty of any wrong doing, Mr. President.

Trump: Yeah, sure. Me neither. *[Laughs heartily]* Don't forget, Hunter, nobody is ever guilty…of anything…not until they're caught and convicted. That's the way I've operated for years. Until you're convicted, it's just stuff that some other people think you shouldn't have done. Like payin' off porn stars.

Hunter: But I didn't do what they say I did.

Trump: That's okay, Hunter, baby. That's okay. You keep tellin' that story. That's good. Tell it often enough, and everyone'll probably believe you. Nearly everyone, except maybe the prosecutors. They have no sense of humor, you know that, right?

Hunter: But I didn't use campaign funds for personal reasons. I really didn't.

Trump: Yeah, yeah, yeah. And I didn't collude with the Russians. I was never gonna build a Trump Hotel in Moscow. I love my son, Eric. I was always faithful to all three of my wives. And my tax returns will show I have nothin' to hide. Right?

Hunter: What are you saying, Mr. President?

Trump: Hunter! Come on. It takes one to know one. I spent my campaign money pretty much the way I wanted to.

	After all, it's MY campaign money. Hell, that campaign money you spent was yours to spend any way you liked. You earned it. People gave that money to you. Y-O-U. Just because somebody makes up some damn rules sayin' you can't spend it on vacations or Steelers games or theater tickets—that doesn't make them right. Right? Sad. Sad that anyone makes up those kinda rules and expects anyone else to obey them.
Hunter:	But I'm still in trouble. I'm indicted. It doesn't matter what you think, Mr. President.
Trump:	*[Pause]* I'm gonna forget you ever said that, Hunter. The only important thing in this world *is* what *I* think. What anyone else thinks is bullshit. That's why everyone listens carefully to every word I tweet—even the misspelled words. What *I* think is the single most important thing on this planet…or any other planet. Probably the universe.
Hunter:	Sorry, Mr. President.
Trump:	So I had my guy John Kelly compose some first class excuses for you. He's my Chief of Staff, but he's got nothin' better to do. He's pretty sure these excuses can help get you off the hook.
Hunter:	Excuses?
Trump:	Excuses. Explanations. Who cares? Like that trip you took to Italy. Kelly says you should tell everyone that you were going to the Vatican. *[Unfolds a piece of paper]* Let me read what Kelly wrote. You're gonna love it. Here it is:

I went to Italy to buy a thousand rosaries and have them all blessed by the pope…

The Donald Trump Turkey Shoot

Pope What's-his-name?...Frank?... Covfefe? Hell, I can't remember...It doesn't matter. Let me read the rest.

And I brought them all back to San Diego so I could give these beautiful rosaries—blessed by His Holiness—to all the immigrant mothers who are fleeing oppression in Central America by crossing our welcoming southern border into California. So help me, God.

Hunter: That's a great idea, Mr. President, but I'm a Baptist. Rosaries are a Catholic thing.

Trump: Nobody's gonna care, Hunter. All those lousy illegals comin' across the border are Catholic—or they oughta be. You just gotta link your Italy trip with the Mexican border. That's all. What you tell the Fake News folks and the prosecutor doesn't have to be true.

Hunter: Okay. I'll have my secretary run out and buy some rosaries. Maybe that'll boost my rating with Catholic voters—and maybe get some Hispanics in my corner. What other stories did Kelly compose for me?

Trump: Well, remember that trip to Hawaii?

Hunter: Yeah, that Hawaii trip is gonna be hard to explain.

Trump: Not when you got me in your corner. Kelly says you should say this:

I went to Hawaii to finally put to rest the truth about Obama's birthplace. He wants everyone to believe he was born in the USA when he was really born in Kenya, and it's about time people realized that. I work for the American people. I work to find the truth. That's why I went to Hawaii.

Hunter: Damn, Mr. President, even I'm beginning to believe I'm innocent. That's great. Kelly's a pretty good bullshit artist, isn't he?

Trump: Yep. I've had him in my back pocket ever since he lied about that whacko congresswoman from Florida.

Hunter: Frederica Wilson? The one who wears those cowboy hats?

Trump: That's the one. He lied about her, and I wouldn't let him apologize. So, he didn't. Now he works for me. Does whatever I tell him to do. If you get the dirt on somebody, it doesn't mean anything unless you're willing to use it. I got him to lie, and once you get someone to lie for you, you own them. Look at my former White House Press Secretary, Sean Spicer. He was Mister Honesty until I got him to lie about the size of the inauguration crowd. After that, I owned him.

Hunter: So that's why Kelly stays as your Chief of Staff? You got dirt on him?

Trump: Something like that. It took some doin', Hunter, but I've finally convinced Kelly of one important truth. It doesn't matter what you do. The only thing that matters is what you say you did. Got that? It's worked for me for decades.

Hunter: I'm not sure that's a "truth," Mr. President.

Trump: Got news for you, Hunter. If I say it's a truth, then it's a truth. Got it?

Hunter: Got it, Mr. President. Any other really good stories I can tell the prosecutor?

Trump: Well, Kelly's got a great angle on the Pittsburgh Steelers game. Listen to this:

The Donald Trump Turkey Shoot

I went to the game to make sure all the NFL players complied with the president's expectations that no player should ever take a knee during the National Anthem. I went there to insure that only true patriots get the chance to play American Professional Football.

Hunter:	The NFL folks will probably back you up 100%. Another great idea.
Trump:	You bet. But I gotta say, you got big cojones, Hunter. Big ones. You actually blamed all this on your wife?
Hunter:	Well...yeah...I sorta blamed it all on Margaret...
Trump:	Nothin' "sorta" about it. You said she handled all the money. Cojones, Hunter. You didn't just throw her under the bus, my man, you were driving the bus.
Hunter:	Okay, I blamed her. But that's what wives are for, right? To give us an excuse when we really need one? Am I right?
Trump:	I knew there was something I liked about you, Hunter.
Hunter:	So, how come you haven't blamed Melania for everything so far?
Trump:	Well, can you keep a secret?
Hunter:	Sure.
Trump:	Putin would can my ass if I did anything like that. He really likes Melania. Said if anything bad happens to her, something even worse will happen to me. That's why I'm kissin' his butt every time we get together—that and the pee-pee tapes that Moscow's got.
Hunter:	So that's all true?
Trump:	I'm not sayin' it is. But maybe. *[Smiles a smirky smile]* Maybe I was young and reckless. Once. But it was just once.
Hunter:	How about Stormy Daniels?

The Donald Trump Turkey Shoot

Trump: Okay, twice.
Hunter: And Karen McDougal?
Trump: Okay, three times. *[Gets serious]* Hey, don't say another word about all my other women. Okay? None of my personal business is anybody's business but mine.
Hunter: And Melania's?
Trump: Melania's? Yeah. Okay. Sure.
Hunter: And Putin's?

[Phone line goes dead. End of I.D.I.O.T intercept]

Solum Optimis Verbis

Only Duh Best Woids

Week 85 / Sept. 2 – Sept. 8, 2018

I love words…I love language. If you wade into the sea of language often enough, you find some strange fish swimming in that ocean. Here are two that flopped into my boat after I read an article about "Ten Words Every Book-Lover Should Know." I offer these words now because they feel incredibly relevant to the political morass in which we find ourselves.

Ultracrepidarian, [əltrəkrepə'derēən] *adjective* and *noun*
Adj: expressing opinions on matters outside the scope of one's knowledge or expertise.
Sentence: Donald Trump employs an ultracrepidarian strategy whenever anyone asks him a question about anything.
Noun: Someone who gives an opinion on things s/he knows nothing about.
NOTE: While one may feel free to use a more colloquial phrase like: *Trump? He don't know nothin' about nothin'*, we must always keep in mind our motto: "Only the Best Words." Once or twice, try using ultracrepidarian. It glides easily off the tongue.
Sentence: Donald Trump is the ultimate ultracrepidarian.

Morosoph, ['mōrə säf] *noun*
Noun: a would-be philosopher — a fool who thinks he's more clever than he is.

NOTE: Derived from the French writer Rabelais, where the 'moro-' is from the Greek meaning 'dull' or 'stupid' and the '-soph' from the Greek for 'wise.' Morosophs are foolish for thinking themselves so wise.
Sentence: Morosophs are foolish for thinking themselves so wise.

Writer's Question: Does this sound like anyone we know? Once again, in keeping with our motto, *solum optimis verbis*, we should henceforth reference President Trump correctly. *"President Trump, the morosoph, said today…"* realizing that we are also saying there is no reason to read further. For instance, that complete sentence might read like this. *"President Trump, the morosoph, made several ultracrepidarian remarks to the delight of his idiotic audience."*

Writer's Comment: There are numerous examples of comments made by Donald Trump, our ultracrepidarian morosoph, that simply confirm what we already know. His ignorance is ten miles wide—and we have yet to find the bottom. From now on, I am tempted to write Trump's name thusly: President Donald J. Trump, *DKS.* (Don't Know Shit)

For instance, he once said, *"I went to the Wharton School of Business. I'm, like, a really smart person."* One pundit admitted that he'd misheard Trump: *"I attended the Whoreson School of Business."* This pundit may be excused for getting it wrong. It was a reasonable mistake.

<u>**Trump Rule # 1:**</u> Trust me. Don't trust the Fake Media. And don't trust your eyes and ears.

Remember the first Big Lie by Donald J. Trump, *DKS?* The inaugural crowd? The one we could see? Now we have clear and irrefutable evidence that the crowd attending the inauguration was not only NOT

THE BIGGEST EVER—nor the bigliest ever, if you prefer—but was, in fact, insultingly small. In keeping with this week's vocabulary theme, feel free to insert "measly" or "paltry" in front of the word "crowd."

> *A government photographer edited official pictures of Donald Trump's inauguration to make the crowd appear bigger following a personal intervention from the president, according to newly released documents.*
>
> *The photographer cropped out empty space "where the crowd ended" for a new set of pictures requested by Trump on the first morning of his presidency, after he was angered by images showing his audience was smaller than Barack Obama's in 2009. [The Guardian, September 6, 2018]*

Trump Rule # 2: I know everything. Everyone else is stupid. And they're all out to get me.

Fortunately, we heard from one of Trump's hand-picked, stupid people this week in a *New York Times* op-ed. This person—gender, generally unknown—penned an article about the "Resistance" in the Trump administration. Naturally, Mr. Morosoph Trump sees no irony is his failing to realize that members of his administration hold him in such low esteem. Some salient quotations:

> [T]he president's leadership style...is impetuous, adversarial, petty, and ineffective.
>
> Meetings with him veer off topic and off the rails...[H]e engages in repetitive rants, and his impulsiveness results in half-baked, ill-informed, and occasionally reckless decisions that have to be walked back.

This op-ed came on the heels of published excerpts from Bob Woodward's upcoming book, *Fear: Trump in the White House.*[2] In his book, Woodward quotes Secretary of Defense, James Mattis, who slams the president as having the comprehension of a "fifth or sixth grader."

Yeah, right. Fifth or sixth grade? We could only hope. We all know that's way too high. Maybe third grade—if you give him the benefit of the doubt. Woodward's book joins Omarosa's unflattering portrait of Trump in *Unhinged*, as the latest expose' of Trump's massive ineptitude.

Who Dunnit?
A Silly Sketch, Based on a True Story

<u>Dramatis Personae:</u>
Melania, Trump's wife
John Kelly, Trump's Chief of Staff
Mike Pompeo, Secretary of State

<u>Setting:</u> *A dimly lit room somewhere in the bowels of the White House. There is a table and chairs. Melania enters. She looks around to see if she is alone.*

NOTE: The script also includes the Standard English translation of Melania's lines to help the reader.

Melania: Gooot! I em uh-loan. I ken rehearse ensers to Dawnnie's kveschuns befor I tek lyink test.
            <u>Translation:</u> Good. I'm alone. I can rehearse answers to Donnie's questions before I take lying test.

---

[2] Scheduled to be released on September 11, 2018. Hmmmm. 9/11. Another American tragedy.

[Melania pauses, looks around, sits, and begins rehearsing her lines written on a piece of paper.]

Melania: I dint do. No, Dawnie. I dint do. I be best. I kent rite goot.

Translation: I didn't do it. Not with the stupid pre-nup I agreed to, Donnie. I'm trying my best. Besides, I can still read and write better than you.

[Melania hears a sound, goes quiet, and moves to a corner of the room. John Kelly enters.]

Kelly: Hello? Is someone here? I thought I heard someone talking. Hello?

Melania: Oh, Jawney, eets yew. I vuss so vorry.

Translation: Oh, it's you, John Kelly. I'm glad to have an adult in the room.

Kelly: Melania. What are you doing down here?

Melania: Sem es yew. I prektis.

Translation: Same as you. I'm practicing.

Kelly: What are you practicing?

Melania: Vat els? Lyink. I prektis lyink.

Translation: What else? Lying. I'm practice lying. It's a skill my husband's got down pat.

Kelly: You? You're practicing lying?

[Pauses with surprise]

Me, too. I thought it was only Crazytown upstairs. Well, Mel, that imbecile husband of yours thinks we think he's an imbecile.

Melania: He iss im-bee-sigh-ul. Im-bee-sigh-ul, verst kless.

Translation: He is an imbecile. A first class imbecile. It's well documented.

Kelly: He's worse than an imbecile. If I had my way...

[Kelly suddenly puts his finger to his lips indicating silence.]

Shhhhhhhhhh. Shhhhhhhh. Someone's coming.
[Enter Mike Pompeo.]
Kelly: Mike? Is that you?
Pompeo: Kelly?
Kelly: Yeah. It's me. What's up?
Melania: Hello, Mikey.
[Pompeo spots Melania.]
Pompeo: Melania? What are you and John doing down here this time of night?
[Kelly and Melania answer in one voice.]
Kelly: Practicing!
Melania: Prektissing!
Pompeo: That husband of yours is a real ignoramus.
Melania: Ees troo. *[Nods head vigorously.]*
Pompeo: And we're all in trouble because the New York Times printed some anonymous letter about him. Well, I'll tell you this. I wish I'd written it.
Kelly: Me, too.
Melania: Me, too.
Pompeo: But I didn't.
Kelly: Me, neither.
Melania: Me, needer.
Pompeo: Doesn't make any difference, you guys. Everyone's in trouble. Know what he said to me. "Your CIA better find this goddamn traitor or I find someone else to head up the CIA." When I told him I was the Secretary of State, not head of the CIA, he asked me if there was a difference.
Kelly: Did you set him straight—about the difference?
Pompeo: I was just about to do exactly that, when he said he had to get 18 holes in before it started raining. Said he'd execute the weatherman if he got rained on. Said it was

treason to rain on the president. He's in a really foul mood.

Melania: Ulvays. Ulvays in bet mood.
<u>Translation:</u> Always. He's always in bad mood. It's his nature.

Kelly: Amazing how one op-ed piece could make him so mad. Make him suspicious of everyone. We didn't write that piece.

Pompeo: True. But we all thought the same things plenty of times.

Melania: Da. I tink, tew. When I tink Dawnie, I tink awl bet tings. Stupid, im-bee-sigh-ul, ig…ig…vat yew say Mikey?
<u>Translation:</u> Yes, I think so, too. When I think of Donnie, I only think of bad things. Words like stupid, imbecile, and ignoramus.

Pompeo: Ignoramus. That's the word. He's an ignoramus to the 10th power. And if he gets us all to take a lie detector test, we'll all probably fail. After all, we all wish we wrote it.

Kelly: So which will help us pass the lie detector test? The truth or a lie?

Melania: Don't metter. Dawnie kent tell diffrence.
<u>Translation:</u> It doesn't matter. Donnie can't tell the difference.

Kelly: I wouldn't worry so much. Bob Woodward's book, Fear, comes out on Tuesday, and he'll be so upset with that, he'll forget all about the New York Times article.

Pompeo: Don't count your chickens yet, Kelly. Woodward quotes all of us someplace in his new book. We're calling Trump a jerk, an asshole, a danger to democracy, or even something worse. So after Fear comes out, I don't think we'll need to take a lie detector test. We'll all be unemployed.

Melania: Me, tew?
Pompeo: Bad news, Melania. You've been unemployed since Barron was born.

[Curtain.]

𝕾𝖔𝖑𝖚𝖒 𝕺𝖕𝖙𝖎𝖒𝖎𝖘 𝖁𝖊𝖗𝖇𝖎𝖘

Lies & Damn Lies… Sorry, No Statistics

Week 89 / Sept. 30 – Oct. 6, 2018

NOTE: I have some observations I'd like to share because our political universe has just been turned upside down. For my part, I shall do what I can to right it come November 2018. For now, I write letters to the editor. Here are two of them:

Dear Editor,

I find Republican caviling at the Brett Kavanaugh hearings baffling. Set aside the allegations that the Supreme Court nominee might be a sexual predator—an attempted rapist when he was in high school. According to published reports, Kavanaugh's criminal acts happened while he was "stumbling drunk"…and a teenager. So, to be kind, let's also set aside that he was a stumbling drunk…and a minor.

What I find baffling is why anyone in 2018 would decide to disenfranchise women regarding the governance of their own bodies. Roe v. Wade has been settled law for 45 years. Women's reproductive rights, particularly contraception and abortion, should continue to be inviolate—nobody's business but their own. Nevertheless, Kavanaugh subverted Roe v. Wade in a recent immigrant ruling. He's made his views clear.

In 21st century America, allowing "religious convictions" to supersede another person's individual rights should be considered constitutional heresy. That's why we have the separation of church and state—or rather, the separation of bigotry from law.

The same must be said about LGBTQ individual rights. No one should be able to superimpose narrow-minded "religious convictions" on anyone. We are a democracy, not a theocracy.

Kavanaugh should be rejected because he would be an anachronism. His views are anathema to the concept of individual "life, liberty, and the pursuit of happiness." At least for women.

Dear Editor,

Being fond of metaphors, I have told many people that the lies told by our president and his complicit Republicans cronies in the White House, the House, and the Senate—all the deception and dissembling—are tearing apart the fabric of our democracy. But I was mistaken.

I see now that the lies and deceit have steadily been knit into the fabric of a whole new type of cloth—a cloth that will keep bigots, racists, misogynists, scam artists, and those who would profit from the misery of others, snug and warm.

The rule of law is meaningless when there is no one to enforce it, or when those in charge can ignore the law entirely without consequence, or change it by any and all means.

These are scary times for anyone who is paying attention.

Some Observations about Brett Kavanaugh's Ascension to the United State Supreme Court

Observation # 1:
I know I've spoken about the thousands of lies Trump has pawned off on a credulous public since the day he announced for office. But

it appears that lying is contagious. How else can we account for the Senate Judiciary Committee telling us they authorized the FBI to conduct an investigation into Brett Kavanaugh's past when clearly they did no such thing?

Observation # 2:
The truth matters to a great many people, but it appears to have no meaning whatsoever to the Republican Party. While the President was saying that he wanted to get to the bottom of things, wanted to get to the truth, he deliberately limited the scope of the mind-numbingly brief, one-week-only, FBI investigation. Whatever facts or conclusions might be adduced by a longer, truly thorough investigation were thwarted.

Observation # 3:
The Republican members of the Senate knew the truth of what was happening, but they made enough noise—via Jeff Flake [AZ], and Susan Collins [ME]—to distract us from the scam they were truly running.

Observation # 4:
I think the Republicans draw straws to see which of them will be permitted "to appear brave" in the eyes of Democrats—even briefly. During the Kavanaugh hearings, Jeff Flake—who criticized the bogus, one-week delay for an FBI investigation—and Susan Collins—who professed to be agonizing about choosing a liar like Kavanaugh—simply diverted our attention. Democrats harbored the Republican-engendered hope that perhaps there was a real chance that these two may actually vote "No"—that they would actually *be brave*. Instead, false bravery only masked their cowardice. Lisa Murkowski, of course, was the designee who could not only appear brave, but act brave by voting "No." Of course, since the fix was in.

The vote was rigged. Remember, it's easy to vote "No" when it has no effect.

Observation # 5:
Apparently, lying to Congress is not a crime. Boofing? The Devil's Triangle? Barfing? Kavanaugh wanted to appear angelic, but it was clear from hand-scrawled yearbook commentary and the testimony of those *who knew him when* that he was not what he purported to be. He was not an angel.

I, too, went to 12 years of Catholic School—but that was back in the 60s when boofing had not yet been invented. I didn't drink or engage in threesomes, either. But there were times when I got "too big for my britches"—a favorite phrase of my mother's. When I did, she would turn to me and say, "Settle down, young man, your halo is getting a bit tight."

Observation # 6:
Absolute power corrupts absolutely. [I didn't think that one up on my own.]

Observation # 7:
Are any of you as puzzled as I am that the Republicans have deliberately chosen to ignore the #MeToo Movement—especially as it informs the whole Brett Kavanaugh debacle? Do Republicans think that "This, too, shall pass?" Do they believe that American women will be happy to return to hearth and home; happily cooking meals, mending socks, and watching afternoon soaps; happy to be the sexual play things for men who cannot control their libidinous desires? With every fiber of my being, I hope that the female vote this November proves the folly of the Republican position.

Observation # 8:

I'm not really a betting man—I don't mind spending money, but I do hate losing it. Nevertheless, I'll wager five dollars with any of my readers that the Supreme Court will overturn *Roe v Wade* before the next presidential election in 2020. Let me know if you're willing to take that bet. I'll be happy to lose.

Observation # 9:

Did any of you realize the scope of the president's powers? Hardly a day passes without the Donald causing some kind of mischief or harm, and we are usually told he has that power to do what he is doing—to the detriment of us all.

Solum Optimis Verbis

The Country Bumpkin and The City Trumpkin

Week 92 / October 21 – October 27, 2018

Somewhere in D.C. A farmer and the Prez. are carrying bags that say "Trick or Treat."

Bumpkin: You goin' trick-or-treatin' looking like that?
Trumpkin: Looking like what?
Bumpkin: Like that. Like a pumpkin.
Trumpkin: I don't look like a pumpkin.
Bumpkin: You look like a pumpkin, sure enough.
Trumpkin: What the hell? This is the way I always look.
Bumpkin: Really? So you like lookin' like a pumpkin?
Trumpkin: Stop saying that! I don't look like a pumpkin. I look like the President of the United States.
Bumpkin: *[Laughing]* Yeah. Sure. If the president was born in a pumpkin patch. Your face reminds me of a joke I once heard when I was a kid.
Trumpkin: What joke was that?
Bumpkin: If my dog had a face like yours, I'd shave his butt and make him walk backwards.
Trumpkin: That's not funny.

Bumpkin: Well, it ain't as funny as your face, that's certain. Or your hair. Not as funny as you look. I gotta admit, that's a great look for Hallowe'en. Major league scary. You'll probably get lots of candy.

Trumpkin: *[Grimacing in frustration]* Why am I talking to you? You don't know shit.

Bumpkin: Well, you're dead wrong there, Pumpkin Man. Nobody knows shit better than I do. I been a farmer for years.

Trumpkin: A farmer? Everybody knows I love farmers.

Bumpkin: Sure you do. That's why you imposed tariffs that screwed U.S. farmers royally, right? I can't sell my soybeans any more. They're sittin' on the dock. But China's not buyin'. Cause of you. They're gonna rot 'cause of your stupid decision.

Trumpkin: You'll just have to be patient. I'm winning the tariff war.

Bumpkin: Winnin'? Well, Pumpkin Man, me and my fellow farmers are losin' while you're winnin'. Our crops gotta get sold soon.

Trumpkin: Wars take time.

Bumpkin: Time we don't have. Crops spoil. And makin' matters worse, just this week John Deere announced a price hike. That makes us casualties of your stupid war.

Trumpkin: So? Why's that my problem.

Bumpkin: It ain't your problem. It's mine…and other farmers. Apparently nothin' is ever your problem. You put a tariff on steel, just like that. *[Snaps fingers]* But you don't need no tractors or farm machinery. So it ain't your problem. Some thinker you turned out to be. If brains were dynamite, you wouldn't have enough to blow your nose.

Trumpkin: You can't talk to me like that.

Bumpkin: Sure, I can. I can talk to cowards anyway I want.

The Donald Trump Turkey Shoot

Trumpkin: You callin' me a coward?

Bumpkin: Damn straight. I ain't the first to say so neither. Don't talk to me about "a war." You didn't never go to fight in no wars. Not like my Daddy. You never fought in Vietnam because your Daddy gave Uncle Sam a blowjob, and now you're happy to fight a war that has no consequences for you.

Trumpkin: Sure…go ahead…blame me. It's the Democrats fault. You know.

Bumpkin: Sure just like Puerto Rican relief efforts from Hurricane Maria.

Trumpkin: That's right…

Bumpkin: 'Spose you think Puerto Ricans ain't no more citizens than those folks comin' up from Central America.

Trumpkin: You said it, not me. But…yeah, that's right.

Bumpkin: How about helpin' all them folks sufferin' from damage from Hurricane Florence or Hurricane Michael…?

Trumpkin: That's expensive. People shouldn't be living where they might be hit by a hurricane…

Bumpkin: Or a tornado?...

Trumpkin: Yeah.

Bumpkin: Or an earthquake?...

Trumpkin: Yeah.

Bumpkin: Or a drought?...

Trumpkin: Yeah.

Bumpkin: Or a forest fire?...

Trumpkin: Now you're seeing it. Most of those tragedies—hurricanes, floods, droughts, tornados—they're a problem only because the Dems are complaining about global climate change. You know that, right? There wouldn't be any global climate change if the Dems would just shut the hell up about it.

Bumpkin: So we wouldn't have none of this 'cept for the Democrats sayin' so?

Trumpkin: Not exactly. But we wouldn't be worrying about it if they'd just keep quiet. The Dems talk about it and then everybody expects me to do something about it. And doing something—sending relief to hurricane victims or places torn apart by tornados—that takes time and costs money.

Bumpkin: Well, as far as I can see, it's Halloween every day with you as our president.

Trumpkin: What do you mean by that?

Bumpkin: Well, it's gettin' scarier each and every day. And who knew that when someone elected you and said "Trick or Treat" that it would be one long trick—and never any treats.

Hallowe'en Limerick

There once was a President Trumpkin
Was quizzed by an old country bumpkin.
"Is that hair of yours real?
I know it's bound to conceal
Vast emptiness. That's really sumpin."

Solum Optimis Verbis

An Un-Armistice Day in France

Week 95 / Nov. 11 – Nov. 17, 2018

Trump didn't serve in Vietnam because he had bone spurs. He has an excuse for almost everything he's failed to do. And nothing is ever his fault. That's why I've penned a…

Trumpian Ditty
for
Armistice Day in France

1

I flew to France, oh yes I did,
To honor our war dead—
But it was raining just too hard,
So I stayed inside instead.

2

I couldn't go and get all wet—
My hair would look a fright.
So I sent John Kelly, my chief of staff,
That'll have to be alright.

The Donald Trump Turkey Shoot

3

But the Twitterverse has ridiculed
My choice to stay indoors,
They wanted wreaths on long-dead guys,
Who died on France's shores.

4

The dead are losers, we all know,
I simply can't respect 'em.
Lovely wreaths won't bring 'em back.
So they really can't expect 'em.

5

No one seems to understand
That I'm under such a strain.
There's lots of things I will not do,
Like theater in the rain.

6

This Mueller thing has me in knots
And now I've lost the Congress.
It's getting scary at the top,
Thanks mainly to the Con-Press.

7

They call me liar, idiot, fool,
There are things that they don't know.
They're gonna feel so very bad
When I end The White House Show.

Solum Optimis Verbis

Piggy-Bank Government

Week 99 / Nov. 18 – Dec. 15, 2018

from *It's Only [Your] Money* Department

<u>Dramatis Personae</u>
Donald Trump   President
Melania Trump   First Lady
Betsy DeVos   Secretary of Education
Scott Pruitt   EPA Secretary (former)
Steve Mnuchin   Secretary of Treasury
Ryan Zinke   Secretary of Interior

President: I've asked all of you to come here to this ultra-super-secret meeting tonight for one reason. Can you guess?

DeVos: You like how I'm doing my best to destroy public education? *[She smiles broadly]*

President: I do, Betsy, but…

Pruitt: He loves the way I've helped to degrade the environment. Clean air and clean water are way overrated. Coal is king! Down with solar!

President: You done good, Scott, always my little cheerleader…and with your help and Zink's advice, National Parks will probably become a thing of the past…but…nobody's guessed correctly, yet.

The Donald Trump Turkey Shoot

[Everyone falls silent into "thinking" poses. They all look like they are thinking really hard. It also looks like it's painful.]

Mnuchin: I know! I know! We're all getting a pay raise? Maybe a bigger expense account?

Zinke: No! Even better! We're finally cutting Puerto Rico loose and letting it drift off into the Atlantic. Right?

President: I see you're still upset with the whole Hurricane Maria, power grid mess, Ryan. But, no, we've gotta keep Puerto Rico. If we let it go, Lin-Manuel Miranda would make a stink—probably write a musical about all of us...which would be a hit... and we'd all look stupid.

Melania: Not me. I be best.

President: That's right, Mel. You be best. Go stand in the corner and be best, okay?

[Melania goes to the corner. Everyone strikes thinking poses again.]

President: Still, no idea? Well, I'd like to welcome each and every one of you to the first annual Spendee Awards.

All: The Spendee Award?

President: That's right. People are always giving awards for people who save money—as if that's a virtue or something to be proud of. This award is for people who find inventive ways to spend taxpayer money—and spend lots and lots of taxpayer money, to boot. Before we leave here today, someone will walk out with this fine award. *[He holds up the trophy]* I had it designed especially for us. Pretty impressive, isn't it?

All: *[Making noises saying, "Sure." "Oh, yeah." "Way to go." "It's unique, that's for sure." Comments like that.]*

President: So, who thinks they deserve the First Annual Taxpayer Spending Award—the Spendee?

The Donald Trump Turkey Shoot

Mnuchin: *[Proudly]* I spent more than $1,000,000 on military flights. That's a lot of moola.

Pruitt: Yeah, but you're flying steerage when you fly military. I know. I spent $58,000 on military flights, myself. But I spent more than $105,000 on first class flights last year. First class! As I always say, 'If you don't go in style, don't go.'

Mnuchin: It's not just how you go, you know, Scott. I took my wife on that eclipse-viewing plane ride. On the taxpayer dime. Watched the whole thing from 30,000 feet. It was amazing.

President: Hell, Steve, I watched the eclipse from the porch of the White House. Without special glasses. When you're famous and powerful nothing can hurt you. You all know that, right.

All: *[All reply rather unenthusiastically. "Oh, right, Mr. President." "Whatever you say, Mr. President." "Of course, of course, power makes you invulnerable."]*

Zinke: Do helicopter rides count?

President: That depends…

Zinke: I took three of 'em for $53,000. Took friends along, too.

President: Nice try, Ryan. Nice try. But I gotta say, 53k is chump change.

Zinke: Hey, how about the $138,000 I spent on new doors for my office?"

President: Okay. That's better. 138k—for office doors?

DeVos: Come on, you guys. If you're hoping to win a Spendee, you'll have to come up with more than eclipse jaunts and office doors. You gotta spend in the millions if you hope to win.

Mnuchin: I suppose you've spent millions?

Pruitt: *[Mocking tone]* Yeah, right. Millions. She's the damn Secretary of Education. What'd you do, buy apples for the teachers?
[Everyone laughs]

DeVos: Go ahead. Laugh. I got you guys beat cold. How does $5.3 million and $6.8 million sound to you?

All: For what?

DeVos: See-cure-it-tee!!! Security! You want costs to spin upward—out of control? Spend your money on security. Spent $5.3 million in 2017 and $6.8 million this year.
[She looks proud. Puts her hands on her hips striking a superhero pose.]

Pruitt: That's not fair. Mr. President. That's cheating. Sure it's millions of dollars, but even I spent $3.5 million on security before you invited me to leave when the public got too pissed off at me spending their hard-earned tax dollars. There should be a category for spurious spending. Totally needless spending.

Zinke: Like office doors?

Pruitt: No, Zinke. Everyone needs office doors. But I spent money on a sound-proof booth in my office. It's a total waste of money but really cool. Cost $43,000. And I spent $1,200 on twelve fountain pens. Talk about wasting money…I'm better at it than anyone in this room.

President: Hey, Scottie, we're getting' out over our skis with remarks like that, aren't we? You think you're better at wasting money than ANYONE in this room?

Pruitt: Except for you, Mr. President.

President: Which is why I'm the winner of the First Annual Spendee Award. Everyone is okay with that, right? I spend like there's no tomorrow.

DeVos:	*[Whispering loudly to everyone but the President]* If Mueller has his way, there won't be a tomorrow. *[Everyone laughs. Except the President]*
President:	You like your job, Betsy?
DeVos:	*[Chastened]* Yes, Mr. President.
President:	Good. If you don't behave yourself, I'll make you my new chief-of-staff. *[Everyone takes a deep, horrified breath]* Then you'll have your hands full of Mueller. You'll get subpoenaed. You'll have to testify. And you'll probably spend years in jail. *[Everyone goes quiet.]* Just so you know, every time I go to Mar-a-Lago it costs $3.6 million. Even better, the government is paying me because I own the damn place. So I make money every time I go there. That's why this Spendee Award belongs to me…and Melania. What are you doing in the corner, Mel?
Melania:	Being be best.
President:	Well, you can't be best without me. Am I right? *[Addressing all his sycophants.]*
All:	You be best, Mr. President.

THE DONALD TRUMP TURKEY SHOOT

The Saudi Ditty: The Donald Trump Song

The Crown Prince he murdered Khashoggi.
I knew it...but I looked away.
It's prob'bly bad business
If I act as a witness
And Jared said that was okay.

So I act as if nothing has happened
Like I can't trust my own CIA.
As a leader I'm willin'
To put up with some killin'
If helps me to get my own way.

It's amazing the power they gave me,
(A man who can't tell wrong from right.)
I support the Crown Prince,
Don't care who I make wince.
I'm ready to put up a fight.

I'm a man with no conscience or morals.
All laws are for somebody else.
It really is funny—
I'm just after the money.
So buckle up your safety belts.

The Donald Trump Turkey Shoot

The Official (but Superfluous) Donald J Trump Chief of Staff Application Form

Name: _____

Pseudonym: _____

1. Do you think Jared and Ivanka make a cute couple?
   Yes ☐   No ☐

2. Have you ever been convicted of a crime?
   Yes ☐   Almost ☐   Never Convicted ☐   Not that I Recall ☐

3. Do you hold any beliefs and convictions?
   Yes ☐   No ☐   Probably ☐   Convictions? ☐

4. Do you have a lawyer?   4. B   Is he/she any good?
   Yes ☐   No ☐   Why? ☐   Yes ☐   No ☐   Why? ☐

5. Can you do anything I ask without asking questions?
   Yes, Master ☐   No, Master ☐   WTF! ☐

6. Would you mind working for a criminal?
   Yes ☐   No ☐   WTF! ☐

7. Would you mind working for a con artist and practiced liar?
   Yes ☐   No ☐   How practiced? ☐

8. Can you spell impeachment?
   Yes ☐   No ☐   Why? ☐

9. Do you believe a sitting president can be indicted? How about a standing president?
   Yes ☐   No ☐   What's indicted? ☐

10. Can you sit as still as my VP Mike Pence?
    Yes ☐   No ☐   For how long? ☐

11. Can you send your mind out for a walk when I'm conferring with shady people?
    Yes ☐   No ☐   Mind? Do I need one? ☐

Solum Optimis Verbis

Stuck on the Wall

Week 103 / Jan. 6, 2019 – Jan. 12, 2019

Business Insider
January 10, 2019

"Trump backtracks further on border wall promises, says he 'never meant Mexico would write a check'"

Yep, that's what Trump said that he said…or didn't say. In case you missed his comments during his tour along our southern border on Thursday, let me provide one quote which I provide here verbatim:

> *When during the campaign, I would say Mexico is going to pay for it, obviously I never said this and I never meant they're going to write out a check…*

Unbelievable, right? My most cogent response to Trump's claim that "obviously I never said this" is "Huh?" If I responded with less skepticism, I'd end up believing that

Douglas MacArthur never said, "I shall return." What he really said—what he really meant to say—is "I'll be back… probably with Arnold Schwarzenegger. But I can't be sure. Don't hold me to it, okay?"

The Donald Trump Turkey Shoot

Or

Abraham Lincoln never said "Four score and seven years ago." What he really said was "A while back—pretty sure before I was born—probably when cavemen and dinosaurs roamed the earth together in search of a right-wing Christian church—I really can't remember so let's call it ancient times…"

Apparently we have reached the point when the president didn't really say what he actually said. (Or at least he claims he never said what he said.) Nor did he say what millions of people heard him say hundreds of times, either—even though his devout followers at his campaign rallies echoed those exact words, exactly as he told them to. His exact words—"Mexico's going to pay for the wall"—have been captured by video and audio devices of every description since his campaign began. What he actually said is now stored in digital amber. It's right there in black and white—as well as in full color.

But he didn't say it…or so he says. (All evidence to the contrary.) Or maybe he did, but it's all been part of

The Trump Presidential Reality Show
(It looks real, but it's pure fiction.)

Because of Trump's extensive TV experience, I expect we'll all be told shortly that the whole "Mexico will pay for it" scene was just one of those dream sequences we see inserted into the plots of our favorite television dramas. It looks real. It feels real. But then the main character wakes up and discovers it was all a dream and he never said it.

I hope that's right, because I've been trapped in a bad dream for more than two years, now, and I would love to wake up and find that

Trump never said "Mexico will pay for the wall," and that Hilary Clinton was elected.

What frightens me most is that I'm afraid I'm wide awake.

There is only one thing to conclude from this presidential comment: We must add "incoherent" to the list of "in" words that describe Trump: incompetent, insipid, insane, in-a-hell-of-a lot-of-trouble. That last one is my personal favorite.

The Wall
Another SNL-style Sketch

Dramatis Personae
Chief of Staff, Mick Mulvaney
President Donald Trump

Mulvaney: Sir, I just got off the phone with Mexico again. President Obrador reiterated what he's said before about paying for the wall.

Trump: Reiterated?

Mulvaney: Yes.

Trump: Reiterated?

Mulvaney: Sorry, sir. Sorry. *[Whispers]* "Reiterated" means "repeated." President Obrador repeated what he's always said.

Trump: Well, why didn't you say that? *[Mulvaney looks a bit perplexed.]* And what did he say this time?

Mulvaney: Uh, sir, he said, "No."

Trump: That's all. Just "no?" No negotiating? No bargaining? No give-and-take?

Mulvaney: No, sir. Just "No."

Trump: Did he say "No" with a capital "N" or a lower-case "n?"

Mulvaney: Pretty sure it was all caps, sir.

Trump: Hell, if I all I wanted was a "No," I'd ask Pelosi to come over to the White House. That woman is nothing but no's. Any chance we could get some other country to pay for it—maybe not Mexico—but some other country? The Republicans are starting to blame me for this government shutdown.

Mulvaney: Well, sir, you did tell Chuck Shumer that you'd take responsibility for the shutdown.

Trump: I never said that.

Mulvaney: It's been broadcast almost every day since you said it, sir. You can't deny you said it.

Trump: Mick, don't be an ass. Of course, I can deny it. It doesn't matter what you say if you don't mean what you say. I almost never mean what I say. I thought you knew that. I never meant that I wanted the blame for the shutdown, or that I wouldn't blame the Democrats for the shutdown.

Mulvaney: How about China?

Trump: No, they're still pissed at me for the tariffs.

Mulvaney: How about Russia?

Trump: Probably not. Putin said he'd pay for the wall if I got all the sanctions lifted, but those folks in Congress get all squirrely when I bring up Russia about anything.

Mulvaney: Hey, what if we blamed Obrador for the shutdown? After all, he's the one who should be paying for the wall.

Trump: But he said "No."

Mulvaney: Exactly. He said "No." This problem wouldn't exist if he'd said "Yes." See where I'm going? *[Pauses. Trump doesn't understand.]* You tell the American people in a prime time Oval Office address, that you're declaring a national emergency because Mexico backed out of paying for the wall that you said they'd pay for.

Trump: Okay.

Mulvaney: Then you send troops to the Mexican border and threaten to annex all the Mexican states along the US-Mexico border. Kinda like we did with Texas back in 1836.
Trump: Okay.
Mulvaney: Then the UN will get involved—send peacekeepers to patrol the border—
Trump: Okay.
Mulvaney: And then we won't need the wall because the UN will be in charge of our border security. America is saved. And you saved it.
Trump: You might be onto something there, Mick.

———◆———

Best new comic line I saw this week from Steve Colbert: *Donald Trump is suffering from a Border-Lying Personality Disorder*

𝔖𝔬𝔩𝔲𝔪 𝔒𝔭𝔱𝔦𝔪𝔦𝔰 𝔙𝔢𝔯𝔟𝔦𝔰

The State of the Miserable Union

Week 104 / Jan. 13, 2019 – Jan. 19, 2019

It is 2019, and we are deeply immersed in Trumpian theater—better known as Theater of the Absurd. Unfortunately, with Trump in the Oval Office, the absurd has become real.

Consider: The government shutdown is absurd. 800,000 federal workers are not receiving paychecks because Trump's vanity project—aka, *The Wall*—has been rejected by the Democrats. It's absurd because a significant percentage of those not receiving paychecks are still expected to show up for work. It's also absurd because, for the first two years of his presidency, Trump had a Republican Congress and a Republican Senate and they never moved to pass any "Build the Wall" legislation. But NOW it must be funded? The idea of a wall—a physical barrier separating the US and Mexico—was absurd all by itself, but then Trump compounded the absurdity.

"...the play's the thing wherein I'll catch the conscience of the king."

The Washington Post
January 14, 2019
Trump Denies Working for Russia…

Trump's Chief of Staff attempts to help his boss fashion a proper response to the question: Have you ever worked for Russia? It is a fool's errand.

Mulvaney: What did you say to the reporters who asked you if you were working for Russia?

Trump: I told those Fake News folks that was the most insulting question I'd ever been asked.

Mulvaney: I'm sure it was, sir, but here's the problem. Your response didn't answer the question. It would be as if I asked you if you'd ever had sex with a porn star, and you told me that you were offended by the question.

Trump: Well, of course, I'd be offended by the question.

Mulvaney: I know, Mr. President. I know.

Trump: I'd be offended because porn stars love me. Everyone knows that. They love being with me. Can you blame them? I'm a well-endowed president. Well-endowed. Just ask…

Mulvaney: Stop, Mr. President. Please stop.

Trump: Why?

Mulvaney: Well, sir, let me put it this way. There are right answers and there are wrong answers…

Trump: *[Interrupts]* You bet there are. And my base will love it when they realize that the right answer is that beautiful women—even porn stars—find me irresistible.

Mulvaney: I know, Mr. President, but…no disrespect intended… shouldn't that be your wife?

Trump: *[Angry]* Can it, Mulvaney! You're my Chief of Staff—not my marriage counselor. The only thing Melania has done is build a wall between my bedroom and hers. Melania says Slovenia paid for it, but I'm pretty sure Mexico paid for it. Pretty sure.

Mulvaney: I understand, Mr. President. But for the moment, let's work on the question about Russia, okay? Reporters are going to keep asking—and Mueller might be asking soon.

Trump: Okay, Mick. You be the reporter and I'll be the president. Ask me the question.

Mulvaney: Okay. Get ready, Mr. President. You are walking toward your helicopter, Marine One, when you stop to answer questions being shouted by reporters.

Trump: Good. Ask away…wait…wait. Which network are you from?

Mulvaney: Does that matter, Mr. President?

Trump: Hell, yes, Mick. If you're from CNN I'll tell you to shut the hell up, call you Fake News, and accuse you of undermining the Constitution of the United States of America, the one that was given by God Himself to Moses in the Old Testament.

Mulvaney: Mr. President, take a deep breath. Good. Take another. Now sir, you didn't answer the question, did you? I know insulting reporters is your favorite sport—and it sure makes for great TV…

Trump: Damn right it does…

Mulvaney: —but remember, sir…remember…answer the question. And don't bring up Moses and the Constitution, okay?

Trump: Was it Abraham?

Mulvaney: *[increasingly exasperated]* Maybe. I don't know, Mr. President. We'll call Franklin Graham later today, okay.

	He knows which of the Founding Fathers brought the Constitution down from the mountain in Israel. We'll call Franklin. But right now we've got to figure out an answer that will satisfy the media folks.
Trump:	Sorry, Mick, I get carried away.
Mulvaney:	*[Pauses]* Mr. President, have you ever worked for Russia?
Trump:	Why would I work for Russia?
Mulvaney:	Sorry, sir, that's not an answer. That's just another question.
Trump:	I don't even speak Russian.
Mulvaney:	Sir…
Trump:	And I don't need the money—not like Manafort did—but I do like their hotels…and the Russian women. Oh, Mick. The girls they sent to my room. Va-va-voom!
Mulvaney:	Sir…
Trump:	Besides, I like Putin. And he likes me. We're big on liking. We both like being liked. What's wrong with being friends with enemies? Maybe Putin doesn't get along with the CIA, but then neither do I. We talk a lot. Well, I talk a lot…and he's a good listener…he takes plenty of notes…
Mulvaney:	Sir, STOP!
Trump:	Did you just yell at me?
Mulvaney:	Sorry, sir. Sorry. When anyone asks you about Russia, please, just say "No."
Trump:	Who do you think I am, Nancy Reagan?

Treasonous Traitor Trump Tries to Trick Americans

[A desperate poem in four-couplets]
There's really no disputin'
That Trump is friends with Putin.
He's always callin' Moscow
'Cause Putin's got the know-how
To undermine the U.S.
And cause us all big distress.
So Trump has got to go now,
I really couldn't care how.

USA Today
January 16, 2019
…Trump Asked to Deliver
State of the Union in Writing…

Nancy Pelosi has dis-invited Trump from presenting his State of the Union address before a joint session of the House and Senate. While the State of the Union has traditionally been given in the House chamber of the United States Capitol, Trump may only speak there at the invitation of the Speaker of the House, Nancy Pelosi. Pelosi believes this year's government shutdown raises security concerns for the assembled government. The Senate chamber lacks the space to accommodate the entire Congress.

Therefore, Speaker Pelosi has suggested that Trump simply write out his speech and forego the usual, live, public presentation. "Unlike some politicians, Mr. President, my colleagues and I know how to read," Pelosi said. Trump has not yet responded to Pelosi's unvitation.

Should the president accept Pelosi's suggestion to submit a written State of the Union, the Speaker has a very specific set of requirements. In her letter to the president, Pelosi explained,

The Donald Trump Turkey Shoot

The State of the Union is not a campaign rally. It is a serious assessment of where the United States of America is as a country. Therefore...

1. It must be available to ALL newspapers, and may not be published on Twitter.
   [Pelosi: "If this takes an Act of Congress, I think I'm up to that. No twitter-speak from a twidiot."]

2. Everything in the State of the Union must be provably true.
   [Pelosi: "If that means he has nothing to say, then we all benefit. Silence is golden."]

3. Nothing in the State of the Union can be a lie.
   [Pelosi: "It may be the first and only lie-free day in his administration. One can hope."]

4. Every claim made in the State of the Union must be fact-checked by The New York Times, The Washington Post, Reuters, and CNN & NBC News.
   [Pelosi: "Alternative facts, fictional facts, fact-wishing, and fact-phishing will all be eliminated."]

5. All statistics will be subject to fact-checking and prior approval and may not be part of the "damn lies" category.
   [Pelosi: "As Stephen Colbert pointed out, 'Trump has a Border-Lying Personality Disorder.'"]

6. The State of the Union must be "brag-free."
   [Pelosi: "This means that the entire speech will be ghost-written."]

7. The State of the Union must be "insult-free." No insults—aimed at colleagues, companies, cities, countries, or foreign leaders—will be permitted.
[Pelosi: "Let me repeat: This means that the entire speech will be ghost-written."]

8. The State of the Union must not praise our enemies—or the leaders of adversarial countries.
[Pelosi: "Need I say this again? This entire speech will be ghost-written."]

9. The speech must be grammatically correct with proper punctuation and correct spelling.
[Pelosi: "Duh! Donnie boy ain't reel giftud when tawkin' 'bout grammer and spelink."]

10. Consider writing the State of the Union while wearing a bright-orange jumpsuit.
[Pelosi: "It's never too soon to prepare for one's next occupation."]

What follows is the State of the Union speech...
if left strictly to Trump. I call it:

Donald Trump—State of the Union—Off the Cuff

[Sit up straight. Don't slouch. Smile. Really smile.]

Good evening,

I'm speaking to you from the Oval Office tonight because Nancy Pelosi won't let me into the big room over in the Capitol Building. I don't think that's fair. I don't. After all, I'm the President of the

The Donald Trump Turkey Shoot

United States. I am, I am, I am. No one thought I could win, but I won. You bet I did. I won bigly. I won with the biggest margin ever in the Electoral College. Biggest ever. And I beat the odds even when Hilary Clinton got almost three million more illegally cast votes in the popular election.

It's true. I've talked with lots of people who have told me that they saw cheaters everywhere. Everywhere. The polling places were full of people voting and voting and voting. Lots of people told me they saw some people vote as many as five times. Five. That's not fair. But has anyone done anything about it? No! They're always going on and on about me and the Russians. I don't know any Russians... well, I do know Putin, but everyone knows him so that shouldn't count.

I won without any help from the Russians. I didn't have any help from anyone. Nobody helped me. Nobody ever helps me. Not even the Russians. And, by the way, there was no collusion. I don't care what Mike Cohen says, or what Paul Manafort or Rick Gates or Mike Flynn say—or Stormy Daniels either. How can you trust people like that? I'm a great judge of character, and I know when you can't trust someone. There was absolutely no collusion and I should be in the big room.

It's absolutely unfair to me...and to all the American people who don't get to watch me in the big room. But Pelosi's running the show now, and she's one of those stubborn Democrats out to ruin the country.

So, I'm here in the Oval Office and I have my family here with me—except Melania and Ivanka...and my sons Don and Eric. They're off somewhere—I'm not sure where, they didn't tell me. But they're doing important work. Very, very important work. Somewhere else…but not here. So important they couldn't be here tonight. They wanted to be here. Everyone knows they wanted to be here, but sometimes you just have to do what you have to do. But I see Jared. He's here. Hi, Jared.

[Wave at Jared who is off camera.]

So I'm here to talk to all of you tonight about the State of the Union. I should be doing this in the big room but I'm not. As for the State of the Union…we're closed…until I get my wall…or fence…or barrier. I don't care what they call it. So we're closed. You can blame Mexico.

Good night. God bless America—except maybe he shouldn't bless the Democrats. We're done, right?

[A microphone is accidently left open.]

I gotta go watch the replay on FOX News and see how I did. I hope I didn't look as dull as I did the other night when I made my first Oval Office speech. Jared, get me two Happy Meals and a Big Mac.

𝔖olum 𝔒ptimis 𝔙erbis

Fantasy Becomes Reality

Week 109 / Feb. 17, 2019 – Feb. 23, 2019

Little Donny Trump

Little Donny Trump decided he was tired of all the neighbor kids sneaking into his yard to play. They'd crawl under hedges, vault over the short chain-link fence, or shimmy up a tree next to wherever the fence was too high to jump over. Then they'd leap onto the lush grass on *his* side of the fence. This made Little Donny especially mad. *It isn't their yard,* he'd fume, *it's mine.*

"Sure, I have a bigger yard than those guys do—but it really is small as far as big yards go. It's only a measly fifteen acres. Fifteen acres. That's all. That's really small for a kid as rich as me, but I deserve it 'cause I'm rich. Yeah, I know, I know. Those little sneaks don't have any yard at all, but that's because they're poor. Why should that be my problem?" he'd say, to no one in particular.

He talked a lot to himself because, as he often said, "I'm the bestest audience anyone could ever have. No one has ever been a better audience than me—not ever."

Nope, Little Donny did not like sharing. "Sharing's for losers," he said.

"And you're not a loser," his audience-self replied.

"Goodness," he'd squeal, "I am the best audience ever."

Little Donny knew those other kids—the sneaker-inners—were all losers especially the black kids, the Hispanic kids, and, yeah, the camel jockeys. He hated all of them.

Not only do they sneak into my yard, they don't even look American, he thought. *Americans should look like Americans. It should be a rule. When I'm president, that'll be my first rule.*

So he went to see his Mom while she was having her nails done and her hair curled.

"Mommy, I need to talk to you," Little Donny said climbing up on a chair next to his mother.

"Watch your feet, Little Donny. You have mud on your saddle shoes. Don't put your feet on the chair," she said while examining the new nail polish on her left hand. "We are not barbarians, Little Donny. Only poor children put their dirty shoes on a clean chair."

"That's what I wanted to talk to you about, Mom. All those poor kids keep sneaking into my yard. And I want it to stop."

"Are their shoes dirty?"

"How should I know?"

Little Donny's mother shot him a withering look.

"Okay, yeah, sure. They probably have dirty shoes."

"And you don't want them bringing those dirty shoes into our pristine environment, do you, Little Donny?"

"I don't know what pristine environment means, but Dad is loaded with money, and we have the bestest grass this side of Kentucky, the cleanest water anyone has ever seen in a swimming pool ever, and a basketball court where all the hoops have nets and no one has to worry about dodging cars between jump shots."

Donny waited for his mother's response.

"Didn't you forget something?" she asked in a slightly menacing tone.

Donny took a deep breath.

"Oh, yeah," Little Donny said in a flat monotone. "We also have the most beautiful tennis courts in the entire United States of America where I can watch beautiful babes in short skirts run after a bouncing ball."

"And who's the most beautiful babe of all?"

"You are, Mom," Donny said, his face glowing a bright red.

"That's my good Little Donny."

She inspected her nails again, holding them up to the sunlight streaming in through the window.

"And what do you plan to do about the urchins?"

"About *what*?"

"Someday, you'll want to have the best words, Little Donny. Words like 'urchins.'"

"Sure, Mom. So, what are urchins?"

"It's all those poor, unwashed tykes with dirty shoes sullying our pristine environment."

"You know what, Mom? I didn't understand a single thing you just said. You might as well be speaking British...or another foreign language."

His mother gave him a frustrated look.

"Sometimes I worry about you Little Donny," she said grimacing. "I really do. You don't seem to want to learn anything—not even new words."

"Who needs new words when I've got money? Money talks. Talks loud. Everyone listens to money. Money is the best word. And who needs to learn stuff? When you're rich, people think you're smart."

"That's not entirely true, Little Donny. Being rich and being smart are not the same thing."

"We'll see about that," Little Donny said. "Someday I'll be so rich that people will make me president. They'll say, 'If he's so rich, he's gotta be smart. And since he's smart, he oughta be president.' That's what they'll say."

"I'm happy to hear you're going to be president someday, dear, but what are you planning to do right now about the kids sneaking into the yard?"

"I've been thinking, Mom. I think I need to build a wall. Walls work, right? Everyone knows walls work. Right now there's just hedges and a few fences—mostly low fences. I have to make it really hard for those kids to get in."

"Do you think we really need a wall?"

"Are you kidding? There are mobs of kids comin' every day. There are whole caravans of kids with dirty shoes. You should see'em. And they're probably bringing all kinds of diseases. Just yesterday, I saw two kids sneeze as they jumped the fence. They sneezed without covering their mouths—and neither one was carrying a monogrammed handkerchief. That's disgraceful. They're bringing germs...and they don't look like any Americans we've ever seen...so I think we need a wall."

Little Donny's Mom could see her son was serious. "Well, you'll need money if you want to build a wall."

"I'll get Daddy to pay for the wall."

"If you learn nothing else, Little Donny, you'll learn that your Daddy never became a billionaire by building walls for other people. He became a billionaire by having someone else pay for the walls that he wanted to build."

"Well, I don't want to use my allowance," Little Donny whined. "I only get $100,000 a year. I need my money for really important things."

"Oh, Little Donny, you'll find out soon enough that no one wants to pay for a wall. That's because walls almost never work. Who told you that walls work?"

"I saw it on TV. On some show—I don't remember which one 'cause I watch a lot of TV—Dad says it keeps me out of trouble." Little Donny giggled. "There's this wall in Europe somewhere. It works just fine."

"You mean the Berlin Wall?" his mother asked.

The Donald Trump Turkey Shoot

"I don't know. Maybe. I really don't remember. I don't like keeping facts in my head. I'm not into facts. They just clutter things up in my head and confuse me."

"I think you mean the Berlin Wall. Not only do the Soviets have a wall separating East and West Berlin, they have guards—armed guards who shoot anyone who tries going over the wall."

Little Donny's face brightened. "That'd be a great idea, Mom. We could build a wall, and we could put armed guards to shoot any kids who climb over it. Especially if they don't look 100% American. Great idea."

"I understand your enthusiasm, Little Donny, but it isn't legal to shoot people like that. And guards cost money, too."

"That money thing seems to be a problem. But I don't know why. I've got lots and lots of money and I can't imagine that I'll ever run out of money. Dad gives me money whenever I need any, right?"

Little Donny's mother shook her head, "No."

"I wonder how those fence-jumping kids live without money. How is that even possible, Mom?"

Little Donny pondered such things for few nanoseconds every day.

His mother broke into his fleeting reverie.

"Well, Little Donny, you could probably hire some of those kids—the ones who play in your yard without permission. Give them a job. They're probably here in this country illegally, so they'll probably work for next to nothing. Less than minimum wage."

"Minimum what?"

"Never mind, Little Donny. Here's what you need to know. The people who build things often cost more than the materials you need to build those things. If you get supercheap labor, you can probably get a wall built."

"Thanks, Mom. Even better, I'll tell 'em I won't pay them until after the wall is built, and then once it's finished, I won't pay 'em.

How about that?"

"Now you're thinking like a corrupt billionaire, Little Donny. I'm so proud."

"When I'm president," Little Donny announced, "I'll build walls everywhere. And I'll make it legal to have armed guards shoot anyone coming over those walls who I don't want coming in. 'Cause I'll be president. That's like a king, right? A king can do whatever he wants."

"The president of the United States isn't a king, Little Donny," said his mother.

"Really?" said Little Donny, his eyes narrowing. "You're kidding. Hmmmm...King Donny, the Magnificent. I like the sound of that. Maybe *that's* the first thing I'll change."

Solum Optimis Verbis

The Nicknamer-in-Chief

Week 122 / May 19, 2019 – May 25, 2019

Nicknamer-in-Chief

Unless you've been in a coma—or perhaps wished you were in a coma dreaming of chocolate ice cream rather than a demented presidency—you realize that our president has sought to demean almost everyone around him by offering his adoring supporters…aka the "Witless Nitwits"…as well as the rest of America, a full array of nicknames. The most recent nickname seems to be "Sleepy Joe" Biden. In the pantheon of Trump's most notable nicknames, how could we ever forget these classics?

"Cheatin" Obama
"Crooked Hillary" Clinton
"Crazy Bernie" Sanders
"Head Clown Chuck" Schumer
"Low-I.Q. Maxine" Waters
And that infamous, stand-alone moniker for Elizabeth Warren
"Pocahontas"

Of course, he's been equally mean-spirited to members of his own party.

The Donald Trump Turkey Shoot

"Little Marco" Rubio
"Low-Energy Jeb" Bush
"Dumber-than-a-Box-of-Rocks Rex" Tillerson
"Lyin Ted" Cruz
"Leakin' Lyin' Jim" Comey[3]

Therefore, in the spirit of mutual nicknamability, I would like to offer several New-But-Very-Appropriate Nicknames for The Trumpster. Let's begin by acknowledging that Trumpster rhymes with Dumpster, and that of late, The Trumpster Dumpster appears to be smoldering. Perhaps we'll have a full-blown Dumpster fire in the White House. Uh-oh. Wait. I feel a few couplets forming in my brain:

Trumpster Dumpster Full of Fire
Trumpster Dumpster Full-of-Ire
He's mad the courts won't rule his way
Or let his lies hold final sway.

Thanks for letting me get that out. I feel much better now. Of all people in government who deserve nicknames, Donald Trump leads the list. In fact, he's so high on the list, he deserves as many nicknames as we can possibly imagine—hopefully, as pejorative and demeaning as those he coins for others. So, in the spirit of insulting jabs, let me offer the following

S.O.B.-in-Chief

Any man who would tolerate, much less craft, an immigration policy that would separate children from their parents, or callously allow detained children to die while in custody of ICE, deserves this name… and it ought to be written out in full and hung on the

---

[3] James Comey was a registered Republican

White House door. I suspect Melania has already put such a sign on Donald's bedroom door.

Criminal-in-Chief

Let me confess. I have NOT read the Mueller Report. But among those who have read it are more than 900 former prosecutors—both Democrat and Republican—who assert that the President indeed deserves this nickname. They all signed a document asserting the Trumpster's criminality for obstruction of justice. Of course, the Republicans in Congress and the Senate have pleaded illiteracy, a trait they share with the president, which certainly helps explain why they still think the Trumpster is a wrongly-accused, lovely human being. Synonyms: *Illiterate-in-Chief,* i.e. he's the leader of his Witless Nitwit followers.

Get-Nothing-Done-in-Chief

Trump has declared he's going to take his football and go home if he doesn't get to make the rules. He's told Democrats that he won't do anything—no legislation, no nothing—until investigations into his blameless self, cease.

> *"I'm completely exonerated," he sputtered. "No Collusion. No Obstruction. So there! So there! So there!" he said while stomping his foot and sticking out his tongue. Then he turned, wiggled his vast rear-end, (perhaps it's only half-vassed) and walked away.*

Nada-in-Chief

Trump told us all he'd "build a wall, and Mexico will pay for it." He didn't say it just once. Nor twice. Nor thrice. He said it scads of times. Actually, to use scientific nomenclature: Scads^2. It's akin to all the years I wanted to build a back deck and have my neighbor pay for it. But, as you might expect, my neighbor selfishly refused. Ah, well. Anyway, the much un-needed, Mexico-funded wall along our southern border is largely a figment of Trump's demented imagination. Thus, he is granted a Spanish-language variation of the *Get-Nothing-Done-in-Chief—The Nada-in-Chief*

Nichts-in-Chief

When Trump hears the words "international relations," he imagines a perverse sexual tryst with a Russian hooker in a Moscow hotel. Yep. But we know that's not the proper definition of "international relations." Such words encompass all the critical agreements that Trump has managed to trash, like the Iranian Nuclear Deal and the Paris Climate Accords. So, in fact, our president is not doing something. And he's not doing nothing. He, in fact, is doing "less than nothing." He withdraws from important deals crafted by other administrations, denigrates NATO, and rattles the American sabre at Iran. Therefore, he has earned the German-language equivalent of the *Get-Nothing-Done-in-Chief—The Nichts-in-Chief.*

From *the Impromptu Poetry* Department

The Trumpster Dumpster

The Trumpster's mean to everyone
For each he coins a name.
All I can say 'bout Donnie Boy
Is he's one Gigantic Shame.

Donald Trumpster's like a dumpster
His mind is full of trash.
He'd willingly do anything
To get his hands on cash.

The Donald Trump Turkey Shoot

He'd lie, he'd cheat, he'd steal it all
But Congress just won't let 'em.
When it comes to helping average Joe's,
He'd rather just forget 'em.

"They're all so poor, not rich like me.
They're worthless that's for certain."
Perhaps the Dems will help us all
By bringing down the curtain.

The Trumpster thinks his wealth's a shield.
He thinks he's out of reach.
But if all of this were up to me,
I'd vote, "Oh, yeah! Impeach!"

From the Alternative Musical Lyrics Department

They Call the Trump, Pariah

from the musical,
<u>Paint Your ~~Wagon~~ White House</u> "They Call the Wind, Mariah"
with apologies to Lerner & Loewe

Pariah, Pariah,
They call the Trump, Pariah.

Down in D.C., they got a name
For scams, and cheats, and liars.
The scammer's Don, the liar's Trump,
And they call that cheat, Pariah

Pariah blows the facts around
And sends the truth a-flyin',
His words don't stand on solid ground
And always he's a-lyin'.

Pariah, Pariah,
They call the Trump, Pariah.

Before I knew Pariah's name
And heard him always whinin',
I loved our good old USA.
Now for those days I'm pinin'.

But then one day Trump took an oath,
An oath he would not honor.
And now we're lost, by storms we're tossed,
I fear we may be goners.

Pariah, Pariah,
They call the Trump, Pariah.

Happy Memorial Day!

My father was a WWII bomber pilot, flying 35 missions with the 8th Air Force. My uncle Ed Scannell was a sergeant commanding artillery with Patton's Third Army as it swept across France and into Germany. My brothers, Bill and Mike, both fought in Vietnam with the United States Marines. They truly should be thanked and remembered. But...but now we have President Bone Spur. Ah, well.

Solum Optimis Verbis

Ignorance is (Presidential) Bliss

Week 130 / July 14, 2019 – July 20, 2019

From *the Simple Truth* Department
This week I sent an editorial letter to the New York Times, and when they didn't print it, I sent it to the Seattle Times. Although the letter was under their 200-word limit, I fear that it was probably too smarmy—too truthful?—to actually make its way into print. Even now, I fail to understand why everyone isn't completely outraged and seething from the shameless, callous, libidinous, and hurtful conduct of our president. This man, who uses the word "disgrace" to describe so many others, is the biggest disgrace ever to occupy the Oval Office—which we should properly re-name, the Offal Office.

To the Editor, The Times,

As the second Democratic Debate looms, I write to my fellow citizens regarding Donald Trump:

Some say he's smart. Some say he's ignorant. The two are not mutually exclusive. He has an instinctive, low cunning; a determination to preserve himself by any means necessary. He's had to develop that instinct because he knows so little.

And his lies? He lies so often precisely because he is so profoundly ignorant. He's ignorant of so many things—ignorant of U.S. history (and all the things that pertain therein, including racial issues and gender issues), ignorant of the U.S. Constitution, ignorant of governmental processes, ignorant of the needs of the American people, ignorant of international alliances and their impact on the safety of the U.S., ignorant of international threats, ignorant of society's norms (ironically, ignorant of Christian norms), and ignorant of the truth.

Worse, he dismisses his pervasive ignorance as "fake news." Worst of all, he has no use for truth.

Remember this, as you listen to informed and truthful Democratic candidates, who want a better world for all Americans. Even the worst Democrat is better than "Lyin' Donald."

from *the Aided and Abetted* Department

Republicans are shameless…and shameful because they are shameless. They masquerade as religious zealots, spouting pro-life rhetoric, while undermining and destroying the lives of those who seek asylum. Shouldn't pro-life mean that we all support all those who are alive?—seeking always to make their way easier and more tolerable. But it is vital to remember that pro-life enthusiasm only applies to the unborn. Once born, that human being is at the will of any ill-wind that blows. And it is the Republican Party blowing ill-winds these days. As I said, S-H-A-M-E-L-E-S-S. (All caps, no redemption.)

from *the Scientists Must Be Idiots, Right?* Department
United Press International

Adrianna Navarro, Accuweather.com

July 19—After a month of blistering heat waves across Europe, relentless rising temperatures in India, and sweltering temperatures in Alaska, last month *was the hottest June on record,* a new report by the National Oceanic and Atmospheric Administration said.

Trump: That's it, Mick. We've got to get rid of NOAA.

Mulvaney: But they help track the weather. Help track things like hurricanes and tornadoes, Mr. President.

Trump: So what? NOAA makes me look bad when I tell everyone there is no global climate change. When I say something is a hoax, I want it to stay a hoax.

Mulvaney: But what if climate change is real, sir?

Trump: Then reality is a hoax, Mick. In fact, reality is already a hoax. I say that racism is patriotic and millions of people believe me. I tell them that they'll be better off with my tax plan—the one where only me and my rich friends benefit—and they believe me. I tell them I've got a better healthcare program—as if I care at all about their health—and they believe me. Like I said, reality is a hoax.

Mulvaney: But the people still want NOAA, sir. They need an organization like that.

Trump: Okay, Mick. We'll just move the entire operation to Puerto Rico. Anybody wants to work for NOAA, that's where they'll have to live.

Mulvaney: But Puerto Rico is still recovering from Hurricane Maria. NOAA can't move there.

Trump: You're wrong, Mick. Of course they can move there. I fixed Puerto Rico good as new.

Mulvaney: You did? When did that happen?

Trump: Just now. Didn't you learn anything from what I just said? Reality is a hoax.

Solum Optimis Verbis

Songs from the Optimist's Heart

Week 140 / Sept. 22 – Sept. 28, 2019

from *Extortion-Is-Us* Department
Well, it has begun. I don't know if this is the beginning of the beginning, the end of the beginning, or the beginning of the end. Whatever it is, it's different than the emotional malaise that's infected the body politic ever since Trump came to office.

Our idiot president tried to shakedown the Ukraine…and he's been caught. It's only the latest violation of the US Constitution and his oath of office—so whether it will have any effect on his actually leaving or being impeached remains to be seen.

Trump says he wants to stop corruption in the Ukraine…so he says. He also said he was going to drain the swamp—but admitted later that "Draining the swamp" was only a slogan, pure Madison Ave. malarkey. Or poppycock? Or balderdash? Maybe bullshit? Or the next bald-faced lie among more than 12,000 lies in less than three years?

Imagine Trump *stopping* corruption. He *is* corruption, personified. What is the biblical quotation about "seeing the mote in your brother's eye?" [Matthew 7:3]

Responding to the language I've heard on the news today—September 25, 2019—I decided to rewrite the lyrics to a portion of Gregory Abbotts' song, *Shake You Down*, released in 1986. In the interests of all, I offer two versions.

My Anti-Trump Version / Take You Down

Trump, I've been watching you.
You're a sleaze-bag that's for sure, now Donnie,
That's nothing new,
You've been one, your whole life that's for sure, now Donnie,
I see that smirk on your face
(Smirk on your face)
And what it's telling me,
That you know, that you're a dreadful disgrace
I'm glad you'll be gone from our democracy.
Now Donnie,

[Chorus]
You're out of your mind.
Trump we're gonna take you down.
Gonna make you feel that you gotta leave.
Yes, we're gonna take you down.
Send you packin' back to New York.

Trump, won't be missing you,
And you make me feel so bad inside.
What can I do?
I can tell you've got no pride.
Oh, Donnie,
Just get out, (just get out)
It'll ease my mind.
Oh, Donnie,
That's the best remedy (Yes it is.)
You're nothing but a big ball of slime.

[Chorus]
You're out of your mind.
Trump we're gonna take you down.
Gonna make you feel that you gotta leave.
Yes, we're gonna take you down.
Send you packin' back to New York.

Trump Version
(Trump singing "Shake You Down"...badly)
Dems, I've been watching you.
You're on a witch-hunt that's for sure, now honest,
That's nothing new.
You've wanted to even up the score, now I'm right,
You just can't stand all my lies.
(Can't stand all my lies)
Know what that's telling me?
I know, that you'd love my demise
But I'm not leavin, I'm ruling by decree.
Now, boys,

[Chorus]
I'm messin' your mind.
Dems, I'm gonna shake you down.
Gonna make you know that I'll never leave.
Yes, I'm gonna shake you down.
Gonna make your lives a mis'ry.

from *the Good Riddance* Department
If music from the 1980s isn't in your wheelhouse, let me offer a song from the 1990s. I've rewritten the lyrics to the song, *You're in Love*, by the band Wilson Phillips. The new title is, *You're Impeached*. Let me apologize for not rewriting the whole song.

THE DONALD TRUMP TURKEY SHOOT

You're Impeached
Open the door and get out,
I'm so glad to be rid of you.
Don't know how long it has been
Having good feelings again.
And now I see that you're unhappy,
Oooh, it just sets me free.
And I'd like to see you in prison jams.
Just like you should be.

[Chorus]
You're impeached.
That's the way it should be.
Your impeachment makes me happy.
You're impeached.
And I know
That it's just what you should be.
Oooh, it's enough for me to know
That you're impeached,
Now you've gotta go.
Cause I know
You're impeached.

Solum Optimis Verbis

Lying: It's What Republicans Do

Week 146 / Nov. 10 – Nov. 16, 2019

I garner a great deal of satisfaction in ~~demeaning and~~ satirizing Trump. I deleted the word "demeaning" in the previous sentence, because I recognized that nothing I write, say, or do, demeans Donald Trump. He demeans himself entirely on his own. As a truly immoral, unethical, Constitutionally-ignorant & constitutionally stupid, and deceitful man, Trump needs no push from me. He demeans himself whenever he talks. With him, it is all self-dealing and personal greed. In fact, I bet he's looking for a corporate sponsor for his 2020 campaign.

And now a word from our sponsor: [Think insurance]

If you're a Republican serving in the Unites States Congress or Senate, you lie to the American people about everything: about tax relief for the middle class, about saving manufacturing jobs, about affordable healthcare, about the horrible treatment of immigrants and asylum seekers, about Trump's betrayal of the Kurds, about Trump's abominably immoral behavior. You lie: that's what you do.

But if you want to save 15% or more on insurance, just do what Donald Trump does. Only pay 80% of what you owe.

Only 80%. Even better, don't pay the insurance company anything at all and threaten to take them to court if they don't insure you, your home, your auto, and Air Force One. It's what a cheapskate, pretend-billionaire like Trump—well, he's not really a billionaire, true?—it's what he does.

Writer's Advice: Be Prepared: Impeachment Notice

Whatever alcoholic beverage you typically enjoy in your celebratory stash, I'd advise stocking up now. Personally, I have six bottles of beer—a yummy amber—that I made this past summer at *Gallaghers-U-Brew* in Edmonds, Washington. For Wendy I have a 14-year-old bottle of scotch, *The Balvenie, Caribbean Cask*.

It matters not at all if you have expensive tastes or a pedestrian palate—nothing will taste better than what you are drinking when Trump is sent packing. That beer will taste better than beer has ever tasted.

Stupid Is As Stupid Does
An Absurd Donald Trump Sketch

Trump is in the Oval Office with his Chief of Staff, Mick Mulvaney, and his lawyer, Rudy Giuliani. Trump is agitated and walking back and forth across his office floor.

Trump: What is a quid pro quo, anyway?

Mulvaney: As far as Republicans are concerned, it's quid pro so, Mr. President. We're all saying, "So what? What's the big deal, anyway?"

Trump: Thanks, Mick. But my faithful flunkies may be saying quid pro so, but the Dems are saying quid pro quo. So what is that, anyway? Is that a Canadian phrase? French, maybe?

Mulvaney: No, Mr. President, it's a Latin phrase. It means "this for that."

Trump: This for that? Like in negotiations? I'll give you this, if you give me that? Right? What's all the fuss about, it's good, old-fashioned, horse-trading. They want to impeach me because I'm a veteran horse-trader? I told everyone when I was running for president that I was probably the greatest negotiator they've ever seen. The absolute best. Nobody's even second when it comes to me as a negotiator.

Mulvaney: You're not being impeached for negotiating or horse-trading, sir.

Trump: No, I'm being impeached because I'm the best ever negotiator. Ever. Right? The best ever horse-trader. Ever. Just watch any episode of "The Apprentice." Everyone's mad at me because I had the best reality show ever made for television. Ever. And now my presidency is the best ever reality show in the government. My ratings are so much better than the Democrats. More people would rather watch me than the Democrats. I get the ratings, right?

Mulvaney: That's true, sir. People watch you every day because no one ever knows what you're going to say.

Trump: I keep them on the edge of their seats, right? Because I have every possible angle covered, right? First I say I didn't do whatever it is they say I did. Then I say I might have done it—but you'll have to ask my lawyer. Then I say I did do it—whatever "it" is—but it doesn't matter because I'm the president and I can do anything I want. Just check the Constitution. Article Two says, "Trump can do anything." That's the part of the Constitution Melania doesn't like very much.

Mulvaney:	Yes, sir. But you scare the hell out of 'em, too, sir. Everyone's waiting for you to say something like, "I think maybe I didn't do it. Not on purpose anyway." Or something like that. Of course, everyone in the White House is waiting for you to say, "You're fired."
Trump:	[Laughs] I've been doing that quite a bit since they crowned me president, haven't I? That's my favorite tweet, you know. "Rex, you're fired." "Jefferson Beauregard Sessions, you're fired." Firing people is fun. If I had my way, I'd fire every disloyal Democrat and every evil Republican…
Mulvaney:	Evil, sir?
Trump:	Mitt Romney for starters. I need people I can trust, like Vladimir Putin.
Mulvaney:	I wouldn't say that out loud, sir.
Trump:	If I can shoot someone on 5th Avenue in broad daylight, I can say that Putin and me are brothers as loud as I want. That's how powerful I am. Just to be clear, quid pro quo isn't a crime, right? You can't find any laws against quid pro quo because there aren't any.
Mulvaney:	That's true, Mr. President, but there are laws against extortion. Laws against blackmail. Laws against bribery.
Trump:	Blackmail? Extortion? Bribery? Are those synonyms for quid pro quo?
Giuliani:	Not really, sir. Those are crimes.
Trump:	Yeah, but they're not real crimes. Come on, Rudy. It's just business. That's how I've always done business in New York. It's the way I've done business in Panama where I have the best hotel those Panama people have ever seen. It's also the way I'm trying to do business in Turkey…
Giuliani:	And Russia, Mr. President.

Trump: That's true, Rudy. Vlady understands how these things work. You don't see any investigations into Putin, do you? No. He has 100% of his people squarely behind him. 100%. That's almost everybody, right?

Giuliani: Pretty close, Mr. President. Pretty close.

Quote of the Week
from Kate Cohen, *The Washington Post*
Loyalty is dumb; party loyalty is dangerous.
That's the point of loyalty.
It by-passes the brain.

Solum Optimis Verbis

"I'm Like, A Smart Person"

Week 159 / January 26 – February 1, 2020

from the *Fictional History* Department

I was about to say, "After last week, there can be no doubt of Trump's guilt…" and then I caught myself in mid-sentence, realizing that there are millions of people who would disagree with my assertion, and possibly many millions more who simply don't care if Trump is guilty. After all, these are the same people who have either overlooked or dismissed his sexual escapades, his racism, his xenophobia, his cruelty to children at our borders, his cozying up to autocrats like Putin or Kim Jong Un, his shameless bullying on Twitter, his denigration of a Free Press, his insulting our allies, and his ignoring global threats like climate change. If a person can ignore those things, ignoring Trump's guilt in extorting the Ukraine for personal gain is child's play.

Most astonishing to me is the willingness of so many to ignore The Trump Lying Machine—with lies big and small, lies that obfuscate, misdirect, and confuse the American voter—or lies told out of sheer, unadulterated, full-blossom ignorance. I'm convinced our "very stable genius" has an IQ hovering somewhere around room temperature. (Please note: It's winter and his thermostat is broken.)

Let me illustrate. On January 23rd, while in Davos, Switzerland, Trump was talking about protecting human resources like inventor and entrepreneur, Elon Musk. Trump went on the say,

> *"We have to protect Thomas Edison and we have to protect all of these people that came up with originally the light bulb and the wheel and all of these things. And he's [Musk] one of our very smart people and we want to cherish those people,"* Trump said. *"He's done a very good job."*

By all means, let's protect Thomas Edison, the father of the light bulb who died 88 years ago on October 18, 1931. I'm not sure how we might protect the man—or woman?—who invented the wheel, but let's do that, too. According to archeologists, the wheel was invented by a clever Sumerian (not an American) sometime around 3500 B.C.—or 5,520 years ago. As I'm sure Trump and his advisers will tell you, "History is easy if you just make it up."

On the basis of these comments—and referencing an encyclopedia of inane, stupid, or indecipherable comments made from the day Trump announced his presidential candidacy—I can only conclude that our president is essentially brain dead. His brain allows him to do little more than inhale, exhale, excrete, copulate, and boldly lie where no president has lied before. Knowledge and thought are not part of the Trump equation.

We all know there are only two articles of impeachment, but I have one very simple question that I'd like to pose to every Republican. *How many bad, senseless, mindless, hurtful, traitorous, and evil things must a president do before you would consider removing him from office?*

from the Trump Liars Hall of ~~Fame~~ Shame Department

Because lying has become the new Republican norm, my wife has suggested that we should henceforth refer to the current administration as the "Trump Badministration" or the "Trump Sadministration." Both seem appropriate.

I thought it might be useful if we compiled a list of all the liars in the Trump Badministration, both past and present, either walking around, indicted but free on bond, or in prison. With the exception of the president and his family, I've compiled these names in no particular order.

Members
Donald J. Trump, President
Donald J. Trump Jr., son
Eric Trump, son
Jared Kushner, son-in-law
Mike Pence, Vice-president
Stephen Miller, proud, scary, Nazi-loving immigration advisor
Mitch McConnell, evil senator [R] Kentucky
Rudy Giuliani, foolish, loquacious, rogue presidential attorney
William Barr, blatantly and brazenly dishonest Attorney General
Michael Pompeo, "The Cowardly Lyin'," Secretary of State
Kellyanne Conway, Presidential Advisor
Michael Cohen, former Trump personal attorney
Steve Mnuchin, mindless Treasury Secretary
Betsy DeVos, inept Secretary of Education
Wilbur Ross, former Secretary of Commerce
Tom Price, former Secretary of Health and Human Services
Michael Flynn, corrupt former National Security Advisor
Rick Perry, former Secretary of Energy
Kirstjen Nielson, cruel, former head of Homeland Security
Jeff Sessions, racist, former Attorney General
Lindsay Graham, duplicitous senator [R] South Carolina
Jim Jordan, arrogant and nasty representative [R] Ohio
Louie Gohmert, amazingly dim-witted representative [R] Texas
Doug Collins, incoherent representative [R] Georgia
Devin Nunes, traitorous representative [R] California
Matt Gaetz, clueless representative [R] Florida

The Donald Trump Turkey Shoot

Jay Sekulow, White House Defense Team
Alan Dershowitz, White House Defense Team
Pat Cippolone, White House Defense Team
Pam Bondi, White House Defense Team
Jane Raskin, White House Defense Team
Eric Herschmann, White House Defense Team
Michael Purpura, Deputy WH Counsel
Scott Pruitt, former head of the EPA
Steve Bannon, former Senior Advisor
Sean Spicer, former "Big Crowd" WH Press Secretary
Sarah Sanders, former WH Press Secretary
Stephanie Grisham, former, virtually-invisible, WH Press Secretary
Kayleigh McEnany, new, "Lie-from-the-Start" WH Press Secretary
Hope Hicks, former WH Communications Director
Newt Gingrich, Republican & FOX News gadfly

NOTE: My list is clearly incomplete. But I make no apologies. I never dreamed so many grown-ups would be capable of lying so audaciously—forever sullying their reputations.

from the *Renaming the Grand Old Party [GOP]* Department

Government of Pirates
Grand Obstruction Party
Greed Over People
Group of Predators
Gutless, Obnoxious Politicians

Solum Optimis Verbis

Theater of the Absurdest

Week 170 / April 12, 2020 – April 18, 2020

from *The Buck Doesn't Stop Here* Department
President Harry S. Truman placed a sign on his desk: *The buck stops here*. He understood the importance of his job, and he took responsibility for everything that happened during his tenure in office—happily accepting the credit and bravely accepting the blame.

But not Trump. He wants all the credit but none of the blame. His presidency is a reality show—one in which Trump would sooner fix the blame than the problem. Since January 20, 2017, we've come to realize that television performance skills are far more valued than genuine leadership skills. He's interested in reviews, not results.

Unfortunately for all of us, Trump's leadership abilities are a great deal like COVID-19—invisible but lethal. We always knew Trump was incompetent, but we were hoping to avoid the kind of crisis where his ignorance, ineptitude, incompetence, and lack of empathy would be so starkly apparent. Well, chickens have come home to roost. The crisis is here.

Trump said he was sure the coronavirus was going to disappear—like a miracle. It didn't. Faced with the COVID-19 outbreak in the country he was elected to govern, Trump has done almost nothing. Tragically, there is just so much Trump could have done, should have done, but hasn't done. Is his lack of effort a political calculation? Is it laziness? Or is it just rank incompetence?

Trump has taken no meaningful or timely action against the spreading novel coronavirus. In a bizarre twist, Trump brazenly trumpets what a great job he is doing while his minions nonsensically extol his "bold leadership"—even as Americans die by the tens of thousands. Trump is hubris on steroids.

As I said, his leadership is invisible, his negligence lethal.

Below I have imagined what a conversation between Trump and his newest Chief of Staff must sound like as Trump's fears and misgivings grow each day. Will Trump pay a political price for shifting blame and responsibility to the various states? Trump proved us right. He failed to be the leader that we all knew he could never be. Thousands of vulnerable Americans have died under the careless leadership of this carping, whining, do-nothing president. Will real science, and an even more real and recurring COVID-19, undermine his reelection? So many questions—so much to answer for. So much to do for a man who would rather play golf or manufacture lies while "playing president" on television.

Dramatis Personae
Donald Trump, president
Mark Meadows, chief-of-staff
Setting:
The two men are in the Oval Office. Alone. Meadows is looking over Trump's shoulder.

Meadows: That was a great point you made at the televised coronavirus press briefing on Friday, Mr. President.

Trump: You bet it was. *[Trump seems surprised]* You mean where I said I wasn't going to wear a mask like the CDC recommends? What did I say?

Meadows: No, that's not what I was referring to. But I completely understand why you don't want to wear a mask, sir.

Trump: Yeah. I'd look silly with a mask on. I can't afford to look silly, can I? America sees this face every day, and I don't want to look silly. Besides, if I wore a mask, my Secret Service detail might not recognize me. After all, most of those Covfefe-19 masks are blue—and my face is orange.

Meadows: That's COVID-19, sir, not Covfefe-19.

Trump: Tomato, potato. Everyone knows what I mean. What's that 19-thing all about, anyway? Why nineteen? Is that how old the virus is? *[Laughs]* I went out with a nineteen-year-old once—maybe six or seven years ago. *[Pauses. Looks suspiciously at Meadows]* Remember, Meadows, you're not to tell Melania what I just said. Understand? I told Melania that the nineteen-year-old was thirty-five. She'd be plenty upset if she knew she was nineteen.

Meadows: Mum's the word, Mr. President. My lips are sealed.

Trump: Good. I don't want to have to fire another chief-of-staff before the next election.

Meadows: The election! That's exactly what I was talking about, sir. Remember when you said that we needed people to show up in person at the polls to vote? Remember that? You said—let me consult my notes so I quote you exactly — you said, "A lot of people cheat with mail-in voting."

Trump: That's true. Nothing's ever been truer. They cheated by the millions during the last election and I still won. Millions cheated. And I won. Won big. That's definitely true. At least, I feel it's definitely true. And all presidential feelings become true. We know that's true because I just said it. Ask Jared. He always agrees with me.

Meadows: I'm sure he does. However, the Governor of Washinghton State called to disagree, sir. He called me and said, "Voting by mail is the best way to insure that all

Americans will be able to exercise their Constitutional right to vote. Please tell the president that he is wrong."

Trump: Wrong? Me, wrong? When have I ever been wrong? Who is he to call me wrong? What's his name? Innee? Outee?

Meadows: It's Inslee. Mr. President. His name is Governor Jay Inslee.

Trump: You got that wrong, Meadows. His name is Governor Snake. I've seen plenty of snakes in my time. So what else did Governor Snake say?

Meadows: Let me consult my notes, sir. He sent this e-mail and said I should read it to you verbatim. *[Pulls out a folded sheet of paper]* "Washington State voters vote by mail and will continue to vote by mail. Washington State voters will never have to worry about standing in long lines to cast their ballots. Because of mail-in ballots, no Washington State voter will ever have to contend with rogue viruses, the vagaries of bad weather, or the fear of lost time on the job. Better still, all Washington State voters can vote from the comfort of their own dining room tables where they can discuss the issues and candidates on the ballot with those they love. Concerning the issues about mail-in ballots, the president is dead wrong."

Trump: I told you he was a snake.

Meadows: I'm not sure how that makes him a snake.

Trump: Look, Meadows. Some elected officials—guys like this Governor Snake—are more interested in the welfare of their people than they are in getting re-elected. How stupid is that?

Meadows: *[Shrugs sheepishly]* People expect you to lead during a crisis, sir.

Trump: Yeah, well, I'm leading. Doin' a great job, too. Everyone I know tells me what a great job I'm doing. I get phone calls. Lots of phone calls. Phone rings and rings. Rings off the hook. I'm doin' great. Everyone says so. I get on TV every day and tell people that we're doing great. I lead the U.S. for two hours a day. Well, almost two hours. Sometimes only ninety minutes, but that's leadership right? Making everything happy and upbeat. I'm not bumming anybody out…like Birx and Fauci…

Meadows: Perhaps if you just told the American public the facts, sir…

Trump: Are you out of your mind, Meadows? This is no time for facts. The facts are depressing. Here's the secret to really leading, Meadows. If 250,000 Americans die in this pandemic, you've gotta tell everyone that's great news. You gotta tell'em it coulda' been way worse. Way worse. You gotta make 250,000 dead seem like a good thing.

Meadows: *[Confused]* I'm not sure that 250,000 dead is ever a good thing, sir.

Trump: You're not gettin' it, Meadows. Sure, 250,000 dead would be a catastrophe, but who wants responsibility for that? Not me. You gotta turn catastrophe into victory. *[Meadows looks confused again]* Look, let's say a million die. I say, "Wow! Only a million? That's great! It coulda' been worse. Way worse." The numbers of dead don't matter. What matters is how people look at me, whatever that number is. I want them to see me as their hero. Their savior. Is that too much to ask? And don't forget, making me look like everyone's savior is job one for every Republican. That's how I'll get re-elected.

Meadows: Isn't that a little dishonest, sir?

Trump: Look Meadows, I don't need any namby-pamby advisors here. That's why I got rid of Kelly, and Priebus too. Those guys wanted me to act like a grown-up. I finally told'em, "No way. Who wants to be a goddamn grown-up? Grown-ups are expected to obey the rules. I hate rules. Rules are for people who think that rules actually mean something. They don't. Rules don't apply to me. They never will, and I'm not about to start obeying rules now." That's why I fired 'em.

Meadows: But how can you make 250,000 dead Americans sound like a good thing, sir?

Trump: *[Looks at Meadows as if he's an idiot]* I just spin the facts that have to be spun—I create what Kellyanne calls "alternative facts." It's like magic. I'll just *say* that 250,000 dead is a good thing, not a bad thing. If anyone says it's bad—I'll stop 'em. Stop 'em immediately. Tell 'em it's good. Tell 'em only fake news folks think it's awful. Then I stick in phrases like, "Be glad it's *only* 250,000." I'll keep using that word "only." Great word. *[Trump repeats it rapturously]* Only. Only. *[Back to reality]* And short, too. Easy to say. So I say it lots of times.

Meadows: That's genius, sir.

Trump: Then you say, "If it hadn't been for the president's bold leadership…"—that's Mike Pence's favorite phrase. He says it all the time. "Bold leadership." Great phrase. Great PR. Great sound-bite. The fake news guys hate it. I love it. Use that "bold leadership" line. Make me look good, Meadows. Got it?

Meadows: Do you really think people will see that as the truth, sir?

Trump: *[Shoots Meadows a withering look]* You want the truth? Here's a truth for you. If the whole country gets mail-in ballots, no Republican will ever get elected again. And you'll be out of a job. So I cheat. I lie. I've been cheating and lying my whole life—that's how I got elected. And the best cheaters and liars always win. Don't you ever forget that!

from the *Fake News* Department

Trump seems genuinely afraid of a free press; afraid of journalists who remember what he actually said yesterday, or a week ago, or a month ago, or years ago. He seems afraid of journalists who call him on his lies, falsehoods, and deceptions, even as he addresses the country with his lies, falsehoods, and deceptions. That's why he continually calls them FAKE. My friend AJ took a moment to enlighten me about what FAKE really means when applied to news and news organizations by Trump. Behold, the acronym.

> Factual. Accurate. Key. Educational.

No wonder Trump hates F-A-K-E News.

from the *Trump AA Meeting* Department

<u>**Dramatis Personae**</u> *(in order of appearance)*
Anonymous Counselor   Kellyanne Conway   Mitch McConnell
Bill Barr   Donald Trump

<u>**Setting**</u>
Somewhere in the bowels of a government building in Washington, DC. A nondescript meeting room with a dozen chairs in a circle. Four chairs are occupied and the Counselor sits opposite the four.

Counselor: We have a new person with us at AA this week. He'll be addressing us in a moment, but before he does, let's share what we've begun to understand since we've started coming to AA; how we've begun taking control of our lives. Miss, why don't you begin?

Kellyanne: *[Stands up]* Hi, I'm Kellyanne *[She grimaces]*...and I'm an asshole.

All: Hi, Kellyanne.

Kellyanne: *[Takes a deep breath]* I'm still new—I mean, new to AA. *[Another deep breath]* I've been an asshole for more years than I care to remember. *[Pauses]* I thought I'd begin by reciting Step One of AA's Six Step program. I've committed it to memory, okay? *[Closes eyes and recites]* "We admit we were addicted to leading lives as unmitigated and despicable assholes—and that our lives had become unmanageable."

Counselor: Very good, Kellyanne. We all heard her, right? Who here admits they are unmitigated and despicable assholes? *[Kellyanne, Mitch, and Bill raise their hands. Only Donald Trump sits, unmoved]* Excellent. Identifying, admitting, and embracing your terrible reality—that you've permitted yourself to victimize both yourself and others by becoming an unmitigated and despicable asshole—that's always the first step.

Kellyanne: Yes. That's Step One. The all-important first step. A journey of a thousand miles begins with the first step. You must take that first step. *[Growing slightly hysterical, begins to cry]* Without a first step, you can't have a second step. Without a first step, you remain an unmitigated and despicable asshole, victimizing yourself and others. *[Begins to swoon]*

Counselor: *[Jumps up to help Kellyanne]* Thank you, Kellyanne. Would someone get her a glass of water? Cold water.

Mitch: Where's Brett Kavanaugh when you need a nice cold beer to calm yourself?

Bill: *[Jumps up to help the Counselor]* Brett Kavanaugh? The Supreme Court's supreme asshole? Yeah, he's been an asshole way longer than any of us. Ever since high school. Probably longer. I don't have any water or beer, but I've got some vodka. Would that help? *[Digs a pint bottle out of his pocket and hands it to the Counselor]* I never come to an AA meeting without my vodka.

Mitch: *[Stays in his chair]* Hell of a lot better than water. But if you're going for the hard stuff, there's nothing better than Kentucky bourbon. *[Digs a pint of bourbon out of his pocket]* Best bourbon in the world.

Counselor: Here you go, Kellyanne. Take a deep breath. Now take a swig of this. *[Hands Kellyanne the pint bottle of vodka]* You got a bit excited. *[Kellyanne swigs bottoms-up]* Whoa, slow down. Slow down. Don't drink, too quickly.

Kellyanne: Thanks. *[Wipes her hand across her mouth]* Gosh, that's good. *[Takes another swig]* I'm feeling better already. *[She sits down unsteadily]*

Bill: Well, since I'm already up here, I'll go next.

All: *[General sounds of agreement]* Sure. Go ahead. You bet.

Bill: Hi, my name is Bill, and I'm an unmitigated and despicable asshole.

All: Hi, Bill.

Bill: I see Kellyanne is feeling no pain. *[Laughs]*. A couple of stiff drinks always keeps me from feeling like an asshole.

Mitch: Not really. It just keeps you from noticing how big an asshole you really are. *[Mitch takes a swig of his bourbon. Kellyanne stands up a bit wobbly and takes another swig of vodka]*

Bill: Hey, save some of that for me. *[Takes back the bottle from Kellyanne]* Kellyanne started us off pretty well—Step One is that all-important first step. *[Shakes head sadly. Takes a swig]* I never liked calling myself an asshole…even though everyone else knew it was true. *[Deep breath]* Hey, where's Rudy this week?

Counselor: *[Interrupting]* Bill. Bill. What's our rule?

Bill: Sorry. *[Recites rule]* "We never talk about the assholes who aren't here."

Counselor: That's right. While we can be concerned about the assholes who aren't here, we cannot help them unless they help themselves.

Bill: *[Laughs]* Yeah, if all the local D.C. assholes who needed to be here attended all the meetings, this place would be crowded out the door.

Mitch: That's so true. D.C. is full of assholes. We just happen to be the biggest and the best. *[Mitch takes another swig of his bourbon]*

Bill: I only mentioned Rudy because I'm afraid he's having a relapse. I'm worried that he thinks life isn't worth living if he can't be an unmitigated and despicable asshole.

Kellyanne: I know just how he feels. Sometimes I feel the same way.

Counselor: That's not all that unusual, Kellyanne. And Bill, I understand your concern. Perhaps that's the perfect entrée to Step Two. *[Nods to Bill]*

Bill: Me? Right. Good. Step Two. Let me see. Step Two. Oh, yes. "I've come to believe that powers greater than ourselves could restore our humanity."

Counselor: And what are those greater powers, Bill?

Bill: Honesty and decency.

Counselor: And have we been practicing honesty and decency?

Bill: Sure. *[Shrugs his shoulders]* Well, kinda. I didn't realize it would be so hard.

Mitch: Yeah, really hard. Especially when it comes to doing something honest and decent for the American people. That's really hard. Screwing people over comes more naturally to me. *[Mitch takes another swig]*

Counselor: *[Speaks directly to Mitch]* You're right. But we're all here because we have to overcome those urges to be unmitigated and despicable assholes. We must use honesty and

The Donald Trump Turkey Shoot

	decency to defeat those urges. I know it's hard. *[Pause]* Perhaps we should all take a moment to welcome the newest asshole in our midst. *[Nods at Donald Trump]*
Donald:	Me?
Counselor:	You have the floor.
Donald:	*[Stands up, moves to the center of the circle]* My name is Donald…and I'm an asshole.
All:	Hi, Donald.
Donald:	*[Shrugs his shoulders. Begins slowly]* I like being an asshole. I'm good at it. My father always said that I should stick to what I'm good at. I'm lousy at most things. I'm a lousy business man. I'm a lousy leader.
Kellyanne:	A lousy husband.
Mitch:	A lousy father.
Kellyanne:	A lousy human being.
Donald:	*[Glares at Kellyanne and Mitch]* That's enough out of you two. You really are assholes. *[Gets back to his explanation]* Here's the thing. I really don't like other people, so I don't give a damn about honesty and decency. Why would I want to be honest and decent? Honest, decent people get screwed their whole lives…by people like me… because they expect that somehow, someday, some way, I'll be honest and decent, too. *[Laughs]* Some people have been waiting for more than three years for me to be honest and decent. They call it "presidential"—whatever the hell that means. Never gonna happen.
Counselor:	*[Confused]* Then why are you here?
Bill:	Probably because Melania sent him.
Kellyanne:	*[Slurring her words]* She thinks he's an asshole.
Counselor:	That's enough. Let him talk. Never interrupt someone when he's making an asshole out of himself. *[Turns directly to Trump]* So…Melania thinks you're an asshole…?

Donald: That may be true—but what does she know? She's a woman. I'm here because I'm a genius. A very stable genius. *[Starts to speak conspiratorially]* If people think I'm trying to stop being an asshole, they'll give me the benefit of the doubt. Honest and decent people always do that. And that's good for me because that means I can get away with being an asshole for a whole lot longer than I could if they knew I was an unrepentant asshole.

Kellyanne: *[Kellyanne stands up and slurs her words]* Dammit, Donald, that's not fair. That's the same reason I'm here. I figured I could pull the wool over the eyes of a whole lot more people—including my husband, George—if they thought I was trying to be honest and decent.

Bill: Yeah, that's why I'm here.

Mitch: Me, too.

Donald: Honesty and decency may play okay on the Hallmark Channel—or on the Disney Channel—but assholes rule the world. Don't you ever forget that. Assholes rule!

All: *[Jump up in unison]* Yeah, assholes rule.

Counselor: *[Astonished]* Assholes rule? Assholes rule? Are you kidding me? Assholes crap all over people and never clean up their mess. You people are crazy.

Donald: *[Walks over to the Counselor]* You only think we're crazy because you're honest and decent. That's how all honest and decent people always view unmitigated and despicable assholes. Let me tell you something. Assholes rule 'cause we can cheat. We don't have to play by the rules. There are no rules. But honest and decent people have to play by the rules. Be fair. Be nice. *[In the Counselor's face]* Honest and decent equals loser.

The Donald Trump Turkey Shoot

All: Yeah, loser. *[They push the Counselor away and gather around Donald and pat him on the back. Donald preens and folds his arms and glares at the Counselor]*

Donald: Let's get out of here. Honest and decent people scare the hell out of me.

All: *[General agreement]* Me, too! Alright! Let's get outa here! *[Exit all assholes]*

Counselor: *[Left standing alone. He picks up the empty vodka pint bottle and moves to the door of the room. Puts his finger on the light switch as he talks to himself]* I was wondering if I needed a drink to get over all the unmitigated and despicable assholes in this administration. *[Shakes his head]* Shameless and unrepentant, too. *[Deep sigh]* But then I realized, there's just not enough alcohol. *[Turns off the light]*

Solum Optimis Verbis

Epilogue: The Morning After

November 4, 2020

Yup, this was the way to do it. And about time, too.

The country had watched, and the world had watched. There could be no real question now as to where the USA was headed. He was sure the people would follow him when he showed them the way. There were a few doubters, of course, but he expected they'd come around. It was time to really get things in gear.

He knew he could do it.

Solum optimus populi—Only the best people.

Appendix / The Trump Nursery

Little Boy Trump © 2017 [with apologies to *Little Boy Blue*]

Little Boy Trump, so infantile
You tell your big falsehoods, and keep your big smile.
Where is the truth that we treasure so dear?
It's under your fake hair, dormant, I fear.

Will you tell truths?
Oh no, not you.
For if you do
They won't sound true.

Spicey, Spicey © 2017 [with apologies to *Cobbler, Cobbler*]

> Spicey, Spicey, tell my lies,
> To the press that I despise.
> They'll run to check up our false words,
> That fill the news like slimy turds.
> Words untrue, and oh so false,
> Till they're dancing my lying waltz.

Come to the Window © 2017 [with apologies to *Come to the Window*]

Come to the window
Ivanka, with me,
And look at the people
As dumb as can be.

There are two journalists
Who print my lies,
Like two little kids.
Unwise, so unwise.

And two TV pundits
Full of gullibility.
I smile so nicely
In my lying spree.

Get a Glass of Whiskey © 2017 [with apologies to *Draw a Pail of Water*]

Get a glass of whiskey
Cause I'm feelin' frisky.
This prez needs a girl, so his privates unfurl.
She must be a ten and shine like a pearl.
This orange womanizer
Ignores his good advisor.
One rush! No blush!
Pray thee, fine lady, I just want your bush.

The Donald Trump Turkey Shoot

Donald Ran a Little Scam © 2017 [with apologies to *Mary Had a Little Lamb*]

Donald ran a little scam
And fleeced some pupils bad.
His university was a fake
Their learning curve was sad.

They took him off to court one day
Cause he had broke the rules.
He settled and was forced to pay
The cash he stole from fools.

Hickory, Dickory, Trump © 2017 [with apologies to *Hickory, Dickory, Dock*]

> Hickory, dickory, Trump
> I'll give my polls a bump
> With the Russian scam
> I'll be the man.
> Hickory, dickory, Trump.

Hickory, Bickory, Bet © 2017 [with apologies to *Hickory, Dickory, Dock*]

Hickory, bickory, bet
Our Trump runs up the debt.
Congress debates,
Our debt inflates.
Hickory, bickory, bet.

With My Connection © 2017 [with apologies to *Hey, Diddle, Diddle*]

>With my connection
>I won the election
>(I won the popular vote)
>The people they laughed to hear me say,
>"Don't you love when the facts are rewrote?"

Oval Office, Oval Office © 2017 [with apologies to *Frere Jacques*]

Oval Office, Oval Office,
Is for sale! Is for sale!
To the highest bidder, to the highest bidder,
Ka-ching, ka-ching. Ka-ching, ka-ching.

Donnie Trumpie © 2017 [with apologies to *Georgie Porgie*]

>Donnie Trumpie, orange guy
>Groped the girls and made them cry.
>When the girls went to the courts
>They finally got him in the shorts.

Here We Go Round the Legislators © 2017
[with apologies to *Here We Go Round the Mulberry Bush*]

Here we go round the legislators,
The legislators,
The legislators,
Here we go round legislators
'Cause we ain't got no ethics.
This is the way we launder cash,
Launder cash,
Launder cash,
This is the way we launder cash
To keep our Putin happy.

This is the way we make fake news,
Make fake news,
Make fake news.
This is the way we make fake news,
With Kelleyanne and Spicey.

www.ingramcontent.com/pod-product-compliance
Lightning Source LLC
Chambersburg PA
CBHW070836160426
43192CB00012B/2207